Never Rush Your Fences

by

Karen A. Stansbury

Lakeland Terrier Press, LLC

Lakeland Terrier Press, LLC
P.O. Box 181
Washington Depot, CT 06794

Cover cartoon by Dave May, Custom Cartoon Art
Cover design/layout by Deb Tremper, Six Penny Graphics
Logo design by Kelli Mincey, Cre8tive Mind Designs

Printed in the United States of America

Never Rush Your Fences is a work of fiction. Names, characters, places, and incidents either are the product of the author's imagination, or are used fictitiously. Any resemblance to actual persons, living or dead, events or locales is entirely coincidental.

Also by Karen A. Stansbury

Inside Leg, Outside Rein

Eyes Up, Heels Down

Stay Balanced!

CONTENTS

If men were angels, no government would be necessary. If angels were to govern men, neither external nor internal controls on government would be necessary. In framing a government which is to be administered by men over men, the great difficulty lies in this: you must first enable the government to control the governed; and in the next place oblige it to control itself. A dependence on the people is, no doubt, the primary control on the government; but experience has taught mankind the necessity of auxiliary precautions.

James Madison

All eyes are opened or opening to the rights of man. The general spread of the light of science has already laid open to every view the palpable truth, that the mass of mankind has not been born with saddles on their backs, nor a favored few, booted and spurred, ready to ride them legitimately, by the grace of God.

Thomas Jefferson

I went to the woods because I wished to live
deliberately, to front only the essential facts of life,
and see if I could not learn what it had to teach, and
not, when I came to die, discover that I had not lived.

HENRY DAVID THOREAU

When much in the Woods as a little Girl, I was
told that the Snake would bite me, that I might
pick a poisonous flower, or Goblins kidnap me,
but I went along and met no one but Angels.

EMILY DICKINSON

Dedicated to Professor Martin B. Margulies

Who taught me Constitutional Law

CHAPTER ONE

Residual Hauntings

"You told me you wanted adventures!" Luke shouted.

"Really?" I bellowed back. "Was I sober at the time?"

Luke grinned. "We can slow down if you like."

"No thanks! I like a challenge!"

Perthshire, Scotland. The majestic raw terrain of the Highlands. We were galloping on saddle horses along an old carriage road that hugged the periphery of a golf course. A trout stream sparkled beside the path on our right. The hotel, more like a Baronial style castle, was just visible above the dense tree line to the west.

"That's the spirit!" Luke replied. "Let's try the cross country jumping course." We veered east toward the bridge, our horses nickering with enthusiasm.

To the land of the bens and the glens!

This was my third trip to Scotland, and once more I was bewitched by the wild, mystical beauty of the terrain. The landscape of mountains and valleys, punctuated by deep sea lochs, clusters of small islands, and ubiquitous flocks of sheep, appeared to my painter's eye as washes of cobalt violet, ultramarine blue, burnt sienna, and sap green that I was never able to simulate with a brush. It has been said that the abundant glories of nature are often too painful to behold for long. This is how I have always felt about Scotland.

Half an hour later we stopped our horses at a golf cart crossing. Four elderly men, arrayed in various tartans, buzzed by us and crossed the bridge.

"Not terribly concerned about safety around here, are they?" I asked, as we trotted back to the barn.

"Historically? No," Luke replied. "I'm sure that we'll hear more about that tonight."

I grinned at him. "We still have a few hours before dinner, Luke. Any ideas?"

"None that involve my putting on that kilt again."

"But you have such a great big sword to go with it!"

"My *claidheamh mòr?*"

"Is that what we're calling it now?"

Dinner was served in a large paneled room which surrounded its occupants with faded tapestries of ancient battle scenes, and panoramic views of the terrace, with the golf course beyond. Luke and I were working on our salmon with grilled potatoes and vegetables, when a middle-aged couple was seated next to us.

"How old is this hotel?" The woman asked.

"The brochure says 1843," her husband replied. "It was originally a country home—shooting and fishing parties."

"Kind of an odd feeling about the place—don't you think?"

"What do you mean by odd?" He asked, scanning the list of single malt whiskeys.

"There's a heaviness in the atmosphere—kind of damp and oppressive. Especially on our floor. And all those noises last night—did you hear them? People going up and down the stairs for hours. Banging on the walls and windows, like someone was throwing rocks from below."

"We're three stories up, Kath," her husband scoffed. "Take a look at the menu, will you? I'm starving, and the waiter's headed this way."

Luke put down his wine glass and asked me in a low voice: "Did you hear anything last night Emma? It *was* noisy, I thought."

I decided to sidestep his question. "Why?"

He glanced over to our neighbors. "Just as this woman says," he replied, quietly. "Especially the explosive sounds from the windows. I also heard bells ringing, overhead. Not electric—more like a hand bell."

"Is this unusual for you?"

"What do you mean?"

I danced around the question again. "Do you normally hear noises at night?"

Luke frowned. "Occasionally—at the farm. Certainly not like this."

The waiter appeared with the dessert menu, and the subject was dropped.

The hotel was hosting a public book signing event that night in the old ballroom. At least two hundred chairs had been set up in rows, facing a stage. Author Hector Lawson was introduced as a famous local historian, and ghost hunter.

"My specialty is clan legend," Lawson began. "And here in Perthshire, the MacGregors and the MacLarens are among the most evident. The battles over land through the centuries have been brutal and bloody, and the dramatic, turbulent energy from Scotland's past has left its mark. It is still all around us.

"Some history first," he continued. "I'll be talking about the various kinds of hauntings in a bit.

"For more than one thousand years, Highland Celtic society centered on the clan system, through which close-knit family groups relied on loyalty to each other and to their autocratic clan chief for survival. The members bore the names of their chiefs, and wore the checked wool cloth denoting each tribe, known as tartan. They were warriors who followed fierce codes of nobility, and hospitality.

"The most common perception of Scotland as a nation is evoked by the Highlands—ominous mountains half hidden in the mist, rugged valleys filled with heather, the playing of bagpipes. It is a sparsely inhabited place, which experiences some of the harshest weather conditions in Europe. Life here moves at a slower pace, and the people—perhaps reflecting the spirit of the land—are strong and self-reliant.

"Clan MacLaren is one of the oldest clans in Scotland, but the clan's power went into a decline very early in its history. Regardless of their many misfortunes, however, the MacLarens have managed to preserve their line, and the Clan has since reacquired its ancient rallying place at Creag an Tuirc—translated as 'the boar's rock.'

"Most famous for military acumen, many of the MacLarens became mercenaries—soldiers for hire. During the Wars for Scottish Independence the MacLarens fought for King Robert the Bruce at the Battle of Bannockburn, near Stirling, in 1314. This victory drove out England's much larger forces, and won Scotland her independence. Nevertheless, war with England continued for another four hundred years.

"The MacLarens and the MacGregors were prominent in Balquhidder, here in the Midlands region. The MacLarens were once plentiful and powerful, but war with their neighbors throughout the generations diminished their hold on their land, and their numbers and status died out. Clan MacGregor, known for its aggressive tactics, probably contributed the most to the decline of the MacLarens. In 1558, having been ousted by the Campbells, the MacGregors attacked the MacLarens at Balquhidder. The grave of Rob Roy MacGregor, the famous eighteenth century outlaw hero, lies in the kirkyard in Balquhidder village. The words 'MacGregor Despite Them' are etched into his headstone.

"Clan MacLaren was allied with the Stewart family, and the MacLarens suffered major losses as a result of their support of Bonnie Prince Charlie and his Jacobite forces."

"Not terribly impressive back then, were we?" Luke whispered. "We were either wiped out by the guy next door, or we were backing losers."

"Of course," Lawson continued, "after the Battle of Culloden in 1746, which tolled the death knell for the old clan system and the seven hundred year era of regional government, Scotland was oppressed by the English for decades. All clan property was forfeited to the Crown. 'No land, no clan.' Thousands of people were 'cleared' from their homes to make way for the more profitable business of raising sheep. Many Highland customs, such as the playing of bagpipes, wearing tartan, and even speaking the Gaelic language were forbidden. Ironically, in the war for American independence, members of Clan MacLaren fought on the side of the English king."

"I see your point," I whispered back.

"For the Americans in the audience, you may not be aware that your Declaration of Independence, as drafted by a gentleman named Thomas Jefferson, was modeled on a document originally signed here in Scotland on 6th April in 1320—the Declaration of Arbroath. An eloquent appeal to Pope John XXII for recognition of Scottish freedom, it is considered by many to be the founding document of Scotland, and the first real movement toward the concept of constitutional monarchy in Europe. The Scots—famous for their suspicion of authority and their contempt for showy extravagance—declared that they would never submit to the English. 'We fight not for glory, nor riches, nor honour, but only for that liberty which no true man relinquishes but with his life.'"

Lawson paused. "Right. Now that you have an idea of the centuries of blood letting throughout Scotland's history, let's talk about the different categories of hauntings that I have highlighted in my new book. The two most common types are 'intelligent' and 'residual' hauntings.

"Earthbound spirits, known as ghosts, have a consciousness, and may interact with humans. They are distinct personalities, and as a result may appear to be anywhere from friendly to quite scary. There are many reasons that a spirit may decide to remain on our physical plane. It might have a strong connection to a person, place, or thing. In my experience, ghosts can be attached to such items as clothing, furniture, cars, or even jewelry.

"Ghosts can be nosy, gossipy, and greedy—just as they were when alive. They can hear what we say, and they observe everything. A spirit may stay on the earth to watch over a loved one. Sometimes a ghost's motivation is fear. It may be worried about what sort of judgment is waiting on the Other Side, or perhaps it is merely concerned about the unknown. Usually there is some kind of unfinished business. Occasionally a ghost is concerned about justice, or revenge. Grudges can last for generations.

"Many psychics claim that ghosts don't realize that they have died, and are attempting to continue their lives here as before. I have to say that in over thirty years of doing this work, I have yet to meet a ghost who did not understand that he or she was dead. However, I am always open to learning something new. Remember that ghosts are just humans who have died. They appear just as they did when they were alive. Other than transporting themselves by thought, they have no special magical powers. Many simply hitch rides with humans.

"Ghosts need energy," Lawson explained. "They require *our* emotional and physical energy to stay on the earth. In essence they feed off humans, and sometimes animals, by absorbing our energy. Ghosts are all around us, attracted by emotional reactions which give them a charge—literally. Unfortunately, this phenomenon leaves us with less energy, and the presence of ghosts has a negative impact on humans, often affecting behavior and moods. In extreme cases this draining can make people sick.

"Ghosts get the best energy jolt from anger, and they are capable of using energy to manipulate people and create chaos, thereby promoting negative emotional responses. Earthbound spirits can also disrupt lighting or other electrical items, as well as electronics, just by standing near them.

"Contrary to popular myth, ghosts are almost never found at cemeteries. Why?" Lawson laughed. "No energy. They tend to lurk in high voltage places, such as malls, airports, bus and train stations, gyms, bars, and schools. Hospitals, police departments, and courthouses are especially active. Ghosts seem to have the most energy during a waxing or full moon, and they get lethargic if their stores are running low.

"Perhaps this would be a good time to explain that although I can see and communicate with ghosts—earthbound spirits—I am not able to do the same with spirits who have passed on. Therefore, I am *not* a psychic. I don't get visions of the past or predictions for the future. I can only report what the ghosts tell me. They do this telepathically—that is to say, only I can hear them. I can telepath back to them, but more often than not I speak out loud for the benefit of my clients. The spirit may be speaking in French, or Chinese, or Turkish—whatever. I hear everything they say in English. I don't use any kind of scientific gadget. I don't need to.

"What does a ghost look like? Just like everyone else, except that from a certain angle I can see through them. Often they are wearing out of date clothing, which is the real tip-off.

"When a client calls me in to deal with ghosts, the goal is to send the spirit over to the Other Side—where it belongs. Frankly, I'll do anything to accomplish this, including lying, to get the ghost to go. When it agrees to leave, I ask for the white light to appear, and that's that. I don't know how I'm able to do this, and I don't question it. This is my gift, and it's why I'm here. I've been talking to ghosts for as long as I can remember.

"What are some of the signs that you are not alone? A ghost may move or hide objects, disrupt your appliances, or make noises. Some people experience cold chills, goose bumps, or a feeling of uneasiness. Occasionally people will see orbs, or apparitions."

Lawson paused, and stared straight at me. So did everyone else. Oh no.

"There are various methods of protecting yourself from ghosts drawing on your energy. The easiest way is to surround yourself with white light before you enter a high energy area. Going to the supermarket? Or the movie theater? Visualize the white light, and you will be safe. Other methods include smudging with herbs such as sage and rosemary, or circling your home with sea salt. My new book outlines these practices in more detail.

"Now, the second kind of haunting that we'll be dealing with tonight is called a residual haunting, or psychic imprint.

"Unlike an intelligent haunting, which I've just described, a psychic imprint is an echo, playback, or recording, of past events. The phenomenon does not involve a ghost who is aware of the earthly plane or attempting to communicate with humans. Rather, it is the replaying of vibrations which have embedded themselves in a certain place. The recording is played over and over on a continuous loop for a period of time—sometimes centuries, often at the same hour of the night or day.

"The imprint may manifest itself in a variety of ways, including visual, auditory, or olfactory sensations. The event tends to be one that was traumatic, but can also be life altering in some way, or merely an often repeated occurrence.

"Common examples are observing apparitions walking the same path regularly—up or down staircases, for instance, or along hallways. One may hear moaning, crying, screaming, or heavy breathing. Doors may slam, footsteps may be heard. If a human form is observed, it never interacts with its audience. If anything, it is oblivious to onlookers.

"There is no scientific explanation for these events, and nothing so far has been discovered that removes them. One theory is that the crystals in the earth actually store the vibrations like a battery, and then replay the occurrence.

"In my opinion, psychic imprints are about powerful human emotion. This explains why battlefields are common locations of residual hauntings. Here in Scotland the brutal fighting at Glencoe and Culloden are examples, as are the sites of the Normandy beaches in France—and Gettysburg, Pennsylvania, from the American Civil War.

"No one knows what triggers a residual haunting. It might be the emotional reaction of an onlooker, a similarly traumatic event, or merely the weather. Some people are just more receptive and aware than others.

"Remember, there is no conscious effort of a spirit to communicate with humans in a residual haunting. This is true whether it has been seen, smelt, heard, or merely felt at some level. Unlike intelligent hauntings, there is no danger of energy being siphoned off from humans, or animals."

"In closing, I should tell you that there are some who claim that *all* hauntings are imprints—that ghosts are never sentient. Frankly, I think this theory is nonsense. I've conducted hundreds of clearings over the years, and just about every ghost I met was able to relay information about something that happened *after* he or she had passed. How could an imprint do that? But again, I'm always willing to be proved wrong."

Lawson glanced around the room. "I'll take a few questions before my book signing begins," he said.

"What about children?" An Englishwoman asked. "Do you see many young ghosts?"

"Not until they were about four when they died," Lawson replied. "I have an idea about that—perhaps the really little ones have no reason to stay around. They remember life on the Other Side, and they're happy to return."

A man in the back asked about ghost animals. "The ones I come across are mostly pets," Lawson said, "But I've seen a few horses, and the occasional wild animal. They're tougher to get to move on because I have trouble communicating with them."

"Is there any truth to cold spots?"

"Sometimes," Lawson admitted. "Although in my experience, there's more of a pressure change when a ghost comes into a room. Like a car passing you on the highway. I've found that the larger the number of ghosts, the more energy is drained from humans in any given space. There does not seem to be any regular pattern. Some ghosts simply require more energy than others."

A young woman in the third row stood up. "Are there any ghosts here with us, right now?"

Lawson smiled. "This is a very popular question, and I've promised the hotel management that I would say the following—it is very rare that I walk into an area with this much human history, and it does not have at least one ghost."

I took a deep breath. "I count three," I whispered to Luke.

"What?" Luke turned and looked at me in shock. "How do you know that?"

"Because I can see them too," I replied. "Always could."

Luke ordered a Bailey's on the rocks for me, and a whisky for himself. We sat by the big windows in the bar, overlooking the bend in the river.

"OK, Emma," he began, and there was an edge to his voice. "How long have we known each other? Nearly a year? You couldn't have mentioned in passing that you can see ghosts?"

I worked hard to keep the panic out of my voice. "I'm sorry that you're upset, Luke. I didn't hold back this information from lack of trust, or respect. You already know that I'm into Shamanism, and witchcraft; that I'm telepathic, and empathic, and that I often have unusual dreams. I just figured that I'd let you know the rest in increments."

"The rest? You mean there's more?" Luke swallowed the remainder of his drink and signaled the waiter for another.

"Just the ghosts," I replied. "So far, anyway. This stuff always develops for me over time. I didn't have past life dreams when I was a kid, and I still can't see spirits, or angels, or anything dramatic like that."

"But why didn't you tell me?" Luke demanded. "I live on a three hundred year old family farm. The property must be loaded with ghosts!"

"It is," I assured him.

"Great."

"Look. I was a weird little girl. My family didn't know how to deal with me as it was. I always preferred books and drawing to playing with other kids. I liked outdoor sports that I could do alone, but not team sports. I found it easier to talk to adults, rather than children my own age. When my parents discovered me reading a copy of *Anna Karenina* when I was in third grade, I think they flipped out, and never really recovered. Too many of my dreams turned out to be prophetic. I just couldn't tell them about the ghosts. I was always a head taller than everyone else in the lower grades, and much stronger. It wasn't until high school, when the boys began to catch up, that I felt more like a girl, and less like a freak."

"So you were afraid of my reaction?"

"Yes! Frankly, I'm just careful about telling people. Who'd want to hire a lawyer who could choose ghost hunting as an alternative career?"

Luke processed. "Who else knows? Your sister?"

I shook my head. "Angela knows. So does Sophie. But that's it."

"Can you talk to ghosts too? Like this guy tonight—Hector Lawson?"

"They talk to me. Most of the time I tune them out, but when I'm focused, well, let's just say that I've learned some pretty interesting things." I grinned. "I've found that my gift can be quite useful in court."

"That's why Lawson looked straight at you during his speech! But how did he know?" Luke asked, confused. "He said he wasn't psychic."

"One of the ghosts told him. The one standing near us in the nineteenth century suit. He caught me staring at him."

Luke started laughing. "Never a dull moment with you, is there Emma? I'm in a constant state of *what's next?* whenever we're together."

"But we're OK, right?" I asked nervously. "Has anything changed with us because of this?"

"More in love than ever, not to worry," Luke replied. "No more secrets, though. All right? And please don't feel compelled to inform me of every spook that's hiding in our room, or hanging out in the shower."

"Deal."

Luke signed the check. "Let's go upstairs. I'm ready for our trip to the Hebrides tomorrow morning. I feel like I've absorbed enough ancestral spirit—for quite some time."

That night I dreamed that I am back at Vanderbilt University. It's the end of my freshman year, and I'm studying for finals in the library. Rich, my boyfriend, suddenly appears at my carrel. He dumps his backpack on top of my work, and announces that he can't date me any longer. His high school girlfriend has just been killed in a car accident, and he has to attend the funeral.

CHAPTER TWO

The Irish Play

After nearly twenty years of practicing law on the congested—and financially obsessed—coast of Connecticut, I had divested myself of my marriage, and moved up to Litchfield County, in the northwest corner of the state, to become a country lawyer. Over a year later, it was a tremendous relief that I was no longer commuting the hour plus each way to the Westport office. My law partner Denise Frederickson and I had hired Tina Rosen as a new associate to take my place in Fairfield County, and I had opened a satellite office in Bridge Hollow.

Established well before the American Revolution, the town of Bridge Hollow was a historical landmark that straddled both sides of the Hunterbury River, and was also home to two famous boarding schools—Tallmadge Academy, and Bridge Hollow School. I was to teach classes in Evidence and U.S. History, beginning that fall.

My teenage Mentee from Tallmadge, Carlie Graham, was about to enter her junior year. An ambitious student and exceptional athlete, Carlie and I had become close the previous year, and I had hired her to help out in my new office during free periods from school.

Luke and I returned from Scotland shortly before the start of the fall semester. I was immediately inundated with new projects.

The Bridge Hollow Country Playhouse was putting on a production of *Over Heath and Glen,* a romantic comedy that had done well in Great Britain, and was attracting interest in the United States. The heroine, Amanda, is an American artist in her forties. Healing from a failed marriage, Amanda sets off on a painting tour of Ireland, determined to recover control of her life. In a town near Dublin she meets a local curmudgeon named Alec, who offers to be her driver and guide. Alec is dealing with some emotional challenges of his own, and through a series of humorous misadventures Amanda and Alec fall in love. The story, although not outstanding for originality, was nevertheless a crowd pleaser, chiefly because of its snappy dialogue, its mystical setting, and the dramatic transformations of both characters by the end of the play.

As a member of the theater association, I had been asked to help out with the extra scenery touch ups. Carlie squatted near me, her reporter's notebook clutched in her left hand.

"You think they've got enough green?" Carlie asked, just a trifle sarcastic. "And how many different ways can you paint a rock wall?"

I took the hint. "You don't have to do this. Go interview one of the actors for your article."

The Playhouse had been built in the early nineteenth century, and numerous renovations had occurred over the decades. Approaching the bicentennial of its opening, the theater had endured yet another facelift, and Carlie was reporting on its renewed spirit for the next issue of *The Bridge Hollow News.*

"OK. The guy who plays the innkeeper said he'd have time today. I'll be back for lunch."

At noon I stood up and stretched. I was covered with dust from sitting on the floor for so long, and my hands and arms were speckled with various earth tones. I retrieved my purse, and set off in the direction of the nearest facilities. Behind the stage was a passageway which led to a series of rooms for storing scenery, props, and costumes. The hall then made an L turn, and opened into another wing of the building, which housed dressing rooms and offices. A traditional greenroom was the first door on the left.

I walked in, and was immediately transported to the Victorian era. Old theater posters and cast photos in frames crowded the walls. Brass lamps with green glass globes stood on antique tables, and yellowed scripts were bound in leather and stacked in the bookcase. I picked one up and flipped through the pages. It was Oscar Wilde's *An Ideal Husband*. Notes had been made by hand in red pencil down the margins. The play had been performed in 1921.

Next to the bookcase was a glass encased cabinet, which contained show memorabilia. There were the usual fans and yellowed elbow length gloves. Old playbills. Feather shaped pens, charming china inkwells in amusing shapes, and boxes of theater make-up. In the center of the middle shelf was a gold pocket watch, with attached chain and fob. I bent over to read the faded card, handwritten in beautiful black calligraphy.

> *Gold watch belonging to Hugh Murdoch (1890–1922).*
> *Played Arthur, Lord Goring in Oscar Wilde's* An Ideal
> Husband *at the Bridge Hollow Country Playhouse in*
> *1921. Was arrested, tried, and subsequently hanged for*
> *the murder of his fiancée Fenella Cameron, who played*
> *Mabel. Hunter case with jeweled movement. Interior*
> *of case inscribed "Hold On To Dreams." Fob is the*
> *Murdoch clan coat of arms—two ravens hanging upright,*
> *transfixed by one arrow through both heads horizontally.*

I sat in one of the armchairs. I could hear the actors in the corridor, making their way to their various rooms to get ready for rehearsal, and experienced a flashback to my days at The Warwick Playshop, when college students had been asked to fill in the chorus for professional summer productions. I felt the itch of the fishnet stockings that I wore for my small role in *Annie Get Your Gun*, and the pinch of an ill fitted dress for *Bye Bye Birdie*. Even further back, my debut as Anna in *The King and I*. My high school Drama Club had performed the musical in my sophomore year, and I had belted out *Getting to Know You* in my alto voice, with a determination that enabled me to just barely hit the high notes, night after night.

Thank goodness nobody in Bridge Hollow knew that I could sing.

A disturbance erupted in the corridor. Clare Rowler, the actress who played Amanda, was in distress.

"Has anyone seen my wristwatch?" She barked. "I left it on the vanity in my dressing room."

"What does it look like, honey?"

"It's a Cartier dammit! Gold rectangle. Brown leather band," she snarled. "I've had it forever."

There was a general murmur of forced concern.

"Well, whoever has it, I want it returned!" Clare snapped. "And who the hell has been burning incense back here? I'm allergic to lavender!"

"That was subtle," a member of the cast remarked, a moment later.

"Sure was," replied the voice of the Stage Manager. "I'll check around."

I took a seat in front to watch the dress rehearsal. Carlie had texted me that she was running late for lunch.

The stage was set for the haunted inn scene. Amanda and Alec are sleeping in adjoining rooms, but once Amanda discovers that she is sharing her bedchamber with the ghost of a previous innkeeper, a complicated dance between the two rooms ensues, ending, predictably, with the two of them in Alec's bed.

"This is funny," Carlie whispered in my ear.

"London agrees with you," I whispered back.

"That's some nightgown she's wearing," Carlie remarked. "You can pretty much see everything."

At that moment the current innkeeper and several other guests rush into Alec's room, and more chaos results, as Amanda attempts to explain her screaming. Additional energetic movement of the cast, and suddenly the spaghetti straps of Amanda's negligée give way, and she is standing onstage with nothing but a lace edged thong adorning her person.

"Nice figure," Carlie said drily. "I didn't know that there was nudity in this play."

"I don't think there is," I replied, as Clare shrieked, grabbed her crumpled wardrobe, and sprinted offstage.

I sat next to Lacy Basdin just before the call of the family short calendar in court on Monday morning. She moved her bulging briefcase and flashed me a smile.

"Heavy docket?" I asked, grateful for my one agreement to report to the judge.

"Three contested cases," she said, taking a few deep breaths. "Constant battlefields to contend with." She paused, and added quietly, "here, and at the office."

"I've heard that Esther can be tough to work for," I replied carefully. "I've noticed that she rarely keeps an associate for long. What's it been for you? Over a year? That's got to be some kind of record."

"I've watched ten people come and go since I was hired," she whispered. "Not all lawyers, but the same story every time. Esther starts out treating you like a best friend, and then suddenly, for no reason, you're the enemy, and she doesn't rest until she eradicates you." She shivered. "It's horrible, wondering who the next target will be. I'm ashamed to admit that I feel relieved when it's someone else."

"But you never know when it will be your turn," I finished for her.

"Exactly."

"We all thought it would be easier for you once she was elected to the State Senate. She'd be around less."

Lacy shook her head. "So did we. But instead, she just blasts us electronically while she's in Hartford, and then we all dread the days when she swoops into the office, to abuse us in person. Esther enjoys making people afraid of her—even the clients."

"She sounds like a raging psycho. Why don't you leave?"

"I'm a single mother with a toddler, and my family is my support system. I can't be commuting long distances, and jobs aren't plentiful up here these days." She whispered. "She knows that I need the money. I do a lot of yoga to try and decompress. I live for the weekends. And by Sunday afternoon I'm a wreck, working on files for court on Monday, and anticipating being berated for everything I did wrong once I get back to the office. If it isn't exactly what she would have done—and it never is—Esther gets really nasty. Personal nasty. Sometimes I think that I'm losing my mind, I'm so miserable."

"All rise please!" The marshal announced. Everyone in the courtroom stood as the judge climbed the steps to the bench, sat down, and began going through the calendar.

"Ready with an agreement, your honor," I responded, when my case was called. I looked over at Lacy, and was troubled by the fear in her eyes. Esther MacInerney had a reputation for combativeness, but for some reason clients translated her offensive behavior to good lawyering, and continued to hire her.

Luke and I had tickets for opening night of *Over Heath and Glen.*

"Have you heard about the problems they've been having at the theater?" Luke asked as we drove through town. "The Management is saying that there's a practical joker sabotaging the play. I've even heard the word poltergeist mentioned. At first it was just the lead players who were being attacked, but now it seems as though most of the cast has suffered, in one way or another."

"That explains what happened at the dress rehearsal!" I replied.

"Actors can be superstitious people," Luke said. "Even in the twenty-first century. The cast is starting to refer to this show as 'The Irish Play,' and making *Macbeth*-like gestures to ward off evil spirits."

"Who told you that?"

"One of the owners is an old friend. He's very worried about tonight's opening performance."

"We'll get our money's worth then," I grinned.

We were well into Act One, and the house was packed. A fast paced Irish reel is playing as Alec and Amanda, traveling in Alec's old Land Rover, nearly collide with an offstage flock of sheep (sounds of bleating) and run off the road into a bog. The characters scramble to retrieve their belongings, and the car (cleverly managed from underneath the stage) begins to sink. There is a very funny interchange as Amanda's first priority is her beloved easel, while Alec is clearly, and more practically, concerned about his vehicle. The audience laughed gleefully as Alec attempts to throw Amanda's paint box into the bog after the disappearing Land Rover.

Suddenly, a small lamb with a bell around its neck scrambled onstage, and peered out at the crowd.

"Head's up!" Luke exclaimed, nudging me. "I don't think this is in the script."

"No," I replied. "How are they going to fix it?"

The lights went out to change the set, and when they came up again a few minutes later, the lamb had disappeared.

The play continued.

Amanda and Alec are walking along the coast toward a fishing village, with the bulk of Amanda's gear strapped to various portions of Alec's anatomy. They argue, as Amanda wants to stop to paint the picturesque town, and Alec's one and only goal is locating a tow truck. The tone is becoming slightly more romantic, as they have lunch at a pub that overlooks the sea (mystical Irish tunes and sound effects of pounding waves).

The farcical theme returns, however, as one of the pub patrons offers his team of draft horses to haul the Land Rover out of the bog, and Amanda works at her easel near the beach. Heavy hoofs clip clop

across stone as Amanda smiles to herself and sets her palate. In the next scene, Alec returns with his vehicle showing signs of abuse, but still running. He and Amanda convince the morally rigid landlord and his wife that they are on their honeymoon, in order to spend the night in the only available room for miles. As the first Act closes, it's clear that our heroes are about to put themselves, and the audience, out of their collective misery, and consummate the relationship.

Just as the lights went down there was a loud crash, followed by screams. The audience laughed appreciatively.

At Intermission Luke bought us two glasses of sparkling wine, and we managed to find a small table on the porch.

"OK," he said, handing me my champagne flute. "Let me see if I've got the plot of this thing nailed, Emma."

"Shoot."

"Amanda is a control freak who has just unloaded an unhappy marriage. Do we know why it was unhappy, by the way?"

"She alludes to the fact that her husband was indifferent to her needs, but beyond that, no."

"She probably drove him to self medicate," Luke concluded, "but we may find out in due course. Alec, on the other hand, is a cranky sourpuss, who won't give Amanda an inch on any topic, and disparages everything she stands for."

"But still sleeps with her," I reminded him.

"True," Luke conceded. "Are we aware yet of Alec's issue, or issues?"

"Not really. He mutters a lot, and his accent is difficult to understand sometimes. So far I've gleaned that he's a songwriter who has lost his Muse, and doesn't think much of women in general, or of American women in particular."

"I got that too. Who wrote this play?"

"No idea. Probably a Brit."

A large balding man in a dark blue suit moved over to our table. Luke got up, and introduced us.

"Emma, this is Jerome Forester, one of the owners of the theater. Jerry, this is Emma Carbury."

"A pleasure, ma'am," Jerry said, pulling over a chair and sitting down. "What do you think of the play?"

"It's a lot of fun," I replied, truthfully. "I can't remember when I've enjoyed a performance this much. The actors' comedic timing is perfect."

Jerry frowned. "They're not feeling too jolly just now, I'm afraid. I'm sure you both heard that parting crash as the curtain came down."

"Not in the script?" Luke asked.

"No. Nor was the little baa baa by the bog. A section of the set got loose, and almost crushed Tom Colman, who plays Alec."

"Is he all right?" I asked, my mind immediately leaping to the legal.

"He's fine, and the curtain will go up on schedule." Jerry paused. "I just don't know what's going on with this playhouse," he said. "But if it continues, someone's going to get hurt."

Amanda and Alec are touring a medieval castle. Several diverting incidents occur whereby priceless antiques barely escape destruction by Amanda, who is a hazard to any item that is not nailed down. After Amanda has knocked a fellow tourist into an ancient well, Alec decides to remove her to a safer location.

In the next scene they stop at a local fair, and Amanda has a reading done by a fortuneteller. She is informed that she is at a major crossroads in her life, and that she must consider her options carefully. Dazed, Amanda emerges from the psychic's booth, to find Alec presenting her with a prize that he has just won tossing coconuts. They stare at each other with enlightened appreciation, just as Amanda's cell phone rings. It's her ex husband, and he wants her back. She agrees to cut her trip short and return to the States. Alec's shoulders slump, the lights come down, and the scene shifts.

Alec and Amanda are moving down the Shannon River in a hired cabin cruiser. Amanda is sketching in the bow. Alec is leaning over the stern, looking pensive. (Sound of water lapping at the gunwales). He sighs, and makes his way toward Amanda. He proceeds to tell her the story of his life.

"Here we go," Luke whispered to me. "Bet you dinner that he was left at the altar just before Act One, which is why he hasn't been able to write any new music."

"Damn, you're good," I said, as Alec's sad tale unfolds.

"If the boat sinks, I want my money back."

But the Fates finally appear to be smiling on Alec and Amanda. The play ends at Dublin Airport, when just as Amanda is about to check her luggage, Alec swings her easel from his back, produces a ring, and proposes.

"When did he have time to go to a jewelry store?" I protested.

"Maybe it belonged to the ex fiancée," Luke replied, "and he carries it around with him as a memento."

The curtain comes down as the engaged couple argues about where they're going to live; in Ireland, or back in her hometown of Baltimore.

"Not exactly Jane Austen," I remarked. "But I was amused throughout, which is unusual."

Luke and I were invited to the cast party, as guests of the Management. The event was held at the home of one of Jerry's business partners.

"Actors make me nervous," I admitted to Luke in the car. "They build careers on faking emotions for audiences. How can one possibly take them seriously in a social setting?"

"I know," Luke agreed. "It's amazing when you think that most of the time these people can barely stand each other."

"It's why I rarely look at DVD extras," I said, as we walked to the front door. "I prefer the manufactured fantasy, not the reality. I don't want to think about some shattering love scene set in the nineteenth century, surrounded by cameramen in jeans and a director making them repeat the same lines, over and over. How do they do it?"

"Training," Luke replied. "And, I would imagine, a certain degree of emotional tune out."

"My point exactly," I concluded, as we stepped inside.

I have never been a fan of modern architecture. The house was a colossus in white stucco, and the furniture was leather and chrome. Glass tables adorned with unrecognizable sculptures and stark floral arrangements were placed at various positions throughout the rooms. The floors were covered with faux animal skins. Enormous unframed modern art canvasses were suspended from the ceiling, and the fireplace, with no mantel, was gas burning.

"Yikes," I muttered to Luke. "Where's the bar?"

The cast arrived as I restored myself with another glass of champagne.

"Town Hall is well represented," Luke said, indicating a gathering of Bridge Hollow officials by the appetizer table. "Do you know any of these people?"

"Just the Selectman," I grimaced. "And the Town Attorney. I had a rather heated discussion with them regarding a land use case several months ago. They were less than helpful."

"Unfortunately I deal with most of them regularly because of my work," Luke replied, "and they've seen me. Let's get this over with."

"Luke!" First Selectman Chester Shea extended his hand. "Do you know our Chief of Police? Ernie Marino, this is Luke MacLaren—the best landscape architect around. We've been trying for years to get Luke's help with town property."

"It would be a conflict of interest," Luke explained, patiently. "I have to testify in front of land agencies for my private clients."

"Always the professional!" Town Attorney Norman Daley chuckled sycophantically.

I finished my champagne and gazed longingly at the bar.

Luke made the introductions. "This is Wendy Bowman, the Town Treasurer, and Leonard Abel is Chair of the Conservation Commission."

"Ah yes," Abel said, grasping my hand. "You're new to the area, aren't you? Recently up here from the Gold Coast?"

"Correct," I replied. "A little over a year."

"I hear that you're popular with the students," the Chief of Police remarked. "My daughter Suzanna is looking forward to your U.S. History class."

"So you're the famous Evidence teacher!" Wendy Bowman exclaimed, too loudly. "I know about you from a few of the Tallmadge Board members. Because of you a big crisis was avoided last year."

"Yes," I said quietly. "And I'm sure that the TA Board would prefer to keep it that way. Please excuse me."

"We'll hold Luke for just a moment, though," Chester Shea replied. "I've been hoping for a chat with him for some time."

I had my flute refilled and took a seat by the doors that opened out to the garden. It was a lovely evening. The fragrance from the flowering hostas was intoxicating. A familiar voice floated in from beyond the hydrangeas.

"I want to know what's going on, Alan!" Clare Rowler, who played Amanda, was vehement.

"So do I Clare!" Alan Moore, the director, sounded annoyed. "But the backers are nervous. Until we get this crazy situation straightened out, they're not even going to consider our next move."

"Are we getting any attention from Broadway? How long are we stuck doing backwoods towns like this?"

"I'm not in the loop, Clare. You have to talk to the producers."

There were sounds of rustling branches. I assumed that Clare was exercising her considerable charms on her director.

"I'll see what I can do," he said finally, breathing heavily. More rustling. "But remember, it's not my decision. Ultimately it's the people with the money who make the rules."

Luke appeared at my right with two plates.

"I just had an interesting conversation," he said in a low voice.

"What do you mean?" I popped a stuffed mushroom into my mouth.

"The Town is considering some big changes," he replied. "They've hired an engineer from New York, and tonight they were feeling me out—trying to get me to come on board."

His tone got my attention.

"I told them no," he continued. "But I'm worried, all the same."

"Can you disclose the property in question?" I asked carefully.

He nodded. "We were just there. The big lakefront parcel behind the theater that's open to the public, and maintained by the Town. They're considering breaking it up and selling it off. It's worth a fortune."

We pulled up to Luke's garage just before midnight.

"I'm going to the barn to give Joy a quick kiss," I told him. "I'll be right in."

Walking deliberately in my heels I moved down the aisle until I came to Joy's stall. The lighting was low, but her pink and white muzzle shone in the dark. I rolled the door back and ran my hand along her neck, and then scratched behind her left ear. She delicately removed the mint from my hand, and nickered gratefully.

We both watched as one of Luke's colonial ancestors walked out of the tack room, and disappeared right in front of us.

CHAPTER THREE

Jefferson's Women

My new marital mediation clients arrived at the office just before two. I had them sign the usual agreement: they would behave respectfully to each other and to me; they acknowledged that I was a neutral facilitator and would not represent either one of them; and that neither would call me to testify in the event of a divorce trial.

Marielle was the Type A partner in the marriage. Pete, a big man, sat quietly in his chair. I was tempted to offer him a magazine.

"We've decided that I'm going to quit my job, and help run Pete's business," Marielle announced. "And I want it to be in writing that this was a joint decision, and that it won't come back to haunt me later on."

I decided to reframe the issue. "Your concern is the ability to generate adequate independent income in the event of a divorce?"

She bristled. "Correct. I don't want to hear that I didn't pull my weight in the marriage, in case he runs off with some female half his age, and tries to take the house away from me."

I looked over at Pete. "What is your understanding of the agreement between you and your wife?"

He shrugged. "She's tired of her job, and I need help with the office stuff. It makes sense." He let out a long breath. "But I don't understand all the drama she's generating. In fifteen years I've never let her down. Why do we suddenly need a contract?"

"Marielle?"

"He's at that age," she replied, slapping her hand on the table. "It's been happening to everyone I know. It happened to my mother. I don't want to invest a third of my life in this marriage to be told by some guy in a robe that I didn't contribute my fair share to the group effort. I want security."

I reminded myself that I was not a psychotherapist. "Your decision to mediate this proposed change in your work status is based on the negative experiences of other people that you know?"

Marielle looked confused. "Yes. When you put it like that…. Yes." She registered defiance. Her husband sighed.

"I'm more than happy to help you work out this agreement," I replied, looking at them both. "Shall we get started? Let's begin with details of what you're each doing now. We call it full disclosure."

"Fine!" Marielle snapped. "Let's see if he tells you. I'll bet anything that he's hiding cash somewhere. My father did."

Our Book Club met on Saturday morning, at my house on Lake Washington, to discuss *The Women Jefferson Loved* by Virginia Scharff.

Denise, Tina, and Dottie—from the Westport office of our law firm—drove up together in Tina's SUV. I helped them haul two kayaks down from the roof rack. Angela, my best friend since our Ridgefield High days, pulled up behind Tina with two more boats.

"Let's get started ladies!" Eliot called from the dock, already in her bathing suit. Like Denise, Eliot had been a law school classmate. "I'm really here to play in the water."

"Abby's sitting in my kayak," Tina called.

Abby, my tough little Lakeland Terrier, was enthusiastic about boating. I tucked her under my arm like a football and followed Tina up the flagstone path.

"Did anyone else feel like hitting our third President over the head with a frying pan?" Dottie inquired, as we assembled on the porch.

"I admit that Jefferson's personal life was worrisome from the moral perspective," Angela agreed.

"The big question is—does it change how we feel about him as a Founding Father?" Tina asked.

"He was *certainly* accomplished when it came to fathering," Denise replied, sarcastically. "I counted six births with his wife Martha, known as Patty. And at least seven with his slave Sally Hemings, who was his wife's half sister."

"And aunt to his white kids," Eliot added. She picked up a turkey wrap. "What a family!"

"If it's all true—and there seems to be plenty of documentation to support Professor Scharff's conclusions—then three generations of these people lived on that beautiful mountain perpetuating a lie that is absolutely mind blowing," I commented. "The author writes that Jefferson's ultimate goal was to erect an impenetrable wall to separate his public persona from his domestic life."

"A goal which failed," Denise said.

"Let's start with the obvious," Angela prompted. "Who were the women in Jefferson's life?"

Dottie replied: "His mother, Jane; his wife, Martha; his slave/sister-in-law/mistress, Sally; his two daughters who survived to adulthood—Patsy and Polly—and then his granddaughters."

"As a lawyer it was extremely difficult for me to read this book," Tina admitted. "Although it moved very quickly, and I like Scharff's style."

"What bothered you Tina?" Angela asked.

"What didn't?" Eliot barked. "Childbirth in eighteenth century Virginia was very often a death sentence. Jefferson, knowing that it is dangerous for his fragile wife to become pregnant, keeps knocking her up until she expires from the effort. Then, he drags his daughters to Paris and starts screwing the teenage Sally, who is there as a maid."

"And who would have been a free woman by French law," I added.

"Then Jefferson yanks them all back to Virginia, promising Sally that their children, although born into slavery, will eventually go free," Denise said.

"But Sally remains legally enslaved for the rest of her life." Dottie remarked.

"He refuses to allow his daughters, or granddaughters, any formal education or career training," Eliot continued.

"So that when TJ dies, leaving enormous debt—his unmarried female descendents are homeless, with no means of supporting themselves." Tina said. "They have to rely on the men in the family."

"All because Jefferson felt that it was his duty, as grand patriarch, to look after them all," Denise concluded.

"Lots of love going on there," Eliot snarled.

"OK," Angela said quickly. "There's some pretty serious feeling swirling around this porch." She paused. "I agree that to educated, professional women in the twenty-first century, the Jefferson family story is pretty horrifying. Let's try to approach these issues from a historical standpoint."

"Jefferson, and all of the Founders," I began, "lived in an era when white men with property were deemed supreme, and everyone else was considered unimportant. Society worked for centuries to keep this myth protected."

"Hence the brutality toward African and Native Americans in this country," Denise said.

"And *all* women," Eliot added, still furious.

"I studied this stuff in high school," Tina remarked, "and then again in college. One thing I have never understood—how in the world could these white slaveholding families reconcile the day to day intimacy of having enslaved persons in their homes, and living and working on their land—and then sell them like furniture when they needed to?"

"I don't know," Angela said slowly. "It would take a kind of compartmental thinking that I couldn't begin to imagine."

"I think it's just as Emma said," Denise added. "They were protecting their family status, their way of life, all that they knew. Everything else went under the bus. They had priorities that were set in stone for centuries. Domination and control. Wealth was only the visible rationalization."

"Meaning that they got off on being tyrants," Eliot concluded, grimly.

"Yes."

"They were terrified of slave insurrection, remember," I said. "The cruelty was probably meant as some sort of deterrent for conspiracy and rebellion."

"Maintaining control over the larger population that might rise up and destroy them." Tina remarked.

Dottie said: "For decades historians have commented on the fact that the author of the Declaration of Independence, who wrote so passionately about freedom and happiness for all, bought and sold human property."

"He also kept the white women in his life firmly under his thumb," Eliot noted. "His letters to his daughters, especially Patsy, made me squirm with discomfort."

"She was a surrogate wife to him, you mean," Dottie agreed. "I had the same reaction. You *know* what we'd call that now. Patsy's husband could never compete."

"But Scharff's argument is that TJ loved these women—all of them. Much of what he produced as a Founder, and later as President, was based on his attachment to the domestic side of his life," Denise said, clearly hoping, perhaps unrealistically, to steer the group away from emotionally charged issues.

"There are many definitions of love," I said. "But oppression has never been one of them."

"According to Scharff, Jefferson believed that women were naturally dependent on men," Tina said. "Women were expected to give men their unquestioning obedience—no argument. They were loyal and subservient and even physically submissive. The limited weapons they had at their disposal were manipulation and misdirection."

"Women were passive aggressive," Dottie added. "It was the only way to get what they wanted, if ever. They had to play the game. They learned to live in denial, and to master distance from their enslaved shadow family."

"Jefferson liked his women docile," Eliot said. "Gentle and loving. Excellent wives and mothers. Impeccable hostesses. He really believed that women were happiest when they confined themselves to home and family. Domestic tranquility was top priority."

"Don't ask—don't tell," Dottie quoted.

"And remember the English law of coverture," I remarked. "We touched on it last year when we discussed the Brontë sisters. A woman's property passed to her husband upon her marriage. *Unless* they had a prenuptial agreement."

"TJ's mother-in-law had a marriage contract," Denise pointed out. "And as a result, Jefferson's wife Patty inherited her half siblings after her father's death."

"But why didn't Patty have a similar pre-nup?" Dottie asked. "We know she didn't, because Sally and her family belonged to Thomas after the wedding. Why did Patty give up her rights?"

"Scharff says that Patty *wanted* to marry Jefferson," Tina replied. "But she didn't *need* to—she had a fortune of her own. Maybe she knew that subjecting herself to financial control was the only option she had to make their marriage work."

"It gave Jefferson the upper hand," Eliot snorted. "Which is what made him happy."

"And Patty's significant resources made TJ a very wealthy man," I added. "She doubled his fortune—in land and slaves."

There was a pause. Dottie accepted another chocolate chip cookie.

"Of the six of us sitting here, three are married, and three are divorced. What about it ladies? Would any of you do it again?"

Eliot laughed. "Honestly? I was just thinking how envious I am of Emma's arrangement with Luke. No responsibility. No legal tie. She doesn't have to do a blessed thing that she doesn't want to. And if she decides to back out, the State has no standing to interfere. I'd have to vote no."

"Same here," Denise admitted. "And I love my family. But what is it about being married that is so appealing to people who aren't? Do they seriously consider it to be a secure way to live? It's actually double the trouble. I have to think of everything in terms of 'us,' or 'we.' It's never just about what I want."

"So why are twenty-first century women still getting married?" Tina wondered. "I've been divorced for five years. I date, and I have a terrific circle of friends. I don't think that I'd ever give up my independence again."

"What about you, Dottie?" Angela asked. "Since you posed the question."

Dottie smiled. "I'm very content, frankly. Tim and I understand each other perfectly, and I do as I please most of the time. I sincerely believe that the decision is everything to do with the person you choose. Maybe that was Mrs. Jefferson's reasoning. She was so crazy about her husband that the rest of it—financial control—just didn't matter to her. She had options, and she chose commitment to a man who was emotionally stuck when it came to hearth and home. He wanted the ideal."

"But in the end," Tina reminded us, "Jefferson's goal of an agrarian utopia, for the nation, and especially for his family, failed miserably. Monticello was sold off after his death. His family had to relocate. And thirty-five years later, the country was split by Civil War."

Angela looked at me. "I know what you're going to say, Em."

I nodded. "Karma. The ripple effect. The energy that you send out to the Universe comes back three-fold. Jefferson didn't walk the talk. So his family paid the price."

My new students had assembled around the large conference table on the first floor of Barlow Hall, one of the oldest classroom buildings at Tallmadge Academy. At least half of the group was composed of young men from Bridge Hollow School, located across the Hunterbury River.

"This is an upper level U.S. History course, which will cover in depth the period beginning with the American Revolution, up to and including the War of 1812—our two battles with the British. The emphasis will be on the formation and development of the new Republic, and the political tensions that erupted during that time. We will be examining themes—rather than following a particular timeline.

"I recognize many of you from my last year's Evidence class. New students should note that I expect you to be prepared for every meeting, and that forty percent of your grade is based on classroom participation. Your exams will be take home essays. Having said that, let's talk about government. Thomas Jefferson referred to it as a necessary evil. What is it, and why do we think that we need it?"

Everyone laughed. Adam raised his hand. "Government provides us with protection, through the armed forces. It directs taxation, and commerce. It enforces rules regarding health and education. It manages foreign affairs."

"Those are all functions of government," I replied, "whether or not they are actually carried out. But what is it? What is the definition of government?"

"The branches are the executive, the legislative, and the judicial," Heather offered, brightly.

"In this country, yes. But that still doesn't answer my question."

I looked around the circle of blank faces.

"OK, let's make this simple. Recall the verbs that Adam just used—

directs, enforces, manages. What are some others? How about regulates, restrains, restricts, administers, and determines? Government is Authority. It never creates anything on its own, but serves as a control of productive human energy. Its power comes from the use of force, which is sanctioned by the people being governed. When the same people decide to withdraw their consent, what happens?"

"Revolution," Jon replied. "Violent—or non-violent."

"Exactly. Now the next important question. Is force the same thing as control?"

"Absolutely not," said Suzanna, with feeling.

I was a bit taken aback. "Well done, Suzie. Can you tell us why?"

"Because all the force in the world can't make you do something that you don't really want to do," Suzie answered, her face red.

I recalled that her father was the Chief of Police. "Excellent. Individuals only have control over themselves, not others. Next question. What are the bare necessities for survival on this planet?"

"Life, liberty, and the pursuit of happiness?" Maddie asked.

I sighed. "We're talking about the basics here, Madeline. Food, clothing, and shelter. Does the government provide any, if not all of these items?"

"No," Rob replied.

"Correct. Remember that government is not here to address your needs. Moreover, it has nothing whatever to do with morality. Authority has absolute monopoly, and no competition. Therefore, government has no motivation to please the general public. Nor must it make a profit—it can run on a deficit, and our taxes make up the difference."

Ed raised his hand. "But what about protection, Ms. Carbury? How could we defend ourselves without government?"

I nodded. "Good point. You've all taken European history, right? What entailed the bulk of your studies? Art and music? Sports? Great works of literature?"

Piper grinned. "War. Years and years of it. In nearly every country."

"Aha! And there you have it."

"What?" Several of the students asked together.

"The primary function of government. Big guns. Note that the *kind* of government is immaterial. Monarchy, Communist state, Democracy, Dictatorship. Now think about the American Revolution. What caused it?"

"The Brits oppressed the colonists with too much taxation," Matt replied. "Americans had no voice in the House of Commons."

"Authority. Parliament tried to control American trade—correct? The inhabitants of the city of Boston, full of irate indignation, began a series of rebellious acts that sparked the battles at Lexington and Concord, and subsequently at Bunker Hill, and the colonies were at war with the British Crown." I paused.

"Historically, what have been the superstitions attached to rulers, which supported the use of force in the past?"

"People believed that rulers were so-called living gods," Ted answered, "like the pharaohs, and the emperors in Rome."

"Some were the supposed agents of God," Cassie added. "Like the divine right kings."

"And others were just self appointed tyrants, usually dictators like Hitler," Rob concluded. "Channeling some kind of mystical power—that only they were entitled to."

"OK, so what we're saying is that the Old World folks believed that Authority—in whatever form—controls individuals. Therefore the American Revolution was a World Revolution of sorts. Why?"

"It made people think!" Kim exclaimed. "And whenever we think beyond ourselves, change happens."

"When people can act freely, the release of energy is terrific—right?" I looked around the room. "Awareness, my friends. Submission to perceived Authority is voluntary. It is so easy to distract people by inducing fear. We live in an age of distraction. If you learn anything from me this year, make it that you start to notice everything around you, and analyze what it really means. Consider who is pulling the strings, and why. When we manage to elect ethical leaders in this country—men and women of integrity, look at the good we can do—for the whole planet!

"Recall Thomas Paine's comments on Ignorance—'once dispelled, it is impossible to re-establish it.' Power is simply knowing what works—and what is best ignored. The American Revolutionaries rebelled against the economic controls that restricted their free will—they fought the feudal social order until the British Regulars arrived in Boston to subdue them.

"Let's talk about the feudal system for a bit. Who can tell me about it?"

"The Sovereign is at the top of the ladder," Megan explained. "The rest of the herd buys into the birth status hierarchy, and the pecking order goes on down the line—royals, then aristocrats like Dukes and Earls. Finally, it's the common folk."

"It's all about who pays rent to whom," Suzie remarked. "So basically, the titled gentry are really just big landlords."

"Hence the derivation of the word," Ed said, in exaggerated clipped tones.

"Everyone knows their place in the class system, and their rights and duties as such—within their class, from birth," Kim continued. "You're evaluated by your place in the social order, and there you stay. At least, that's how it was at the time of the Revolution."

"They did not see themselves as equals," I concluded. "The irony here is that the British Government had nothing to do with establishing the American colonies. It was the trade companies—private money making businesses such as the Massachusetts Bay Company—who obtained charters and sailed west in search of profit. The Crown only became involved later, when trade had to be protected, by force. And so finally, before we start with the Stamp Act, the Boston Tea Party, and other such necessaries of the high school curriculum, what is the definition of freedom?"

Cassie raised her hand. "The ability of every individual to exercise self control and self responsibility."

"Superb, Cassandra. And no authority on the planet can withdraw that ability. It is inalienable."

"Which is where we got into a bit of a row with King George III in 1775," Henry added.

"Alrighty then!" I said, when the laughing had died down. "The American Revolution was a war started by individuals who were fighting for personal freedom. Excellent beginning, people. Remember—if you don't fight for the things that you stand for, you don't really stand for them.

"Now let's talk about the fact that the battle for American independence had no leader."

CHAPTER FOUR

Grave Error

Carlie had done some research at *The Bridge Hollow News* on Hugh Murdoch's murder conviction and subsequent hanging. I went through her notes the following afternoon.

> *Hugh Alexander Murdoch, born 1890 near Stirling in Scotland. Attended Cambridge University and trained for the theater. Over six feet tall with wavy auburn hair and green eyes. Reputation as a Lothario; rumored affairs with married women, and actresses in his company on both sides of the Atlantic. Engaged to be married once—to Fenella Isabel Cameron of Bridge Hollow, Connecticut. Miss Cameron was found stabbed to death at her family mansion in Bridge Hollow in October of 1921; Murdoch's pocket watch was found near the body. Cameron and Murdoch had been co-players in a special production of Oscar Wilde's* An Ideal Husband *at the Bridge Hollow Country Playhouse. Murdoch refused to speak in his own defense, was convicted of murder, and hanged in 1922. Miss Cameron was survived by her older sister, Pauline, who discovered the body. Pauline Cameron continued to live in the house alone until her own death in 1974.*

I decided to stop at Sophie's for some insight before going home that night.

Sophie Sullivan's nursery, *Root and Branch*, specialized in growing and selling herbs—culinary and medicinal—plants that Sophie also used to teach her classes in witchcraft on Friday nights. I found her in the greenhouse, dividing perennials.

"Signing up for another session, Emma? We're doing a demonstration on the many uses for lavender this week." She pulled my hair. "Or do you need information?"

"Both. I've been reading about the Murdoch/Cameron murder."

Sophie washed her hands in the big utility sink and sat down at her potting bench. "Oh yes, the problems with the play. I read about it in the paper. Julie tells me that the pranks continue to occur at the theater. So it wasn't a member of the cast from *Over Heath and Glen?*"

"Apparently not."

"And that's why you're here? You don't think that the poltergeist is still—er—corporeal?"

"I don't know. My question is—could it be both?"

"You mean is it possible that a ghost is influencing a living person to create mischief backstage? Absolutely. Have you seen any activity at the Playhouse?"

"Yes of course. The building is two hundred years old, with plenty of history. But nothing that explains the disturbances. And really, how could a ghost get a lamb with a bell to appear in the middle of Act One?"

"Not on its own, I grant you. What has happened since?"

"Lots of little things, mostly in the kitchen and the office. A mixer was left running at high speed with nothing in it. Books were pulled from shelves when no one was in the room. Radios suddenly shut off—ironically when someone is playing a rock station—and then turn on again to a classical program. Chairs are invisibly dragged around rooms in front of people. Reflections of unknown faces appear in mirrors. All the old fashioned door knobs will start rattling at once. Unpleasant smells with no discernable source—the same thing with a wet spot on the rug in the greenroom. And two items that were more serious. First, a large piece of glass flew out of a door and just missed the head of one of the cleaning crew."

"And second?"

"One of the volunteers was taking a nap in the greenroom. She woke up to a horrible suffocating feeling. She said that she was paralyzed with fear—couldn't move or call out. It was as if someone she couldn't see was lying lengthwise on top of her, crushing her body. Malevolent. That was the word she used. This sensation lasted for about a minute and then disappeared. A definite presence she said. Full of rage, but silent."

"Terrifying. Did anyone believe her?"

"I think Jerry Forester did. One of the owners. But he told her to go to the doctor, just in case the whole episode could be explained scientifically."

Sophie smiled. "And she's fine?"

"Not a blessed thing wrong with her. Does anything suggest itself to you Sophie?"

"It sounds as though someone or something was triggered recently, hence the escalating activity. This is obviously an intelligent haunting. Can you think what the impetus might have been?"

"Perhaps one of the actors in *Over Heath and Glen* made an impression. Clare Rowler was picked on more than anyone else—and her watch was stolen! Or it might be the proposed land deal that the town leaders are trying to shove through the Conservation Commission. The park was used by the actor colony for decades—since the early nineteenth century." I had a sudden inspiration. "Could it be the announcement that *An Ideal Husband* is returning this summer—as part of the bicentennial celebration of the theater? It's the first time since Hugh Murdoch and Fenella Cameron performed here, in 1921."

"Or all three. Are you assuming that Murdoch is the perpetrator?"

"It seems logical, doesn't it? His pocket watch was found next to Fenella's body, and there it is, on display in the greenroom of the theater. He played Arthur Goring, opposite Fenella's Mabel. And he was hanged for her murder."

"Ghosts can attach to people, as well as to places and things. They latch on to a person's energy field and attempt to live life through that person. While it is leaching energy from the individual, the ghost may also be sending its own emotions, behavioral patterns—even addictions to the unsuspecting host. If the earthbound spirit had physical issues when it was corporeal, the same symptoms may show up in the person to whom it has attached itself.

"There is no such thing as possession—a ghost cannot enter our physical body. But no entity should be permitted to hitchhike a ride on our energy field. It isn't healthy, and the ghost should be assisted to move on with its journey." Sophie paused. "There's a theory that ghosts aren't actually sentient entities," she added, "but merely echoes that were left behind on the earth's energy grid by people who have passed on."

"I've heard about psychic imprints," I replied, thinking of Hector Lawson in Scotland. But what fun would that be? "Do you agree with this analysis?"

"No idea," Sophie said cheerfully. "I believe that our spirits stay on this plane for a period of time, before we move on, and that some lower vibrational souls just get stuck. But it doesn't matter either way. Negative energy is toxic, and needs to be cleared."

"But what if the echo is positive?"

"Anything's conceivable in this new era of softer and nicer. But while the earth is still making this great shift, I'd be wary of the concept of benevolent ghosts."

"Great. Because they seem to be having their own private cast party right here in our theater."

"It appears so. Remember Emma, a ghost can siphon energy, but it can also stir up chaos, using low vibrational humans to do its dirty work. Be careful."

I was changing into a suit in the office bathroom after my riding lesson when Carlie tapped on the door.

"Annie from the Westport office just called," she announced. "They're sending a new divorce client to us."

"OK. When?"

"Half an hour—driving up from Woodbury."

"Do we have a file on this person? He or she, by the way?"

"She. Just moved to this area from Stamford. Denise has only spoken to her on the phone. I'll put what we've got on your desk."

Carlie buzzed when Jenna Morgan arrived, and I went out to the reception area to collect her. A chilly looking specimen. Slate gray pantsuit and low, square heels. Coarse black hair like a bush around her face, and eyes resembling small brown marbles.

"Ms. Morgan? I'm Emma Carbury. Denise Frederickson asked me to meet with you today."

She managed to make her eyes appear even smaller. "Fine. Well, I don't have much time."

I led the way to my office. Jenna Morgan sat in one of the armchairs that faced my desk. Abby jumped up into the other one and perched in a lady-like fashion.

"Oh. A dog. Must it be here?"

"She'll be fine. I understand that you want to get divorced?"

"I want to stop being financially responsible for my husband. If that means getting a divorce, then that's what I want."

"Let's put some of the basics out of the way first. How long have you been married?"

She shuddered. "Almost fourteen years."

"Any children?"

"One. Alison. She's eight."

"What do you do?"

"I'm a financial advisor with McClennan and Weaver. I've just transferred to the Danbury office."

"And your husband?"

She smirked. "Not much of anything. That's why I want out."

"I see. What has he done in the past?"

"He's a mechanic. Race cars, mostly."

"But he's not working at the moment?"

"No. He's in the hospital."

"Why is he in the hospital?"

"Broken arm, broken rib, punctured lung. Various other things."

"Car accident?"

"You could say that, yes."

"Work related?" This was bloody torture.

"No."

"Ms. Morgan, how did your husband get hurt?"

Jenna casually inspected her manicure. "I ran him over in our driveway."

"Now *that* was special," I remarked to Carlie half an hour later, after Jenna had been escorted to the front door.

Carlie grinned. "Are we taking this case?"

"I need to know if the police are involved first. Honestly, how does Denise attract these people?"

Carlie shrugged. "Maybe she's just a girl who can't say no?"

I laughed, and walked back to my office, singing the first few lines of *I Cain't Say No* from the *Oklahoma!* soundtrack. From behind me I heard Carlie whistle, and suddenly realized my mistake.

"Wait 'til you meet the next client," she commented. "She'll be here at two."

Myra Nathanson removed a big file from her briefcase and spread its contents on my conference table. She pulled out an eight by ten color photograph and held it up for me to see.

"Here's the family monument," she announced, unnecessarily.

43

I caught my breath. The huge stone straddled space for four graves. A simple rectangle of granite, it was elaborately carved with a detailed scene from a golf course. Various figures were swinging their clubs, sitting in carts, and putting. There was even a sand trap, and a view of a pond in the distance.

"The flip side of the stone is the other end of the course. There will be four graves there as well," Mrs. Nathanson remarked cheerfully, producing another photo. "That's my husband Carl and myself in the cart—he's recently deceased. Those two are his brother and his wife. The reverse shows Carl's parents, who have also passed, and his sister and her husband."

"Quite the golfers, aren't you?" I asked.

"Oh, we're all very enthusiastic," she replied. "Or were, as the case may be."

"You said on the phone that there has been some negative feed-back—regarding your family monument?"

"I just don't understand it," Myra replied. "We purchased this group of plots when my father-in-law transitioned. We agreed that we all wanted to be together when the time came. The director at the cemetery approved our plan for one large stone—she had the dimensions and everything."

"Was the director apprised of the—uh—artwork that would be included?"

Myra shook her head. "It didn't occur to us that it would be a problem."

I located the deeds to the burial sites from the pile.

"Apparently you and your family have bought the right to lease the ground underneath the surface of the land for the location of caskets, but not the surface land itself. That is owned and controlled by the cemetery."

"What does that mean?"

"In other words, if they don't approve of what you've done in terms of markers, or plantings, they can have your property removed."

Myra Nathanson registered dismay. "But that stone cost us *thousands!*" She exclaimed. "Isn't there anything that you can do?"

"Who exactly is complaining? The cemetery powers that be?"

"No. Our neighbors on both sides. They're saying that our monument is inelegant, and unsightly. They don't want to have to look at it."

Surely people had more important issues in their lives.

"I'll give the director a call, and see what I can work out."

"I'd really appreciate it, Ms. Carbury," Myra said, agitated. "I can't imagine what my mother-in-law would say about this kind of negative energy swirling around her grave."

Unfortunately, I could.

My watercolor painting workshop was scheduled for the following Sunday. Carlie and I left my house early and took Route 8 south to Bridgeport, and then 95 eastbound along the Connecticut coast.

"How does it feel to be back on the school paper?" I asked her. "Writing town news stories is probably more interesting."

"Maybe," Carlie admitted. "But there's a lot of hormonal drama at Tallmadge. Plenty of human interest."

"Is the new editor treating you well? Are you still getting the features assignments that you wanted?"

"Yep."

"But?"

"There's a guy," Carlie said quickly. "Max Armstrong—he's a junior. He plays right wing for the hockey team, and he's on the BHS paper's staff. We're doing a story together on this year's senior class."

"You're not getting along?"

Carlie frowned. "Sometimes. He's never the same two days in a row. It makes me nervous."

"In what way?"

"On Monday we met for lunch to talk about scheduling interviews for the article. Max insisted that we go to the Tavern, and he picked up the tab. He was super nice to me the whole time. Compliments about my writing, my rowing stroke in this year's eight—even my sense of humor. Then yesterday I ran into him in the library, and he barely acknowledged my existence."

"He *is* sixteen, honey. Was he alone, or with friends?"

"A couple of guys from the team." Carlie scowled. "One of them is a real jerk. Jim Stoddard. He's center, on the first line with Max. Creates a lot of problems with the other guys."

"That probably explains it. You know what I've always told you about dating."

Carlie giggled. "Buy low, sell high, marry bucks?"

"That men don't think like we do—so stop trying to analyze Max as though he's female. If you like him, I'd give him another chance. Life's tough for teenage boys, but it does get better."

"Something to look forward to," Carlie muttered. "Why can't every guy be like Aragorn?"

"If he's your ideal kind of man, I guarantee that you're going to have problems."

"What are you talking about?" Carlie demanded. "He's such a great hero."

I laughed. "I grew up reading *The Lord of the Rings* straight through every summer, and the man who always got my pulse going was Faramir. He does the warrior bit just fine, but he also radiates compassion and wisdom—two characteristics, if you recall, that his older brother, the so-called hero Boromir, completely lacked. Faramir is kind and courageous at the same time."

"Aragorn has all that good stuff going on too," Carlie insisted.

"Maybe so, but he never feels grounded to me. He's either wandering all over Middle Earth in a muddy cloak, or he's suddenly showing up on Arwen's doorstep, brooding over the mistake his ancestor made with the Ring three thousand years ago. I always want to tell Aragorn to suck it up, and get a life. He's ambivalent about being

King, remember, and emotionally remote. He doesn't want to settle down and stay put."

"Yeah," Carlie said slowly. "I get your point. Faramir *does* seem like more of a grown-up, in the movies, at least."

"Read the books," I told her, "and you'll see what I mean. I always feel like Éowyn is the lucky woman at the end of the trilogy—not Arwen."

Éowyn, the cold shieldmaiden of Rohan, whose frozen heart finally heals when she releases her haunting obsession with Aragorn, and instead falls deeply in love with Faramir.

We drove on in silence for a few minutes.

"You wrote for the school paper, didn't you Emma?"

"Not in high school. I was an arts reporter my freshman year at Vanderbilt."

"But you didn't continue?"

"No."

"How come? Too busy with the sorority?"

"A pretty lame reason, really. Our parents all got copies of the paper, and my mother used to give my articles to a friend of hers to edit. I think he worked on some big magazine—I never really paid attention. Anyway, the man would chop up my stories in red, and Audrey would send them back to me."

"Ouch!" Carlie grimaced. "Were the notes helpful, at least?"

"Don't know," I replied. "I just tossed them. But the whole thing was so annoying that I quit the paper after two semesters. Looking back, I wish that I'd stuck with it. I really enjoyed reviewing plays and student openings and artist's workshops."

"Why don't you submit something to *The Bridge Hollow News*?" Carlie suggested, practically. "They're panting for good stories, and you certainly know about art. If they like a piece, every other paper in Litchfield County will pick it up—they're all owned by the same company. It's great visibility for your law firm. I'll give you the name of my editor."

"Speaking of art, I need to prep you with some background on my painting class for today's outing."

"Oh great. So—are we going to be the only people there under eighty, Emma?" Carlie complained. "I'm not going to hear about operations and funerals all day—right?"

"Nope," I replied. "More like grandkids and bird watching."

"Wonderful."

"Chin up Graham. It's a gorgeous location on a beautiful day. The people in my class are lovely, and Pam's a terrific teacher. Embrace the moment, and be your charming self."

"Fine. But if I hear one word about prostates, I'm out of there."

"We'll be on an island, Carlotta. Where do you propose to go?"

We passed New Haven and got off the highway at the Branford exit, proceeding south on Thimble Island Road to the dock at Stony Creek. The class was assembled at nine a.m., just as Pam's husband Phil appeared in their boat. Carlie and I tossed our gear in first, and climbed aboard, while Phil and Roger helped the older ladies. Amy took a cushioned seat next to us in the bow. I introduced Carlie to everyone, and she moved over to make room for Linda, who came on board with the men.

"It's good to see you Emma," Amy said. "Class just isn't the same since you moved north. It's a perfect day for this," she remarked. "Look at that sky."

"Definitely cerulean blue. How was your summer?"

"Very relaxing. We were on Martha's Vineyard for the month of July. It's a house in East Chop that's owned by some friends."

"I've never spent much time there. Most of the beaches are private, right?"

"Yes. So you can imagine how busy the public beaches can be during the summer season."

"I think we're about ready to head out," Phil announced. "Everyone OK?"

We chugged slowly out of the harbor and then picked up speed.

I put on my sunglasses and grabbed the brim of my Nantucket straw hat.

"The Thimble Islands have a lot of history," Roger commented. "Some of it is pretty dramatic."

"There were pirates here at one time, weren't there?" Robin asked.

"So the story goes," Phil replied. "Captain Kidd and buried treasure. You should take one of the guided cruises and hear the lore. They're about an hour and are supposed to be pretty good."

"Any of the islands haunted?" Linda wanted to know.

"Supposedly," Phil replied. "I've never observed anything unusual, but my kids have. They say you can hear the pirates and their oars splashing, as they row their boats into some of the smaller coves."

"To bury their booty?" Carlie asked, wide eyed.

"Among other things," Phil chuckled.

We skirted a tiny island with one house on it. A woman and her son were loading fishing tackle into a rowboat. On the next island, a man in a business suit and carrying a briefcase was standing on his dock, waiting for the water taxi into town.

"About two dozen of these islands are inhabited," Phil continued. "We generate our own electricity and store rainwater. You'll be able to see the solar panels on the roof, as I come around."

The house was located near the point of the island, with three other homes situated to the west.

Pam was waiting for us on their porch. "Come up and have coffee," she said. "I put away some cold decaf in the fridge for you, Emma."

The house was over one hundred years old, built in the traditional beach cottage style, with weathered gray shingle, teal blue shutters, and bright white trim. The porch, which wrapped around the entire perimeter of the building, was wide and shady. The floorboards were stained gray, and the ceiling was painted sky blue. I put our lunches in the cooler and chose two wicker chairs with views to the south and the Long Island Sound. Robin uncovered her carrot cake.

A sea breeze stirred the umbrellas on the patio. I pulled off my hat and tried my ice coffee. Perfect.

Carlie took out a sketchbook and held a 2H drawing pencil poised over the paper.

Pam assumed her position at the large table. She had already roughed out her subject on a three hundred pound watercolor block: a dinghy moored off the next island, with a foreground of rosa rugosa, and seaweed covered boulders.

"I'd like to demonstrate a late summer sky. The weather is certainly cooperating, isn't it?" She wet her paper down to the water line and mixed cobalt blue with ultramarine. "Now remember to use clean tissue every time you blot out the clouds. Don't make the layers heavy; you want a light and feathery feel. Note the very straight line for the horizon. While the sky is still wet, lay in the under painting for the island treetops. This will avoid having fang like edges sticking into your sky."

"Hey Pam, those two trees look like a bikini top!" Roger commented.

Pam stepped back. "You're right. Thanks." She poked one of the trees with her brush and moved the wet paint. "As I've always said, variation is key in a landscape. The eye of the observer should move around the painting on a path that was planned by the artist."

After an hour of watching Pam work, she sent us forth on our own to pick a vista and start painting. Linda and I agreed to bring our umbrellas out to the eastern point of the island. I filled two water bottles, and the three of us climbed down the stone steps to the sandy area by the sea.

"Nice travel painting kit," Linda remarked. "Did you order it from a catalog?"

"No. I put it together myself over time." I located my Composition Finder and began to scan for a subject. "This is a possibility. Look how the water changes color over there with all the reflections from the grass. I can use the sand as the foreground. Do you see anything that you'd like to paint Carlie?"

"I'm thinking the boathouse," she pointed. "I like the purple hydrangeas planted around it. I'll put the upside down kayaks on the beach in the foreground."

We tried to work quickly, as the sun moved and altered our subjects. I mixed combinations of sepia, burnt sienna and Payne's gray to paint the debris that had washed up on the sand. One blue gray stone was strikingly beautiful. I opened my sketchbook and tried to capture its subtle tones in watercolor.

"Try a little terre verte," Pam suggested, right behind me. "We're taking a break for lunch, ladies. Come on up."

"When did you put in the arbor, Pam? I don't remember it from last year."

"In the spring. It was delivered in pieces to the marina. Phil and I hauled it out here in the boat, and we hammered it together. I'm hoping to get roses to climb over it. If I can keep the deer away, that is."

"You have a deer problem here?" Carlie asked, looking around skeptically.

"Oh, yes. They swim from island to island. Like guests at a progressive dinner."

"I've been admiring the new sign," Amy said. The name of the house, Windward Cottage, had been carved into a quarterboard, painted in blue and gold, and screwed into the wall of the shed. "It reminds me of the stern of an old ship."

"That was the idea. I wanted a Mystic Seaport feel to the place."

"Without the crowds," Phil added.

"Yes. But those guided tour boats come by often enough."

We resumed painting at one thirty, and by four, Pam was ready for the wine and cheese critique.

"I like her attitude," Carlie whispered as I handed her some sparkling lemonade. "If you're going to pass judgment on a painting, make sure the artist is drunk first."

I accepted a glass of chardonnay and helped myself to some cheese. Pam had propped up Roger's painting on a table by the back door.

"Roger has interpreted the bucket of flowers that I have on the patio. Notice that he was careful to keep the focus away from the center of the subject. The eye is drawn around the composition from the bucket to the rock wall and then to the water in the background. Well done.

"Carlie," Pam continued, "has painted quite an impressive view of my boathouse, using part of my perennial border in front."

Carlotta beamed. "I'm better with acrylics," she announced happily, "but I have to admit that I enjoy the challenge of watercolor."

"The hydrangeas have real depth," Robin commented. "The various shades of purple are wonderful. And the yellow coreopsis is a marvelous use of complementary colors."

"Yes," Pam agreed. "For those of you who are not aware of that technical point—whenever you wish a color to 'pop' in a painting, put it next to its complement. Purple and yellow are an example. What are the other two pairs?"

"Red and green," replied Linda.

"Blue and orange," added Amy.

"I'm impressed with the small terra cotta pots on the wall. You've gotten just the right shade. Is it pure burnt sienna?" I asked Carlie.

"And some alizarin crimson with a little ultramarine in places."

Pam nodded approval. "Now, here is Amy's interpretation of the same scene that I did in my demonstration. Note how the difference in style produces an entirely different painting. Amy uses small, round brushes, while I tend to use the larger flats. Her details are tighter and more delicate. The lines of the boat are perfect. This is a lovely little piece, Amy. Are you going to frame it?"

Amy looked flustered. "I suppose so," she answered.

I refilled her glass of wine.

Pam pulled my offering out of the heap. "Emma has painted our beach. The sandy path, warm in the foreground, recedes into the distance in blue shadows. The shallow water is a lighter value than the deeper water beyond it, and the sea grasses and the reflections they cast create dimension in the middle ground. I especially like these stones. They look like very careful studies in blues and grays." She smiled. "You used the terre verte. Very nice."

"Thanks."

"Robin chose the house at the other end of the island. This is also a very detailed work. Look at the intricate cracks in the shingles, the light on the porch stairs, and the geranium in the stone urn. The weathered rail fence is very realistic. See how successful she was with the illusion of roundness on a flat piece of paper, with the use of lost and found edges and carefully placed shadows. Excellent job, Robin. You've all done good work today."

"Are you planning to hold classes this winter, Pam?"

"We will probably start up again in early November. I have two shows in October that are going to require all of my attention for the next few weeks. I'll email everyone as soon as possible." She paused. "We understand that the drive is too much for you Emma, but I'll send you the notice anyway."

My painting class had been one of the sacrifices I had made to move up to Litchfield County. "Thanks Pam. If I happen to be in Westport on a day that class meets, I'll let you know."

Pam smiled. "And please come again, Carlie. Any time. I like to teach artists when they're young. They tend to listen better."

CHAPTER FIVE

Luke's Family Plot

"We have one problem in our marriage," Jed announced, with vehemence. "Judith's mother."

Jed and Judith had bought their home in Harwinton from Judith's mother, who was now living nearby in an elder community. Or wasn't, as it turned out.

"The woman never really left!" Jed continued. "She's with us nearly every night, weekends—and now Judith wants to take her on vacations with us. I've had enough!"

"I hate the idea of Mom staying in one of those places," Judith replied, nearly in tears. "I feel so guilty."

"We paid her fair market value for our home! She has plenty of money—she could go anywhere. She just refuses to cut the cord with you." Jed got up and paced around the room.

"So Jed, you feel that having purchased your mother-in-law's property, you would prefer that she not continue to share it with you and your wife?"

"Correct." He opened the French doors, and walked out onto the patio. "You have a nice view of the river here," he remarked.

The man needed some space. I turned to Judith.

"How do you see the situation?"

"I understand Jed's point, and Mom *can* be demanding. We *could* use more privacy."

"She forgets who owns the house now!"

"Do either of you have any suggestions as to how you can alleviate the stress that you both appear to be feeling?"

"How about limiting visiting time each week?" Jed demanded. "And here's a thought—what if Mitzi is off the property by the time I get home? Judith works out of her office in the house, but I have an hour's commute each way. I'd like to come home, kick back, and relax every night."

"What do you think Judith?"

"I suppose that would work," she said, nervously.

"I play sports on the weekends," he added. "Softball, and basketball in the winter. I could text you when I'm getting in the car, and you could hustle her back to her elder hive. With luck I'd never have to see her at all."

"OK."

"No more overnights," he said firmly. "She has a very nice place of her own just eight miles away. No more taking her out to dinner unless you're willing to do it alone. And she sure as hell isn't coming to Hawaii with us!"

After lunch I walked over to Town Hall to do some research in the Town Clerk's office. The vault was empty except for Jeff Murray, the other associate attorney from Esther MacInerney's office, who was sitting quietly in the farthest corner, looking at a map.

"Land use case Jeff?"

"Variance application," he said, grinning. "You?"

"Curiosity, mainly," I replied, dropping my briefcase at the next table. "I was reading some local history and I'm trying to find the site of a building. Famous murder case from the 1920's. Hugh Murdoch and Fenella Cameron. Her family lived here in town."

"I can save you some time," Jeff said. "The house still stands—it's a commercial office now. Esther bought it fifteen years ago. We're one of four professional practices that rent from her."

"Wasn't Miss Cameron stabbed to death there, in one of the front rooms?"

"In Esther's office," Jeff informed me. "It was the formal parlor at the time."

"That explains some things," I muttered. "How is Lacy doing?" I asked quickly.

Jeff's face turned red. "She's got her first trial coming up early next month, and it's a little stressful for all of us right now."

"I can imagine."

Jeff gathered his file together and stood up. "I'll tell Lacy that you were asking about her. Good to see you Emma."

I watched him leave; head down and shoulders slumped. Then I went to the Tax Assessor's office to get the volume and page numbers for the deed to Esther's property.

"Seriously, Emma. You don't have to do this," Luke said, with anxiety in his voice. "I know how you feel about being dragged into other people's family dysfunction."

"You're not dragging me," I assured him. "The fact that you're asking, rather than demanding, is refreshing."

"Well, I really appreciate it," he said, tucking my arm through his. "My siblings are more of a challenge than I can usually handle, and I admit that it will be easier for me if you're there for this meeting. For moral support, and as the voice of reason."

"I love you too," I whispered. Luke smiled and squeezed my hand. We proceeded up the path to the eighteenth century rectory next to the church.

Although we had been together for nearly a year, I had yet to meet a single member of Luke's family. This was partly due to the fact that Luke was as reclusive as I was when it came to mingling with the relatives, and partly, I suspected, because he was worried about my reaction to them.

His concerns were not unfounded.

The MacLaren matriarch in Litchfield County—Great Aunt Beatrice—had finally deigned to exit this life two days earlier. The remaining members of the tribe were scheduled for a meeting with the rector regarding the plans for Aunt Beatrice's send off, and burial.

The Reverend Glen Pettingill was a long time resident of Bridge Hollow, and had seen the Clan through its various life passages over the decades. I shook the old man's hand, and was promptly intro-duced all around.

Luke's sister Francesca, known as Franny. The middle child of the three siblings, she was about five seven, with a curvy build, small hazel eyes, and perfect even teeth in her cold smile. Her husband, Scott Champlin, was tall and thin, with graying hair, and green eyes that darted around continually as he spoke.

Luke's brother Michael was also of the basketball build. He was dressed in a dark suit and power tie, and had an over firm hand-shake and a pompous demeanor. In contrast, his wife Ellen was tiny, with a shy smile and a quiet voice. She was obviously nervous, and glanced at her husband repeatedly whenever she opened her mouth.

Luke had his arm around my waist as I met each of them. A public display of affection? Or merely a preventative in case I con-sidered escape?

"Well, Emma, this is a rarity," Franny commented, her voice icy. "We had no idea that you even existed—Luke only mentioned a few months ago that you were in his life. He never talks about the women that he's dating. We were beginning to wonder about him."

No preliminaries. Excellent. I felt Luke flinch.

"Shall we sit down?" Reverend Pettingill suggested.

We took our places in front of his big desk.

"As you all know," the rector continued, "Miss Beatrice MacLaren was born in Bridge Hollow—on the family farm, in fact—and it was her wish to be buried here as well. The arrangements have been made with Keller Funeral Home per her instructions. There will be a viewing Friday night from five until eight, followed by a service here in the church on Saturday morning at ten. All the other details regarding flowers, hymns, readings, casket, pallbearers, and headstone were approved and financed by Miss MacLaren before her departure."

"She was an exacting old lady," Michael agreed.

Reverend Pettingill handed Franny a sample of the printed service, and outlined for us the plan for the funeral. "Therefore, there is no decision making to be done today. Perhaps you would like to see the burial site?"

We followed him out the side door of the building and across the green to the cemetery.

I have always enjoyed walking in old graveyards. The inscriptions on the markers, sometimes barely legible, were fascinating, and there was something about the promise of peace at journey's end that was particularly appealing.

Luke's family was well represented. There were rows of MacLarens, dating back to the 1700's, when the family first sailed to the colonies from Scotland. Luke pointed to a stone in the corner by a large birch tree. *Zachary MacLaren. 1754–1833. A Son of the New Republic.* We stood staring at it for a moment. Zack's story—a family secret—had helped bring us together the previous year.

The others had gathered in an area comprised primarily of more modern graves. Luke's parents, Samuel and Carol, were buried there, as well as his grandparents, Frederick and Mathilda. The plot on Frederick's right remained unoccupied.

"Your great aunt will be laid to rest beside her brother," the rector explained. He looked around. "It's a beautiful spot, isn't it? You can see the river from here."

"Waste of a valuable piece of property," Michael muttered. His wife flushed with embarrassment.

"I'll be available all week, in case you have any questions."

"That was short and painless," Franny's husband commented at dinner. "Good of the old broad not to burden us with any of the work."

Franny laughed. "Beatrice liked things done her way, Scott." She pulled a document out of her purse. "Here's a copy of her will for each of you," she said, handing one first to Michael, and then to Luke. "I had a meeting with the lawyer who's executor yesterday. Beatrice's money is to be divided between the three of us, and it's a nice amount. She was also very specific about the distribution of her antiques, and her jewelry. The list is attached."

Luke moved closer to me and flipped to the provision in question.

"Beatrice had a substantial collection of valuables," Franny remarked. "The inventory of the furniture alone, so the attorney told me, is worth over two hundred thousand dollars." She paused, and shot a fierce glance in my direction. "The jewelry and silver is worth even more. And almost all of it has been left to Luke."

Luke pushed his copy of the will over to me, and stared at his sister.

"Her reasoning," I reported, in my best courtroom voice, "was that Luke, as the eldest, should receive the bulk of her personal property."

"But he has no kids," Michael growled, "and therefore no heirs."

"On the contrary," I replied. "You and your sister, and your children, are Luke's natural heirs, by law."

"Not if he gets married again," Franny pointed out. I suddenly understood her hostility toward me.

"There *is* that possibility, of course," Luke replied. "But my understanding is that I can will away my property, real or personal, as I see fit."

"Perfectly correct," I said.

"Not the farm!" Michael snapped. "We have a gentleman's agreement. The farm goes to our kids."

"Was that provision included in the contract for sale?" I asked, sweetly.

Luke smiled for the first time. "No it was not. I paid fair market value for the property."

"Then I'm afraid that legally Luke has the right to dispose of the family farm in any way that he chooses."

Michael signaled the waitress for the check. The four of them rose in a body, but not before Franny had lashed out with her parting shot. "How *convenient* that when Luke finally decides to date women again, he hooks up with a lawyer."

We returned to my house to decompress. I made a pot of tea, and we sat in front of the fire, with the doors open on to the porch. Breezes came in from the lake, and a loon called to its mate from the far side of the island. Abby padded in from her perch on the dock, and jumped onto the ottoman.

Luke was scanning his great aunt's will. "There are some amazing pieces on this list, Emma. I remember most of them. Tables, beds, desks, chairs. The rugs alone are worth a fortune. Old silver. Real imported china. What we can't use at the farm, I could sell with the antique dealers in town."

"A wiser course might be to take what you like, and offer the remainder to your siblings. It would help to keep the peace, especially if you'd like a relationship with your nieces and nephews."

"You're right, of course. I'll do that." He looked sheepish. "I'm sorry about today," he said. "Thanks again for your support. I've never been able to deal with drama—especially the kind that my family generates."

"You *did* warn me," I said, handing him the plate of biscotti. "Besides, this is my job. I deal with people like Franny and Michael almost every day."

"But not under personal attack, right? You're someone's lawyer across the conference table."

"Interesting that I felt so protective of you, though," I said, loosening his tie. "I was immediately on the offensive. What do you think that means?"

Luke finished his tea, gave the rest of his biscotti to Abby, and stood up. "I expect it means that I'll be receiving your bill shortly," he replied, grinning, and followed me up the stairs.

Luke and I arrived at Keller Funeral Home at 6 pm on Friday night. "Take some really deep breaths before we get in there," I advised him. "And this is going to sound nuts, but trust me. Imagine there's an invisible wall surrounding you, blocking anything from coming in. Remember *Star Trek?* 'Shields up, Mr. Sulu'? Do that. It's imperative to protect yourself at these events."

Luke gave me an amused look. "All right—I will. Do you expect my recently departed great aunt to be among those present?"

"They always are. Just stick with me."

"I intend to."

We each signed the book, and proceeded into the viewing area. "OK," Luke whispered. "Where is she?"

I surveyed the room. "At the head of the coffin. She looks angry."

"That sounds like Aunt Beatrice. Any reason in particular?"

"I'd have to ask her."

Luke sighed. "Fine. Let's move in. But I'm definitely going to need a big drink after this."

It wasn't difficult to get Aunt Beatrice's attention. She was a tall, stern looking old lady, with short gray hair, and a very direct gaze. She glanced at Luke, and then focused on me.

Are you here with my nephew?

I spoke in a whisper, so Luke could hear me. "We were wondering what's upsetting you?"

Apart from the obvious, you mean?

I love a ghost with a sense of humor. "Luke and I would like to help, if we can."

These are not the proper earrings.

Uh oh. "Luke, your great aunt says that she's not wearing the correct earrings."

Luke was surprised. "Franny said that you wanted to be buried with the diamond clips, Aunt Beatrice. It was in the instructions you left with the funeral director."

Exactly. But these are fakes.

"She says they're costume, Luke. Do you happen to know where the real ones are, Miss MacLaren?"

Luke's aunt gave a sharp nod. She gazed over at her niece, who was busily rearranging the floral bouquets.

Francesca has them in her purse.

I reported this intelligence to Luke. "I'll take care of it," he said. "Not to worry, Aunt Beatrice." We watched him pull Franny aside. There was a short, animated discussion, and then Franny put her hand into her purse, and drew out a small black bag. She thrust it at Luke, and immediately turned her back on him. Luke then moved over to Reverend Pettingill, and there was an exchange.

"Nice man, your nephew," I said to Luke's aunt.

Beatrice sniffed. *You seem much more sensible than his first wife.* She strode off to mingle with her mourners. I met Luke near the door.

"All set, Emma. The Reverend very kindly offered to make sure that Aunt Beatrice is properly adorned before they close the lid."

"That's good. What exactly did you tell your sister?" I asked, worried.

"Just that I could recognize imitation stones when I saw them." He laughed. "Your secret is safe. That's some gift you have, by the way. Have you considered it as a side line job? You know. Working with the police?"

"You mean spending my days with angry dead people, along with the angry live ones? No thanks."

"So where's my dear great aunt? Is she still here? Or did she go

into the light?" He looked embarrassed. "Or what? How does this happen, exactly?"

"Don't ask me! In my experience, they hang around until after the funeral, and then I can't see them anymore. Unless there's a problem. It's never a good idea to go against their last wishes, especially with sergeant-major types like your aunt."

"You mean that she might have stayed behind? Because Franny tried to take her earrings?"

"Yes, exactly. And plenty of them do, believe me."

Luke took my arm. "Emma. Of my numerous departed relatives, who is still at my farm? I really want to know."

"Let me talk to Sophie. She's the expert. Maybe we can get her to come to your property and do a house clearing for you. I prefer to stick to law."

That night I dreamed that my first husband Shawn and I are getting remarried. Several of my sorority sisters are bridesmaids, but when the processional begins, they collectively shake their heads with disapproval. I'm walking toward Shawn, his round, boyish face beaming, and I glance down. The front of my white gown is smeared with blood, my bouquet is in tatters, and I am barefoot.

CHAPTER SIX

Clearings by Sophie

J oy and I had been warming up in Luke's cross country field
for fifteen minutes when Joanne drove in. Our long term goal
was jumping over obstacles on uneven ground. Joy, an Irish Sport
Horse, was a superior athlete. A big gorgeous bay with interesting
white markings, in our early years together Joy had been a power
and speed horse in the professional jumper world. But once I understood the dangerous insanity of showing my beloved mare over huge
fences, I had pulled her out of the circuit, and had hired a dressage
trainer. Joanne and I were teaching Joy to relax and have fun—outside of the ring.

Joanne was drawing on her previous experience with eventing
competitions to help us in the field.

"Joy was pushed too hard and much too fast Em," she explained,
"and at a ridiculously young age. We need to start all over with her.
Nice and easy—little stuff. When it comes to jumping, never rush
your fences. Joy needs to feel confident that we're taking care of her
as much as she's taking care of us. It's all about team effort."

"Hence the concentration on flat work last year?"

"Exactly. We're going to have to undo any bad habits that she
picked up from showing with Frank last spring." We scowled in uni-

son. "And get her back in the safety-first amateur groove with you. Let's start with some big figure eights."

We executed figure eights and serpentines, and then practiced spiraling in and out at the trot. I concentrated on holding my position over the bumps and dips of riding on natural ground. Then Joanne had me pick up a right lead canter. We started with twenty meter circles, and more figure eights. Joy's flying lead changes were close to perfect.

"She does it so easily, even on this rough field!" Joanne enthused. "OK. Let's canter some poles." She laid out some ground poles on the diagonal. "Now, make her wait for the changes until you ask for them. You're in charge."

It was a real balancing act, but I managed to keep Joy in a package. We finished with a beautiful collected canter in both directions.

"Thanks Joanne—I really love working out of the ring—there's such a sense of freedom!" Joy snorted and bumped my knee with her nose.

Joanne grinned. "This is how riding should always be, in my opinion." She started to gather the poles. "As much as I enjoy showing in a dressage arena, it *is* confining. Training out here is a real treat."

I rode Joy up to the barn and dismounted, making a mental note to thank Luke once again for providing Joy with such a wonderful home. After so many years of difficult, and sometimes unhealthy situations, it was a pleasure to see her so happy.

In my office the next morning, Stan Mullins drew a rough map of his farm on a piece of legal paper.

"Here's the barn. You can see how close Grudberg's property line is to our ring. We're separated by a fieldstone wall, and a few bushes and trees."

"And this is where the son—Rick Grudberg—rides his motorcycle?"

65

"In this area, yes. He roars up and down over big piles of dirt and rock. It's also where his father does all the chainsaw work for their firewood business. The noise is unbelievable. And it always seems to start up just as my wife and daughter are bringing their horses into the ring."

"Which spooks the horses."

"Hell," Stan growled. "It would spook me. The kid's done something to the exhaust on his bike—it's way louder than it should be. We think he's ramped it up on purpose. The horses are really freaked."

"Have you tried talking to Julian Grudberg about this problem?"

Stan shrugged. "Yeah, but it's tough. He's our garbage and recycle guy. He takes care of most of the town and I don't want to piss him off. I'd pay a lot more to another outfit from Danbury, or wherever."

"But being polite hasn't worked?"

"Nope. It happened again yesterday. My daughter got dumped and her horse took off on her, which nearly got my wife thrown as well."

"What do you think the motivation is here?"

"Spite maybe. We have a much nicer place, and no garbage in the yard. My wife thinks that the mother is instigating this—she's seen Bonnie pushing Rick out the door as soon as the horses are in our ring."

"What would you like me to do? We have options. I can send a lawyer letter, couched in civility, to Julian Grudberg. Or, I can go directly to the Police Department, or the town, and complain about the nuisance. There's also a State agency—that might be the avenue to take."

"Please do what you think will work the quickest," Stan replied. "I'm really worried that someone in my family is going to get hurt. There's only the two of them, for god sakes. Can't the kid wait half an hour?"

Sophie, her daughter Julie, and Carlie arrived at Luke's farm after lunch.

"Hey Emma," Carlie barked. "How come you told Sophie your big ghost secret, but you didn't tell me? I'm open to this stuff too, you know. I've done spells and things."

Sophie laughed. "She didn't tell me. I figured it out—I saw her react to a ghost that I could see too."

"Oh," replied Carlie, nonplussed for the moment. "What about Luke?"

"Ratted out again, I'm afraid, honey," I explained. "By a long departed Scottish guy in a fake castle. Spook sighting just isn't something I ever talk about, and I don't want to see my personal business in the local news. Are we clear?"

"Absolutely," Carlie replied. "It's all off the record." She hunched her shoulders. "OK. Let's do this thing."

"Lay on, Macduff," Sophie said.

Luke met us in the kitchen.

"Any uninvited guests in this room?" He asked

Sophie glanced over at the enormous fireplace. An elderly woman with a thin face and dressed circa 1840 was seated to the right, near the pantry door. She nodded to me, and then looked inquiringly at Sophie. It felt odd for me to be part of this threesome. I had been hiding my secret for most of my life.

"This is one of your ancestors, Luke," Sophie said. "Her name is Amelia. She never married, and spent her entire life on this farm."

"Why is she still here?" Carlie asked, opening her notebook, and looking at the wrong side of the fireplace.

"Amelia always managed the care of her brother's children," Sophie explained. "And their children after that."

"So what's the problem?" Carlie wanted to know. "Is there some kind of shuttle that appears when you keel over, and if you miss it, you're SOL?"

"Let's see if Luke has any questions," I said.

"Did she know Zachary?" Luke asked.

"Zack was her uncle, apparently. Amelia is the daughter of his brother Benjamin."

"Find out if she's ready to go on, Mom," Julie prodded. It must have been dull for the girls; nothing to see or hear, and no emotional connection to the conversation.

Sophie asked the question, and Amelia nodded. Sophie said a prayer out loud, asking for a safe transition for Amelia. The ghost walked into the fireplace, and disappeared.

"Well?" Carlie asked, annoyed at missing all the action. "Did the white light come?"

"Do you see it Emma?" Sophie asked. "It always appears when I say the prayer."

"No," I admitted, relieved. "Which tells me that this is not my gig to perform."

"But it is for Mom," Julie said, grinning. "She does it all the time."

"What now?" Luke inquired. "Will I notice a difference in the house? My heating bill will be lower this winter?"

"Not yet," Sophie laughed. "You have quite a family gathering here. Let's move into the living room. I saw at least two of your ancestors going in there."

Several hours later, having cleared Luke's farmhouse of a total of six invisible squatters, we went back outside and moved toward the barn. Luke's property managers, Patty Hubbard and her husband Ryan, had brought the horses in from the pasture, and were dropping grain into their buckets. We heard the immediate snuffling and banging noises of enthusiastic equines enjoying the dinner hour. Besides Joy, and Luke's three—Hamish, Penelope, and Nemo—four additional horses that belonged to new boarders were now in residence.

"We got a call from another prospective boarder, Luke," Patty announced. "One hunter and two ponies. I told her that I'd speak to you and call her back."

I waited until Joy had finished her meal, and rolled open the door to her stall. She poked her muzzle into my jacket pocket, expectant.

I shifted to the right, and Joy was able to pull the big carrot out on her own. She munched on it happily.

"All right people," Carlie called impatiently from the tack room. "I'm ready for round seven. Who've we got?"

"Young man in riding boots, probably pre Revolution," I called. "Coming out of the last stall and heading in your direction."

The apparition in question stopped and looked at me. Carlie scurried out the door and stood next to Julie, who giggled. Sophie stepped forward and asked her usual questions.

This gentleman was Alistair MacLaren, one of Zack's cousins. He was born on the farm in 1745.

"What's the deal with this family?" Carlie wondered. "Can't they take a hint?"

Sophie asked Alistair if he was ready to move on.

In lieu of an answer, Alistair suddenly appeared in a blur by Patty, grabbed a grain bucket from her, and shot the entire contents into the air. He then disappeared.

"OK! *That* I saw!" Carlie exclaimed, brushing horse feed off her shoulders and writing furiously in her book. "I'm going to take his reaction as a definite no."

"Esther MacInerney *thinks* she's a mediator," Joel Newman bellowed on the telephone Tuesday morning, "but really she's a bully." He laughed. "As you know Emma, I practice mostly criminal litigation, and I only take family cases when I need the cash. Esther is one of the nightmares, and I avoid accepting files that she's involved in, if I can. Everything's a goddamn battle with that woman, and it's rarely to the client's benefit. I can just imagine what she's like in the State Senate. Frankly, I prefer dealing with criminals. They're more rational."

"So working on a collaborative divorce with her is a joke?" I yipped. "Great. These clients don't have money to blow on lawyers posturing for an audience."

"Watch everything you say to her," Joel advised. "She always has at least one minion with her taking copious notes—usually that poor guy Jeff. He's lasted the longest of any of her slaves—how, no one knows. She's always looking for a way to nail people into their own coffins." He chuckled. "While they're still breathing."

Esther's office, formally known as Cameron Manor, was an enormous Victorian at the top of Wentworth Hill. She had divided the building into four separate professional offices and painted it a somber grayish blue with an even darker trim. I made the climb to the big curving front porch and met my client, who was huddled on a bench near the door.

"My husband's inside with *her*," Doreen remarked. "But I told them that I'd wait outside for you." She glanced upward at the big windows. "I've *never* liked this place. I go around the block if I can. I get all shaky just looking at it."

We were escorted to the conference room by the youngest paralegal, who asked politely if we'd like some coffee, and then left us, closing the door carefully behind her. The room was paneled in dark wood, and was decorated in a curious display of old movie memorabilia. On a side table was an arrangement of business card holders. Esther's cards, placed prominently in front, were housed in a gold leafed case decorated with lapis blue fleur-de-lis. Behind them, in plain plastic obscurity, were those of Jeff and Lacy. I was staring at a framed poster from the original film production of *Wuthering Heights* when the door opened again, and Esther strolled into the room.

A short, stocky woman with shoulder length bleached hair and teeth like tombstones, Esther MacInerney had raised three boys and then attended law school as a second career. Her platform during her campaign for the State Senate had highlighted the fact that she'd had a tough childhood in New Haven, and was now a self-made success in the Bridge Hollow community. "I'm very grateful for my life," she had announced in every speech, "and I want to share that gratitude by serving my neighbors." Her husband Gilbert, a local businessman, attended obligatory networking events with the other members of the staff to keep up his wife's high profile, while she commuted to Hartford three days a week.

She immediately fixed her frosty green eyes on me.

"Ah yes, the newcomer to our town." Forced laugh. Politicians, like actors, made me instantly uncomfortable. Jeff Murray came in quietly behind her carrying a legal pad, and I remembered Joel Newman's words of caution. "It's all about superficial tricks," he had informed me. "Esther plays the pompous rectitude card with the Family Services people, but in reality she doesn't give a hoot about her clients—it's all aimed at boosting her public image. Ironically, she is *not* impressive in court; goes all mealy mouthed—can't handle someone else being in charge. I guarantee that she'll be intimidated by you, so she'll try to crush you. Watch out for the phony charm. It's a manipulation, and when she thinks she's fooled you, that's when she strikes."

It was clear as our collaborative meeting progressed that Jeff had done all the actual research and calculations for the conference. He distributed their version of the Child Support Guidelines work-sheet, and he outlined their client's position regarding distribution of the retirement funds and various other assets. Esther occasionally interjected with a humorous line or story, always at someone else's expense. I began to see the dynamic of her firm. At more than twice the age of each of her employees, she wooed the denizens and brought in the business. Jeff, Lacy, and the two paralegals did all of the work. It was a tremendous responsibility for relatively inexperienced professionals, and I wondered if the money was worth the stress involved.

"If you take a look at our proposed asset split," Jeff was saying to me, pointing to the spreadsheet, "we can balance out the scenarios quite well if they each keep their own 401k and...."

I caught a strong aroma of lavender, like being smothered in someone's linen closet. Suddenly music was playing—Scott Joplin's

71

The Entertainer from the movie *The Sting*. Jeff looked around the room, probably assuming that somebody's cell phone was ringing. No one moved. The music became louder. Esther let out one of her jolly bellows and moved toward a cabinet in the corner. Amongst the other knickknacks was a piano shaped box with an open lid. She shut it, and the music stopped.

"Must have been the cleaning people," she chortled, but Jeff looked startled, and it was several moments before he was able to continue speaking.

Lacy came in the front door just as we were leaving. I heard Esther shout at the office manager that she wanted to see Lacy in her office in ten minutes. Jeff, who was standing to my right, stepped back as though pushed. I resisted an urge to say something to him, and ushered my client out to the porch.

"That was weird," Doreen said, as we walked to the parking lot. "The music box, I mean."

"Like a warning, you think?" I asked, a little grim.

"Definitely. I loved it when you pointed out that Bruce's unvested stock with his company wasn't included in his plus column," Doreen said. "That woman gives me the creeps. There's no feeling in her, like one of those robots. Do you think she knew?"

"Jeff would have included the stock if he had known. He's an ethical lawyer."

Doreen shrugged. "Well, I think the music was a sign. I just hope that I made the right decision to go collaborative, and stay out of court. Maybe Bruce thinks he can pull something without a judge involved."

"Perhaps, although the discovery process is the same. We'll run their proposed scenario by our financial analyst, just to be safe," I replied. But I wasn't thinking about Doreen's husband.

The Bridge Hollow Country Playhouse sent its monthly newsletter via email the next morning. Prominent in the first paragraph was the hiring of State Senator and Attorney Esther MacInerney as legal counsel to the theater.

The second paragraph announced local tryouts for bit parts and chorus of a new musical comedy called *My Girlfriend's Deceased*. Carlie bounced into my office that afternoon.

"You're going to kill me Emma!" She warbled, waving a flyer in my face.

"Why this time?"

"Because I put your name on the list for tryouts. It starts Thursday night at 6pm."

I stared at her in horror.

There were several reasons why I had chosen not to generate offspring in this lifetime.

First, I have never been a particular fan of noise, mess, or smell.

Second, I had practically raised my sister, and felt that any parenting duty owed by me to the Universe this go around had already been fulfilled.

And finally, because my patience level, rarely good, was apt to be strained further by childish antics such as this.

"Really Carlotta? What on earth makes you think that I'm actually going to participate in this ordeal?"

Carlie slapped the flyer on my desk. "The fact that I've already told Luke's friend Jerry—the owner of the theater—that you have an amazing voice. He suggested it."

Tryouts for *My Girlfriend's Deceased* took place in the big rehearsal room in the older portion of the theater. I had changed quickly into jeans and a turtleneck at the office, and arrived just as the director was calling for the potential members of the chorus to come forward to the piano. We warmed up with several well known show tunes, and then began on numbers for the new play. I was repositioned with the other altos to one side of the floor. Several people were thanked for their interest, and left the room. I was asked to sing with a soprano, and then with a young man with a wonderful baritone.

Then came the shock.

The director called my name. "I want you to read for the part of Rosalie Fox—the Professor's wife," she announced, and laughed at the stunned expression on my face. "She's a very funny lady—an attractive forty-something with cougar tendencies. Not a lot of lines, but an amusing duet with the male lead and some good action scenes in the middle of the play."

I contemplated the definition of 'action scenes' for a married vamp, as I was handed a few pages and asked to report back in half an hour.

"You got the part!" Luke informed me on the phone the next morning. "They just posted the cast list, and Jerry Forester called me. I didn't even know that you could sing, Emma, but congratulations."

"Thanks," I replied, "but the truth is that I haven't sung in public since college, and if Carlie hadn't overheard me by accident, I still wouldn't be."

"It's a paid role, anyway," Luke said.

"You're kidding!"

"Nothing huge, but at least the stipend will cover some of the billable hours that you'll be giving up for the next few months. And it's great exposure for bringing in new clients." Luke laughed. "Especially the men. I guess I won't be seeing too much of you in the near future, unless I want to watch you chase some kid around the stage, waving a horse whip."

"It will be good for you," I retorted.

"Oh definitely," Luke agreed. "I plan to take notes."

CHAPTER SEVEN

We the People

" So it's 1783," I began, and my U.S. History students froze, fingers hovered over their electronic devices of choice. "The Revolution is over. General George Washington, the most revered man in North America, stuns his fans by relinquishing military power—and submits his resignation to the Continental Congress. He returns to Mount Vernon and full time farming. Now what?"

"The new thirteen states....." Heather began.

"Which were?"

Matt ticked them off with his fingers. "New York, Connecticut, Pennsylvania, Massachusetts, Rhode Island, New Hampshire, Virginia, Maryland, New Jersey, Delaware, North Carolina, South Carolina, and Georgia."

"They were operating under the very weak Articles of Confederation," Heather continued.

"Congress had zero power to do anything," Adam said, "even to tax, without every state agreeing. There was no President, or Supreme Court, and they had no national currency."

"And no money to maintain an army or navy," Maddie added. "Which must have been scary for them."

"Sitting ducks," Suzie agreed.

"Why was the new American government so lame?" I asked.

"Most Americans considered their local and state governments the only real authority over their lives," Suzie remarked. "The Confederation Congress was as little to them as the Continental Congress had been during the war."

"The former colonists had just gotten rid of King George III," Ed added, "and were terrified of central authority. The fear was total obliteration of the states by the leaders who favored a strong federal government. They were accused of being monarchists."

"They could create another dictator," Piper said.

"Look at how the French ended up with Napoleon after *their* Revolution," Jon pointed out.

"So while Congress knitted doilies, or whatever," Cassie grinned, "hoping for enough members to show up and vote, a serious financial depression was going on."

"Which not only caused the obvious problems here," Piper added, "but made us look pretty pathetic to the Europeans in the mix, especially the Brits, who took their time leaving our shores."

"There was a concern that the U.S. would split up into two or three smaller Confederacies," Megan said.

"So, to strengthen the new Union—and save face," I replied, "what happened?"

"James Madison eventually talked the states into sending delegates to Philadelphia in May of 1787," Suzie explained. "Their sole purpose, or so they thought, was revising the Articles of Confederation."

"At that time John and Abigail Adams were U.S. ambassadors to the King and his court in London. Jefferson was doing his diplomatic duty in France," Rob said, "but fellow Virginian Congressman Madison, a brilliant bookworm with a degree from Princeton, had a plan."

"He shook up conventional wisdom," Jon contributed, "by claiming that large scale republics—and obviously, the U.S. was destined to be huge—were safer and more stable because the inevitable numerous bickering factions would keep each other in line."

"And for that we have daily proof," Cassie pointed out.

I could feel the energy in the room. It was exciting to think of so many historical demigods gathered again in Independence Hall to change the concept of government for the world.

"Benjamin Franklin had George Washington nominated as President of the Convention," I remarked. "The delegates agreed that their discussions would remain secret. Madison's efforts were presented, and they were debated for over three months. What happened then?"

"The Articles were scrapped," Matt laughed, "to the relief of just about everybody. The delegates created a totally new charter—and a radically bold form of federal government. A two house legislature, a national court, and a very strong executive branch. The people would elect their federal representatives directly."

"Basically the system that we still use today," Henry explained.

"Minus the various Amendments," Kim added.

"We'll get to the Bill of Rights in a bit," I told them. "Let's talk about the Chief Executive. As we've said, Americans had no use for another king. How did the delegates resolve this issue?"

"They decided that the only way to avoid legislative tyranny," Maddie began, "was to have the President elected for a specific term of years."

"We only began limiting the number of terms in the twentieth century—after Franklin Roosevelt was elected four times," Piper added.

"Congress had the power to impeach the President," Matt continued. "He was to be the Commander in Chief of the armed forces, which was a pretty big leap of faith for them."

"With Washington sitting there presiding over the delegation?" Heather laughed. "Everyone knew that he'd be the first man elected."

"Then they worked out the various checks and balances that we still have in place," Suzanna added, "so that no particular branch had more power than the other two."

"Certain significant powers were reserved for Congress," Jon said, "including the authority to declare war."

"OK," I said. "Let's discuss the issue of big states versus little states. What was the concern there?"

"Power," Megan replied. "Size of population equaled more votes. Obviously smaller states like Connecticut and New Jersey couldn't compete with the larger fish like Virginia, Pennsylvania, and New York."

"The upper house," Adam explained, "now called the Senate, would give each state an equal number of votes, while the lower House of Representatives would provide the states with proportional representation."

"Aha!" I said. "Now define proportional representation."

"I know where you're going with this," Ed announced. "Slavery. The S-word was the hot topic on the Convention agenda. And many of the delegates were slave owners."

"Including Washington and Madison," Jon reminded us.

"Correct. Recall that the abolitionist movement was gaining strength in the North. The South wanted some kind of guarantee that their way of life would be preserved."

"Or they'd bail," Cassie scowled. "Yeah. Imagine hearing all the wonderful rhetoric about freedom and independence, and finding yourself still enslaved after the war."

"The delegates agreed that three fifths of the slaves in each state would be considered as part of its population," Rob said. "And in the end, they tabled the whole messy issue, deciding that the slave trade would be permitted until 1808—another twenty years."

"Reactions?"

"It's beyond horrible, we all agree. But really, what choice did they have?" Piper asked.

"With the Brits hovering, just waiting for us to fold?" Kim replied. "No choice at all. Survival first. I bet that most of the delegates hoped that slavery would just fade away on its own."

"But as we know, the situation was never effectively addressed," Megan said, "and it split the country in the 1860's."

The entire room was silent for a moment.

"And the moral of that lesson?" I asked.

"Individual freedom will always apply to everyone equally?" Heather asked, a little nervous.

"One way or another," I answered. "But let's return to the Constitutional Convention."

"They debated and debated," Matt said. "The delegates were determined to solve a seemingly unsolvable political problem—to create a centralized federal government while remaining true to the spirit of 1776."

"So they did," Ed concluded, "and the Constitution was signed by its creators in September of 1787. The delegates presented the Constitution to Congress, and it was subsequently sent on to the states for ratification."

"It was a real miracle," Suzie added. "Washington once wrote that the 'invisible hand of providence had been manifest in the enactment of the Constitution.' It had Divine approval, I guess."

"Madeline—would you kindly read the Preamble out loud?"

"We the People of the United States, in Order to form a more perfect Union, establish Justice, insure domestic Tranquility, provide for the common defense, promote the general Welfare, and secure the Blessings of Liberty to ourselves and our Posterity, do ordain and establish this Constitution for the United States of America."

"In the end the Convention created a system of shared sovereignty, allotting specific powers to the states, and to the federal government. But much was left flexible, to be worked out on a case by case basis." I grinned. "The U.S. Constitution is the oldest written charter of a nation that is still in use. It is constantly evolving—which is how lawyers make their money."

They laughed.

"We the People," I continued. "Recall the motto on the U.S. seal:

79

E Pluribus Unum. Out of many—One. Were the framers referring to the universal collective, or just the majority? Or only white male land owners? What was the definition of citizen? Every group is made up of individuals, remember. Is there even such an entity as 'The People'? What could Americans count on freedom to mean?" I paused. "Remember that just because a majority of voters believes that something is so—doesn't make it right. Which brings us to the Bill of Rights. Discussion?"

"The Constitution was ratified by the necessary nine states in 1788, and Washington became the first President in 1789," Ed replied. "With John Adams as his Vice President. Under Article V the Constitution may be amended. The first ten amendments, known as the Bill of Rights, were ratified in 1791. They protected individual liberties."

"Such as?"

"The First Amendment is arguably the all important basis for citizenship in the U.S.," Megan commented. "It covers our freedom of expression—religion, speech, press, assembly and petition."

"Good. The rest of the Amendments?"

"The right to bear arms," Heather continued. "The right to a speedy and public jury trial—with the assistance of counsel in criminal cases—and to a jury trial in civil cases."

"Protections regarding quartering of troops," Henry added. "Americans are safe from unreasonable searches and seizures, and search warrants issued without probable cause. Also double jeopardy—being tried again for a crime after acquittal—is prohibited. No self incrimination in criminal cases—commonly referred to as 'pleading the fifth.' No government taking of private land for public use...."

"Known as eminent domain," Suzie contributed.

"Under the Fifth Amendment no person will be deprived of life, liberty, or property by the federal government without due process of law," Jon said, frowning, "which is then later applied to the states in the Fourteenth Amendment—this gets a little complicated."

"It does indeed," I said, with feeling. "Too much so for the purposes of this course. If any of you are planning to go to law school, see me during office hours."

"We're up to the Eighth Amendment I guess," Megan said. "No excessive bail or fines in criminal cases—no cruel and unusual punishments inflicted."

"Lets out burning at the stake then," Adam remarked.

"Unenumerated rights—rights not specifically mentioned in the Constitution, are retained by the people in the Ninth," Piper finished up. "The right to privacy probably gets the most press—and finally, powers that are reserved by the States in the Tenth."

"Excellent people! We're not going to go crazy on analysis—just an overview. The important point here is the unusual nature of the Bill of Rights. What do I mean by that?"

"These laws tell the U.S. government what it is *not* allowed to do," Kim replied. "The Bill of Rights is more like a Bill of Prohibitions."

"And why is this so crucial?"

"American government is not superior to the individual," Heather added. "It is a limited permission, granted by free individuals, to use force if necessary. And that permission may change—peacefully—if required."

"The United States of America is all about codified law," Ted said, "not perceived Authority, based on Old World superstitions."

"Human rights are natural rights," Cassie concluded. "Every person is born equal and free. And when our collective natural energy is released, we can move mountains."

Carlie and I were meeting Lacy Basdin for lunch at Bostwick Tavern.

"Are you sure that she wanted me to come, Emma?" Carlie asked. "I feel like I'm intruding on lawyer talk."

"Lacy probably feels closer to your age group than mine," I replied, picking up the menu. "She's not even thirty."

"But she has a two year old daughter," Carlie said. "I can't relate to that."

"Good for you. Just be supportive. This isn't going to be a pleasant conversation."

It wasn't. "On the positive side," Lacy remarked, spearing her grilled tuna with purpose, "the situation at the office has brought the rest of us closer together. Jeff says that they never used to talk amongst themselves before I came on board."

"They didn't know who they could trust, probably," Carlie said.

"Yes. Especially the office manager. She's been there the longest. Nearly five years. But even she says now that she's tired of being treated like... I don't know, like we don't really exist."

I experienced an Aha moment. "Like you just don't matter?"

Carlie looked at me suspiciously.

"Exactly. We're those guys at the bottom of the ship, doing all the rowing, while some overseer with a whip walks back and forth yelling 'Pull, you mangy curs!' One of the crew drops dead, they dump the body to the sharks, a replacement is dragged in, and everyone else just keeps on rowing."

"Can't wait to get out into the working world," Carlie muttered. "May I have a taste of your drink Emma?"

I handed her the glass. "I think Esther's a narcissist. And if I'm right, nothing you say or do will give you any worth in her eyes, believe me. You only have value if you make her look good."

Lacy frowned. "A narcissist? Like that guy in Greek mythology who fell in love with his own reflection and committed suicide because he couldn't have sex with himself?"

"Emma's an expert on this stuff," Carlie said wisely, taking another sip of my vodka tonic. I retrieved my glass. "She was married to one of these crazies, so you can trust what she tells you."

"Narcissistic Personality Disorder," I told her. "Look it up on the web. If I'm right, then Esther is clinically insane, and there's probably no cure. The only emotion that she really feels is rage—everything else is manufactured for effect. The main thing to remember is that these people are ultra toxic, and she is sucking the life essence out of you. You have to leave that office."

"I know I do," Lacy said, taking a big gulp of light beer. "It *is* insane. The control is unbelievable. That stupid computer program with all the memos coming up in your face while you work. So disruptive, and usually abusive. Then copies always go into the files, so anyone can read them. She assigns us 'projects' through the computer as well. They turn bright orange if they're not completed by the due date, and then we get more nasty-grams via e-memo."

"Good grief!" Carlie exclaimed, looking at me. "Emma just drops notes on my desk with smiley faces."

"And chocolate chip cookies, if I really need something."

"We're not allowed to leave our desks without hitting the do not disturb on the phone—so everyone knows if you're going to the bathroom, or grabbing something from the fridge. Then there are the never ending nit picky rules; and if you do something that sets off one of her temper tantrums, she makes up new rules! I have to come in at 8 am; half an hour earlier than Jeff—every morning. Even if I don't have court, which is really a hardship with a toddler to get ready for the sitter. And the office meetings! Poor Jeff. He has double the case load I have with all the land use and probate, but he's still expected to be on top of all the litigation files so he can crunch numbers for her power conferences. Esther memorizes everything, and she abuses Jeff if he's not up on even the tiniest detail."

"How old is Jeff?" I asked.

"He turns thirty in a few weeks."

"He seems older than that somehow."

"I know what you mean," Lacy replied, thoughtful. "He's so reserved. But very kind at the same time. He's covered my butt with Esther so much—I'm super grateful. I'm always pestering him with questions, and he never complains. He has a kind of elegant presence about him, and he dresses really well. Do you think he's gay?" She asked me, suddenly.

I laughed. "No Lacy. I definitely don't think that Jeff is gay. I *am* sure, however, that he has some kind of attraction to you."

She looked shocked. "Really? It never occurred to me! He always struck me as being too sweet to be straight."

Carlie snickered. "Oh Emma likes them sweet. You should see her boyfriend! Total hottie who practically falls over every time she smiles at him."

I ignored this less than dignified description of Luke.

"How is he with your daughter?"

Lacy grinned for the first time. "He's amazing with her! I decided to give Clara her own room a few months ago. Jeff helped me paint the walls and the windows, and then he moved all her furniture. He volunteered; I never even asked."

Carlie was stunned. "And it didn't dawn on you that he was interested? God, even I know that a guy doesn't do something like that unless you matter to him—a lot. Has he asked you out?"

Lacy looked confused. "We come here after work once in a while. Lunches during court if we're there together. I took him to dinner after the move. But asked me out? No."

"He's probably shy, and inexperienced," Carlie announced, the seasoned expert on dating. "And he figures that you've got more know-how, since you have a kid. Were you married, by the way?"

"No. Long term relationship from law school that didn't work out. He's in Stamford now."

"Spending so much time together in that office can't be helping either," I commented. "With Esther always hovering over both of you. Must be very emasculating for Jeff. No wonder he hasn't approached you."

Lacy nodded. "I had a dream once that he and I are making out on a couch, when Esther and Gilbert suddenly walk in and ruin everything. I never thought that it had any meaning beyond the firm."

Carlie rolled her eyes.

"The next question," I said gently, "is how do *you* feel about Jeff? Just colleagues? Friends? Or something more?"

"I'll have to process that one for a while," Lacy said, and suddenly laughed. "I don't feel that I'm attracted to him at all—just grateful. I have to tell you though—knowing that Jeff has a thing for me will certainly help me get through the day from now on."

The setting for *My Girlfriend's Deceased* is present day on the north shore of Boston, in a pre Revolutionary War house on the coast.

"Why don't they just say that it's Salem and get it over with?" Carlie complained, as she flipped through my copy of the script.

"Don't know," I said. "Maybe that's trying too hard to be spooky."

Carlie snorted. "Oh come on Emma! This play reads like a modern *The Ghost and Mrs. Muir*, set to music."

"Hmm. Not really. Do you mean the movie, or the sitcom?"

"OK, then it's more like *Animal House*, only haunted."

Early Saturday morning at the theater. The entire cast was assembled for the first run-through of the play. The actors were grouped in chairs around the director, who stood with the choreographer by the piano. The chorus, comprised mostly of fictional medical students, gathered in the background near the breakfast buffet.

Thank god I wasn't required to dance, as well as sing.

Carlie took her notebook and camera out of her backpack, and proceeded to mingle amongst the company, asking quiet questions for the local news.

The hero of the piece is Jonah Corrigan, one of three male graduate students sharing the property, which is owned by the Dean of the medical school, Dr. Fox.

The heroine is Loretta Whitcomb, the ghost of a young woman from the Transcendentalist era, who, not unlike Emily Dickinson,

rarely left home. Having died in her father's house in the 1850's, Loretta decides to stay on. She is fixated on poor Jonah.

As is my character—Rosalie Fox, the Dean's wife.

I glanced over at the assembled actors, wondering which of the young men in the cast was going to be my prey for the next few months.

"He's the one in the blue sweater," Carlie whispered behind me. I jumped about a foot.

"What's his name?"

"Rory, short for Roderick," Carlie replied. "Rory Miller. Twenty-seven. Originally from Alabama. Got a decent part in a show off Broadway last winter, and now he's here. Nice looking, huh?"

"Very," I said, with feeling. "*Please* tell me that he's gay."

"Nope," Carlie snorted. "Is that going to be a problem for you Emma?"

I gulped. "Depends on what the director wants me to do to the man."

"Try not to enjoy it too much." Carlie smirked and headed toward the food.

We worked slowly through the script. To my chagrin, Rosalie comes in very early in Act One, and shows up repeatedly throughout the remainder of the play. This meant that I was expected to be present for most of the rehearsals. It also meant that I would be spending a great deal of time with Rory Miller, who seemed more than up to the challenge of having two older women—one dead, the other married—chase after him for the entire performance, night after night.

Rory and I were scheduled to work on our duet, a song entitled *The Benefit of Experience*, the following week. The choreography, we were informed, though not dancing per se, would be fairly active, with lots of movement back and forth across the stage.

"Better wear sneakers," Rory grinned at me. He was about six feet tall with a runner's light build, dark hair and gray eyes. "You're a local, is that right?" I heard a slight Southern drawl in his voice.

"Correct. Getting cast for this part was a total shock."

"I heard that you had the right look, along with the talent," he said, very charming.

"You're the one with the talent," I replied sweetly, and made my exit.

That night I dreamed that I am in bed with my ex husband. Nick is unusually flattering and kind. "Let's hold hands, and just see how it goes," he says, leering at me. I surprise him by getting up and grabbing my robe. "No thanks," I reply. "I know who you are now. The phony boyish charm doesn't work anymore."

CHAPTER EIGHT

The Spirit of the Land

The sun was just setting as I drove up to Luke's farm, and parked by the barn. Joy was in her stall munching hay. I rolled the door open and stood with her, stroking her neck and shoulder as she chewed.

"Emma?" Luke called from further down the aisle. "I don't want to disturb your time with Joy, but there's something I'd like to show you, when you're ready to come in."

Luke was in the kitchen when I came through the back door. He handed me a glass of wine, and motioned for me to follow him into the newer wing of the house. I had never been in this section of the property, which seemed odd, after a year together. Luke stopped in front of a closed door, and opened it.

It was a small square room, painted in cheerful French vanilla, with tall nine over nine pane windows on two walls that looked out to the barn, and the pastures beyond. There was a tiny fireplace to my left, with built in shelves and cabinets on either side. An antique rug in deep blues and greens covered most of the floor. The few items of furniture were beautiful. In between the windows to my right stood a magnificent secretary desk. The slant top was down, revealing eight small drawers, cubby holes, and a compartment in the middle. The key was in the lock. The bookcase above had glass doors. I walked over to the desk and ran my fingers lightly across the top of the writing surface.

"It's mahogany," Luke said, still in the doorway. "George III. Built around 1790. The chair is a ladder-back Chippendale, about the same period or a little earlier. I'll have to check the inventory about the other pieces."

I wandered around the little room. A bouquet of yellow roses sat on the candlestick table by the chaise, which was upholstered in a faded old fashioned pattern of violets and ferns.

"It's the first of my aunt's furniture to come in, and I wanted this room set up as much as possible before you saw it."

I looked up, surprised. "Why?"

"Because it's important to me that you feel at home here—that you have a place of your own to go. I know how you are about personal space. I thought—well, frankly I was hoping that you'd want to be here in the house more often. And not just the barn."

"You're telling me that this is my room?"

"If you'd like it to be. Yes."

I was ashamed that my initial reaction to Luke's incredible display of understanding and generosity was panic. I knew that this was old behavior for me—triggers from my marriage. Feeling trapped in a man's home that had everything to do with his own history, and nothing whatever to do with me, or our relationship. I realized suddenly that Luke and I spent almost all of our time together at my place on the lake, and that although he had never complained, creating this study for me was Luke's way of addressing the issue.

"Emma?"

"Do you feel like taking a walk?"

He nodded. We strolled past the cornfields and turned on to the bridle path that led toward the woods. The sun was almost gone, but the hills glowed purple to the west, and there was enough light from the various buildings on the farm for us to find our way.

"I guess I've been pretty selfish," I began. "I promised to let you into my life, and I have. But that doesn't mean that I've allowed myself to become a part of yours."

"I know that you're afraid of being swallowed up again," Luke said gently. "Losing your identity, your independence. I understand that it's nothing to do with how you feel about me."

"But it's getting to you."

"Yes," he said slowly. "I think it is."

"And you're sure that the first step toward alleviating my concerns is having me feel safe and at home on your farm?"

"I am. I really believe that if we can get you to separate the two things in your mind, you'll be more at ease."

"An affirmation of 'that was then, this is now,' you mean?" I considered his theory. "It seems like a very sensible solution."

Luke laughed. "You take the drama out of everything. It's one of the many reasons that I love you so much."

"I've always wondered. OK! I can do this! Luke, I accept my lovely little room, with pleasure. Thank you so much."

"You're welcome. Please feel free to consider it your study. Once it's finished, I will never cross the threshold without your permission."

I visually flashed back to the days of carefully locking personal papers and journals in a filing cabinet, so that Nick wouldn't rifle through them when I was out of the house. I felt a sudden rush of gratitude for Luke. Here at last was a true gentleman.

"I'll start moving into my room this weekend. And may I please have an easel in there as well? Watercolor only, and I promise to be careful with the rug."

Friday night Sophie herded her audience into the greenhouse, and began her series of presentations highlighting two important celebrations in autumn—the Fall Equinox and Samhain. Julie and Carlie worked the on-screen computer images from behind the potted herbs.

"The Autumnal, or Fall Equinox here in the northern hemisphere takes place in late September. The term equinox is derived from the Latin word which means equal night," Sophie explained. "Therefore on two occasions in the year—March and September—day and night will be roughly the same length of time. For centuries autumn has been the season to honor the abundance of the harvest as gifts from the earth. For the next few weeks we will be discussing how those celebrations have evolved from pagan ritual to modern observances—particularly in the United States.

"We'll begin with *genius loci*," Sophie continued. "The genius, or spirit of place. In ancient Rome a *genius loci* was the protective spirit of the land. They were depicted as small supernatural beings like fairies and elves, guardian animals, or ghosts. The entities were thought to be very powerful, highly intelligent, and energetically bound to the area which they inhabited. Believers would leave offerings of food to these spirits, to gain their protection for the coming harvest.

"It is commonly believed that everything that exists is alive, and has a spirit. Trees, plants, and animals are here to balance the planet, and filter negative energy from the air. The earth with the elements of air, fire, and water is a living being, itself a life form, as are the moon and the sun, and every heavenly body. All that is alive is connected.

"Today the term *genius loci* refers to the distinctive atmosphere of a location, rather than a guardian spirit, and is often applied to a rural or relatively unspoiled landscape. The modern concept of *genius loci* was made famous by Alexander Pope, the early eighteenth century English poet, essayist, and literary critic, who urged a return to the 'amiable simplicity of unadorned nature' rather than the formal garden, and inspired the cardinal rule for the English landscape style—'in all, let nature never be forgot... consult the Genius of the Place.' That is to say, landscape designs should always be adapted to their location. All gardening is akin to painting a landscape. The artist must remain true to the composition of the subject.

"In the eighteenth century Lancelot 'Capability' Brown, England's most famous landscape designer, described himself as a 'place maker.' Known for his serpentine gardens, Brown broke with formal French tradition and developed the distinctive English style of natural appearing, asymmetric landscapes, complete with expansive lawns, groves of trees, meandering streams, and picturesque lakes."

A montage of half a dozen stately homes and gardens flashed on the screen—gloriously green and peaceful.

"Here in the United States, it is impossible to understand the American Revolution and the shaping of this nation without considering the Founders first as farmers and gardeners. Benjamin Franklin, for example, concluded that while war is essentially robbery, and commerce equals cheating, agriculture was the only path to wealth. Why? Our vast resources meant that we could be self sufficient, which relieved us from reliance on Great Britain. Farming was the key to America's future of freedom and independence. Nature was the backbone of her economy, and therefore, her success.

"The environmental movement in this country began decades before Thoreau and Emerson and the era of Transcendentalism. George Washington's love of America was inextricably intertwined with his passion for gardening, agriculture, and the beauty of this land. Think of some of our most patriotic songs, and the natural images that they invoke. Fruited plains. Amber waves of grain. Majestic mountains. Oceans, prairies, and forests. Nature was the unifying force of the American people. Providing more than the mere occupation of plowing and planting—nature was the transcendent symbol of the United States. Fertile soils and home grown abundance created a distinct identity for a new, vital nation.

"Washington designed the truly American gardens at Mount Vernon," Sophie continued, "as his vision of republican simplicity."

Various views of the famous estate appeared behind Sophie, including the vista from the veranda, down to the Potomac River.

"Using only native trees and shrubs as his brushstrokes, he offset smooth with rough bark, large and small leaves, rounded deciduous shapes with conical outlines, spring flowerings and autumn yellows and reds—creating living landscape paintings that pleased the eye while making his personal statement of independence.

"Like Washington and Jefferson, John Adams considered himself to be a farmer first, and preferred being home in his fields in Massachusetts to any other occupation. Touring famous gardens in England with Jefferson in 1786, he first learned of the ornamental farm. This method of agriculture merged the elements of a working farm with the beauty of a pleasure garden. Both men viewed this combination of tidy furrows with beautiful groves as a symbol for the new American liberty—glorious and bountiful.

"Adams in particular saw the balance of nature as an analogy for the ideal government—offsetting one power with the equal power of another—in the checks and balances system that we still use today. For Adams and Jefferson, farming was an act of patriotism. It was an affirmation of their belief in the future of the new nation.

"Many of the fifty-five delegates to the Constitutional Convention were farmers, or came from an agricultural background. Determined to avoid the gluttony and corruption of Great Britain, Americans aspired to the simple country life, far removed from the hedonistic excesses of Europe. They believed that farmers were the foundation of a healthy society. Merchants, bankers, and money obsessed speculators in the cities had no attachment to the land, or to the nation.

"Recall the theory of Enlightenment—an understanding of nature and how it applies to humanity—and the natural rights of freedom and equality. James Madison argued that farmers were the best foundation of public liberty, and the strongest bulwark of public safety. The father of our Constitution believed that nature was not subservient to the existence of humanity, and therefore we must return what we take from the land to restore balance. Madison was probably one of the first conservationists. He understood the relationship between the earth and mankind, and that a healthy planet was essential for the survival of the human race.

"The Founders worried that without the traditional control mechanisms of monarchy—fear and force—the new republic would be too fragile. The old restraints had to be replaced with moral integrity and self-control. 'Only a virtuous people are capable of freedom,' Benjamin Franklin once wrote, meaning farmers."

Sophie's voice became terse. "As we have seen—even here in Bridge Hollow—vicious politicians breed corruption and selfish destruction of our land.

A nineteenth century map appeared on the screen.

"During Jefferson's Administration, the Louisiana Purchase in 1803, and the subsequent Lewis and Clark Expedition expanded the American glorification of the wilderness. A new emphasis was placed on the untamed vastness of the U.S., and it became an object of national pride—synonymous with its spirited and free people. Landscape artists focused on the Hudson River Valley, Niagara Falls, and the Great Plains as their subjects. Novelists and poets romanticized the American frontier."

Sophie grinned. "So you see in this instance, size *does* matter. Farmers need space, and a passion for the rugged nature of the West became part of our national identity, an attitude which is still prevalent today.

"Let's move on to modern landscaping.

"Landscape architects are advocates for the environment. They work with engineers, architects, and town planners to ensure that the spirit of a place is always considered when land is to be altered.

"Modern landscape planning has seen a revival of the nineteenth century designs. Frederick Law Olmsted, 1822 to 1903, is recognized as the founder of American landscape architecture and park making. A journalist, scientific farmer, environmentalist, and social reformer, Olmsted is most famous for his work on New York City's Central Park, the U.S. Capitol grounds, and his role in the creation of the National Park Service.

"Olmsted was committed to egalitarian ideals. He believed that common green open space must always be accessible to everyone—that retreat into nature was necessary to replenish the soul. Influenced by his many tours of English landscapes, Olmsted's theory was concealment of design in the pastoral or picturesque styles, manipulating natural elements, and utilizing interplay of light and shadow, so that the whole effect enhances the sense of space, and induces relaxation.

"As a native of Hartford, Connecticut, Olmsted found that the exceptional beauty and modestly scaled terrain of Connecticut recalled the gently undulating hills of the British landscape. Memories of rambling through the countryside on horseback with his parents inspired Olmsted's passionate attachment to farming and the land. He spent much time alone, and outdoors. His solitary time in nature provided Olmsted with a lifelong love of the countryside, and an appreciation for its power to heal.

"A colleague of Olmsted once described him as 'an artist, he paints with lakes and wooded slopes; with lawns and banks and forest covered hills; with mountainsides and ocean views.' Elaborate gardening should be avoided, according to Olmsted, as it will disappear in time. Always sacrificing immediate success for future results, Olmsted was known for organization and rare patience, and his ability to visualize his projects years ahead—sometimes generations, before the full beauty of his design was realized.

"The goal of a modern landscape designer is the emphasis on the garden as a means of creating a resting place for the spirit. Like General Washington, we prefer to rely on the use of native plants rather than horticultural rarities to manifest natural art, which is rooted in a sympathetic understanding of the land.

"The first consideration is the particular outline of the tree, bush, or perennial in the delineated space. The massing of texture and height in a garden is more important than the actual varieties of plants that are used.

"The various greens are important as well. They are placed with the intention of creating shadows, contrasts and varying perspectives, depending on the size and type of the garden, and the natural roll of the land. Color has been overemphasized in modern landscapes. We want a sense of tranquil seclusion, and a little mystery and surprise is welcome as well. The best gardens are edited with an experienced artist's eye. One must exercise restraint in the palette of colors, and allow the environment to dictate the design.

"Another goal is symmetry between the architecture involved and the plantings, such as the early building styles of fieldstone farmhouses in Pennsylvania, weathered shingle on Cape Cod and Nantucket, or the Spanish style in California. These structures fit pleasingly into their surroundings, creating a calmness which is soothing to the eye. We often use hedges, terracing, steps, pathways, bridges, and arbors as links, or gateways into the green world. Water is wonderful for both reflection and sound. Above all, one should look for balance in garden designs—tying all of the details and the parts together in proper relation to each other and to a harmonious whole. There's an honoring that one owes to the land. Remember the genius of the place."

Sophie paused. On the screen behind her, Julie replaced the images of modern American gardens with an artist's interpretation of the planet—swirls of greens and blues and earth tones.

"Human life is intertwined with the forces of nature, and nature *must* be respected. The concept of *anima mundi*, or world soul, is ancient. All that is living is connected by an invisible Oneness. We need a balanced and self renewing environment—ensuring biological prosperity and spiritual rejuvenation for all of us. Any deviation will result in physical disorders and natural disasters, I promise you. We are all bound in this web of life. It is now time to abandon the illusion of separation, and give our energy to unity. Remember *E Pluribus Unum*. Out of many—One.

"A final word regarding the healing of this earth. Our culture has taught us to believe that the power of change is always someone else's job. In my opinion we give up too much energy to people whom we deem to be authority figures, who rarely give anything of value back.

"Every individual has the ability to create a better environment. Toxic energy in the form of thoughts and feelings is poisoning us— and the planet. The concepts of scarcity and separation are illusions, invented by humans, used to control the population with fear, greed, and hate. This negative energy is unstable and disruptive. The earth is in the process of a powerful shift—the physical manifestations of which are earthquakes and tidal waves, tornadoes and hurricanes. Humanity must earn its right to remain on this planet. Personal healing is the first step for all of us, and ultimately the cure involves integrating positive energy work with politics and science across the globe.

"The more we honor and respect the spirit of the land, and the spirit that exists in every being, the faster we will restore balance to each other, and to the planet."

CHAPTER NINE

All Hallows Eve

Lacy's voice was calm. Too calm. "Emma. I'm being shunned."

"I beg your pardon?"

"You know. Like what some religions do to members of the flock who break the rules. Excluded. Ignored. Cut off."

"What is she doing now?"

"It started because I gave one of the clients my cell number, and then made the mistake of telling Esther." Lacy forced a laugh. "Information on a need-to-know-basis only, is my new motto."

"She had a problem with that? All of my clients have my cell number. Especially if we have to go to court."

"My point exactly. But you're forgetting the control factor. She can't hover over what I do or say if I'm paying the phone bill and can speak from anywhere. And she can't play her divide and conquer games if we're talking behind her back."

"Is she trying to split you guys up in the office too?"

"Oh sure. It hasn't worked on Jeff, obviously, but the two paralegals are now stiff with me, after months of being friendly. But that's not all. Remember all those ridiculous networking events she kept sending us to? Sometimes three in one week? Plus stupid, waste of gas trips to Bridgeport or New Britain for seminars that taught us nothing, or dinner meetings which accomplished even less. Now my calendar on the computer is blank. All of a sudden. Like I'm not even there. And you haven't heard the worst yet. She's cut off my calls entirely."

"To clients?"

"To anyone. Court personnel. The police department. The private investigator we use. I have to get her permission for each conversation, and keep it short. Emails too. I have to send her a draft first."

"Unbelievable."

"She says I'm too nice, that I don't understand boundaries." Lacy snarled. "This from a woman who regularly makes inappropriate comments in public, and asks personal questions in front of clients. All calculated to embarrass me, and keep me off balance."

"What are you going to do?"

"Ride it out. I can't quit, and she knows it. If she's forcing me to leave she'll have to do just that. I have nothing lined up and I'd need to go on unemployment until I find something new."

"You realize that she's jealous of you, right? You're half her age, attractive, talented. She's taking her rage out on you. Then she feeds off your discomfort."

"I know, but how does that help me? So she's psychotic," Lacy's voice began to shake. "No law against that, right? It's certainly never stopped family litigators in the past. I don't mind telling you that it's getting to me Emma. I have headaches all the time. My stomach is a disaster area. I'm even breaking out like some kid in junior high, and I haven't had a good night's sleep in weeks."

"What does Jeff say about the shunning nonsense?"

"I think he's barely holding it together himself, and he knows that if I leave, it's all on him, and he hates going to court."

"But how has he managed to stay out of Esther's firing range for so long? What's his secret?"

"According to the paralegals his mother is just as bad, and he's used to having a nutty older woman dumping her stuff on him. He knows what she wants, and he just gives it to her. He can be the Esther clone."

"That's not good."

"No, it's not. There's a short distance from there to player. You never know what's real with him—he's always acting a part. Not healthy either way. And I have no interest in hooking up with an emotional chameleon."

So Jeff's interest in Lacy was an occasional energy boost—nothing more. "Look, if I could take you on, I would in a heartbeat. This office is just too new."

"I'm not begging for a job, honest. But if you hear of anything, please let me know." She lowered her voice. "There's something else, Emma. That building. Weird things keep happening. The younger paralegal won't even go upstairs alone now. And Esther's office seems to be the center of the activity. Doors banging shut or swinging open for no reason. Footsteps. Knocking. Shadows where no one is standing. Light bulbs that glow even after they've been unscrewed from fixtures. Electronics that go on and off by themselves. But the worst part is the creepy feeling. It's heavy, almost smothering. I don't know if it's coming from Esther herself, or if she's reacting to it."

"Or both," I replied.

"You've been there. What do you think?"

"A terrible crime happened in that house," I began carefully, "nearly a century ago. That energy is still there, in the woodwork so to speak. Esther is not a highly evolved being to begin with—her vibration is very thick and low. Like attracts like, remember. It may explain why she decided to buy that property in the first place. And a family litigation practice generates lots of useless drama, churning the bad stuff, and keeping it going. I think the sooner you get out of that situation the better, Lacy. It's sick and it's making you sick."

"OK. Thanks. I'll keep trying to find something better."

I put my cell phone in my purse and reminded myself that dark entities always want to destroy the light. I said a protection spell for Lacy, asking for her to find a better paying situation that would make her happy, as soon as possible. After a moment's thought, I did the same again, this time for Jeff and the paralegals.

Halloween in Bridge Hollow. The owners of the Playhouse had cooperated with Town Hall to throw a big spooky bash at the theater. Luke and I had agreed on Highland dress for our costumes.

"Emma never misses a chance to get me into this kilt," Luke said to Sophie in exasperation.

"I'm not at all surprised."

The entertainment began with a guided historical walk through the town graveyard. Over a thousand luminaries lit the path, which wound around ancient trees and headstones for as far as we could see. An actor, in early nineteenth century clothes and cloak, greeted our group at the gate.

"Welcome to Bridge Hollow Cemetery," he said, waving his lantern. "This land was designated as a final resting place in 1747, and many Revolutionary War soldiers and their descendants are buried here. At this time of year the boundary between our world and theirs is thin, and the departed have been known to return to the earth. Kindly follow me as we visit some of them. Watch for low grave markers please, and keep the line of candles to your right."

It was a cold evening, and the stars were unusually bright. The wind blew the leaves on the ground into swirls around our feet. There was occasional rustling in the trees. Luke held the flashlight aimed at the ground as we passed through.

"Emma!" Carlie's voice came from behind us, where she was walking with Julie and several classmates. "Ghosts don't haunt cemeteries—right?"

"Who knows—with all the party minded folks tripping about tonight? Great energy sucking opportunities here!"

"I'll protect you Carlie!" A tall young man exclaimed, valiantly waving a hockey stick. I assumed that this was the mercurial Max. Giggling from teenage girls ensued.

We climbed a slight hill and zigzagged through bushes. Our first stop was in front of a young woman in colonial dress and apron, holding a bucket in one hand. She told us her sad story of little education, endless kitchen toil, too many children, and nursing a husband who came back from the war with horrific injuries.

Our second stop was a middle-aged man, who related his tale of family separated on two continents because of the conflict with Great Britain, and of the eventual reunion of various loved ones in Connecticut in the late 1780's. He had operated the local tavern, now part of the museum, and had died in 1811.

"These actors are pretty good," Luke said, as we proceeded down the hill again. "You really feel like you're back in time with them."

I agreed. "Brave, too. Imagine standing alone in a dark cemetery on Halloween, waiting for the next tour group to file by."

"Hey Ms. Carbury," said a female voice. I turned and smiled. Suzie Marino and Cassie Simmons from my history class were right behind us, surrounded, as usual, by various members of the BHS basketball team. I introduced Luke.

Our fifth gravesite visit was a surprise—Attorney Esther MacInerney, dressed in a heavy ball gown with a purple cloak. Several cries of dismay emanated from behind us, as Esther displayed her frosty tombstone grin. She pulled her hood down and waved a fan dramatically as we approached.

"My name is Maria Barrett Bell. I was the wife of the wealthiest man in town during the Revolution. He owned many of the businesses, and much of the surrounding farmland. I raised money to buy supplies for the Continental army, and organized women to knit socks and make shirts for our soldiers. My husband served on committees for the church and for Bridge Hollow School. We had five children, and three of them are buried here with us. I died in 1798 when our house caught fire, and I was trapped upstairs in my bedroom."

"This is an uplifting experience," I heard one of the boys whisper sarcastically. "Didn't anyone live to a ripe old age dandling grandchildren in this town?"

The tenth and last stop was the town magistrate, who had kept the peace in post Revolutionary Bridge Hollow, and had dispatched several murderers during his tenure.

"Welcome!" The actor called to us. "My name is Josiah Swiggart. If you care to look to your right, you'll see where we hanged young James Abbott in 1801 for beheading his sweetheart with an ax." He flashed his lantern with his left hand, and we saw that a noose was dangling from the big oak tree behind him. "She had decided to marry another man." The magistrate fixed on the crowd, and suddenly pulled Max toward the noose, fitting the rope around his neck. "I enjoyed this part of my job," he said, cackling. The girls in Carlie's group were particularly affected by his impromptu performance.

Max grinned good naturedly. "Yeah, but I'm too tall for this branch!"

The crowd laughed, an owl hooted, and our tour guide led us back to the gate.

We proceeded to the program in the auditorium of the theater, the highlight of which was Sophie's remarks on the origins of All Hallows Eve. Images projected from the light and sound booth were flashed on the walls and the black curtain behind her, and mystical piping emanated softly from the speakers. The house was in total darkness.

"The celebration of Halloween has been reinvented many times over the centuries," Sophie began, "and has its roots in the ancient festival of Samhain, which was observed in the Celtic regions—primarily in Ireland and Scotland. Samhain, or 'summer's end' was an agricultural celebration. An old pastoral harvest feast, Samhain signaled the time for the decrease in the strength of the sun. It was the season for taking stock of the herds and food supplies, and reorganizing communities for the challenging winter months to come. In Celtic lore Samhain took place between the autumn equinox and the winter solstice, and marked the boundary between summer and winter, or light and darkness.

"Most of our information on Celtic practices is based on folklore, rather than historical evidence, but Samhain was also known as a period of supernatural intensity. The Celts were completely dependent on nature, and all its volatility, for survival. With the cold and dark of winter came a thinning of the veil between the seen and unseen worlds, or so the Celts believed. To ward off the spirits from the ancient mounds that were prevalent in the countryside, the Celts built gigantic bonfires to symbolize the sun, and invoked the aid of the gods and goddesses for protection.

"Samhain represented an interval between the two halves of the year, and was said to be suspended in time. The Celts believed that the natural order of the universe was thrown into chaos during Samhain, and that the earthly world became entangled with that of the dead. The boundaries between this reality and the other world dissolved. It was also a time when prophecies for the coming year could be relayed by Celtic shamans through various methods of divination.

"It was said of Samhain that all other boundaries were erased as well. Ghosts could be lurking on the property lines between neighboring lands, or on styles between fences, and it was deemed dangerous to stand on a crossroad or bridge.

"Legend claims that Samhain was devoted to ancestor worship. The Celts supposedly wore masks and costumes and danced around the bonfires, to honor their deceased relatives, and the deities of the fields and flocks, but also to fool any malevolent spirits who may have been wandering abroad. Once home, the Celts would light their hearths with embers from the community bonfire, and place food and drink outside their doors to appease any mischievous roaming ghosts.

"This is one theory as to the origins of trick-or-treating. It also explains the later use of black and orange to symbolize the holiday— black represents the time of darkness, and orange the reappearance of the sun, or longer days, after the Winter Solstice takes place at the end of December. The modern use of Jack O'Lanterns probably began in parts of Ireland and the Scottish Highlands, with the custom of placing candles in hollowed out gourds or turnips to frighten away the dead.

"Once the Romans had conquered the Celts, their traditions mingled, and with the coming of Christianity, many old Celtic festivals were merged with the Church calendar. All Saints—also known as All Hallows—is celebrated on November first, and All Souls Day on November second. All Souls was a designated day for honoring the dead, and midnight vigils were held at gravesites. It was believed that the dead could walk amongst the living on All Hallows Eve, so people would light candles and leave food offerings for their departed relatives.

"The practice of 'souling' evolved as the poor began to move from house to house asking for food and money, and praying for the dead in return, thus speeding a soul's passage to heaven.

"After the Protestant Reformation in the sixteenth century, Halloween in England continued to be associated with the supernatural, although the origins of the festival were lost—but in Ireland and Scotland the traditions continued. In the Scottish Highlands bonfires still blazed from the hilltops, and the natives conducted torchlight processions around their crops to encourage their fertility, and dissuade any interference from ghosts and witches.

"In 1605 Guy Fawkes and his group of Catholic malcontents were foiled in their plot to blow up the houses of Parliament in London. This victory has come to symbolize England's deliverance from Papal control, and later in 1688, with the arrival of William of Orange, freedom from the absolutist rule of King James II. As a result, the Fifth of November is now known as Bonfire Night, famous for rowdiness and pranks, and important as a time for burning in effigy any unpopular leader whose actions have exceeded the scope of his or her authority. Even today, Guy Fawkes Night serves as an occasion when community justice is carried out.

"The holiday became known as Halloween in the eighteenth century, and the celebration continued to be associated with the changing seasons and the agricultural cycle, as well as being an important time for hearing prophecies—the most common being the identity of one's marriage partner."

Sophie paused. "So how did Halloween come to the U.S.? The Puritans of New England were not known for revelry in any form, and they certainly avoided any holiday to do with specters or witchcraft.

"As a result, Halloween did not take off in North America until the nineteenth century, when substantial numbers of Irish and Scots immigrants arrived, bringing with them their old country traditions of mischief-making, wearing costumes and masks—known as guising—and games that were more likely to foretell romantic partners than death. Halloween had evolved as a significant courtship ritual for marriage.

"Since then Halloween has undergone many changes. Today it is primarily a secular community centered festival, although it still retains some links to nature and the harvest—witness the carved pumpkins and gourds that we see around us, as well as the customs of hayrides and bobbing for apples. Halloween is now one of the most important party nights of the year in the United States—second only to Christmas.

"The modern celebration of Halloween shows us that people prefer to have fun, rather than fear. The holiday in effect allows us to mock the pretensions of any power that threatens to control us. Please consider taking this valuable lesson to heart. Fear invariably leads to inactivity, which in turn generates even more pain. Life is all about humor—and fun. We don't need to escape from reality in order to play."

As we clapped, a drum roll sounded, and the black curtain went up behind Sophie. The DJ began the festivities by blasting the opening bars of *Thriller*.

An hour later Luke and I were happily engaged in our own version of dirty dancing to *Slow Ride*—a tribute to the excellence of the margaritas served—when a sound of shrieking suspended the proceedings.

Two of Carlie's classmates had taken over a dressing room for their own private party, and had been interrupted.

"She was all blowy," I heard the girl exclaim. "Like she was standing in the wind."

"She was there in the doorway one moment," the boy with her said, "and then whoa! She was right up in my face. Amazing speed— no human could do that. Asked in a weird accent who we were and what the hell were we doing in her room."

"Then she sort of just plowed right through us—and disappeared!"

"This *is* an active theater," Sophie informed us.

"Marvelous," muttered a tall man nearby. "So pleased to have confirmation."

"Jerry's business partner," Luke explained.

"They're annoyed by the noise," I said, nodding to the back corner of the stage. "It's not exactly Gilbert and Sullivan."

"Disgruntled resident?"

"Man dressed like he's going on safari in 1880."

Then we all heard the crash. It was as though twenty pianos had fallen from a height, very close by. We felt a vibration run through the floor. Several people roared offstage to investigate, but the report came back that there was no evidence of any damage.

"Residual energy," Sophie volunteered. "There must have been a terrible accident here once. I'm getting a visual of heavy scenery on ropes falling—actors being crushed."

The bartender fired up the blender, and the party resumed.

While the DJ was on a break, I took Luke into the greenroom. We sat on the sofa, looking through old playbills. "It's noisy in here," Luke said, glancing around. "Like trees are scraping their branches on the walls outside."

"Two centuries of egocentric actor energy has been absorbed into this room," I laughed. "And it's still bouncing all over. Worse than lawyers."

We moved over to the display case, and I pointed to Hugh Murdoch's gold pocket watch. "I hope someone cleared that thing with sage smoke before they put it here. Otherwise, it's bringing all the energy from the murder into this theater."

"I never thought of that," Luke said, staring at me. "So wouldn't that be true of anything that's old or used? The previous owner's energy—good or bad?"

"Absolutely. That's why there aren't any antiques in my house."

"What about Aunt Beatrice's things?" Luke asked. "They're hundreds of years old, and I've got them spread out in nearly every room."

"No worries!" I replied. "I've cleared the whole farm, and smudged my study twice. We're safe."

We met Carlie and Max at the buffet table in the props room, loading their plates with roast beef and broiled potatoes.

"We're looking forward to your next home game, Max," Luke said. "I've got the schedule on the fridge—Emma and I enjoy hockey."

"Emma used to play, didn't you?" Carlie announced.

"Well, not to say play—exactly. My ex husband did, and I practiced with him, and some of his friends occasionally."

"There's a women's team," Max said, slurring a bit. I looked suspiciously toward his glass.

"At the BHS rink—I know. A friend of mine is a She Lion."

"So you should join them!" Carlie exclaimed. "You can't row in the winter, and you don't like riding when it's cold. Great work-out, and excellent networking potential."

Luke grinned. "So it's settled then. You're skating."

I decided that I needed to be back on the stage with another margarita.

The DJ had just started *Rock Around the Clock* when I saw two Bridge Hollow policemen walk down the center aisle and beckon to Jerry and his partner.

"Uh oh," I said, pointing. Luke twirled me around to look.

"Hmm. Want to hear what's going on?"

"Always."

Luke was back in five minutes. "OK, I know you don't like Esther MacInerney, Emma. But this is just creepy."

I quivered. Probably the tequila.

"Esther was just found by members of the museum staff, who were clearing up after the cemetery tour. She was still by her allotted gravestone. Lights all burned out. She'd been tarred and feathered."

"Excuse me?"

"Well, molasses covered—and feathered."

"So not burned—just really sticky?"

"And bound, blindfolded, and gagged."

"Pretty serious assault then," I replied, trying—but failing—to show concern. "Have they arrested anyone?"

"Not a clue, apparently. They got Chief Marino to come back to the station for this one. He's furious."

"Missing a good party?"

Luke raised an eyebrow.

"OK, you're right, I don't like the woman. She's mean and a fraud," I said, thinking of Lacy. "But she must have been terrified," I added, suddenly feeling compassion.

"People come into our lives for a reason, a season, or a lifetime," Sophie had once said to me. "Everyone is a teacher. You don't have to like them. You don't have to want to be around them. You just have to refrain from judging them. Learn the lesson and move on."

The DJ shut down at midnight, and the revelers began to move slowly toward their cars. Luke and I walked around the building and through the park, down to the lake. The moon was waxing, and it sent cool white streamers of light across the tops of the trees and onto the water. We sat on the bench near the dock, listening to the eerie call of the loons.

"They ought to be taking off about now, shouldn't they?" I asked. "Somewhere warm?"

"A little late this year," he replied, putting his arm around me. We sat quietly for a bit.

"Neutrality is the key," Sophie had said. "If you want to raise your vibration—and we're all being challenged to do that in this new energy—let go of judgment. Then the elevator can move up. Think of your legal scales and Lady Justice. Justice is blind, right? Everyone has a level playing field."

I took several deep breaths, held them for three seconds, and then let them go, asking silently to send energy to Esther MacInerney to serve her highest need.

There was an arbor covered with yellowed wisteria vines to our right. The path from the woods passed through it, and continued behind us, disappearing into the darkness somewhere near the perennial border.

In my semi inebriated state I thought of portals—inter-dimensional doorways.

And just then we heard the sounds of laughter. Luke and I turned as an invisible group of men and women crunched on the gravel path toward us, with the tinkle of glassware and the smell of cigar smoke, and then vanished into the tree line by the water.

We stared at each other.

"So—should I leave some smoked salmon and a bottle of chardonnay outside the back door for Aunt Beatrice tonight?" Luke asked, grinning. "Just in case?"

"It couldn't hurt," I agreed.

CHAPTER TEN

Martha and Abigail

S id and Becca were in their early thirties. Just engaged, they were anxious to work out the financial details regarding their legal union, before the wedding took place.

"I'm comfortable with drafting a prenuptial agreement for you," I informed them, "as long as you each have it reviewed by separate counsel before you execute."

They nodded, and signed my retainer. They had each filled out financial affidavits from the Judicial Department website.

"Are we limited to the subject of money and property in our discussions with you?" Sid asked. "Because we have other concerns as well."

"A pre-nup can say anything you want, as long as you both agree, and there is full disclosure."

Becca shifted in her chair. "We want to talk about sex," she said.

My impression of the mediation process was beginning to improve.

"In what context?"

"Quality."

"And quantity," Sid added. "We keep hearing from our friends that sex starts to drop off, practically from the time that they get back from the honeymoon."

"We don't want that to happen." Becca explained.

"Do you think that entering into a contract regarding sexual relations in the marriage will address your concerns?"

They both nodded.

"How would you like me to word the provision?"

"Something along the lines that we both recognize the importance of physical intimacy in a marriage," Becca said breezily, "and we each expect the other to honor our commitment to keeping his or her end up—so to speak."

"In terms of quality, as well as quantity?" I asked.

"Definitely," Sid replied. "Here," he said, pulling a sheet of paper from his briefcase. "We've spelled it out for you."

"Positions, toys—everything."

Not bad. I considered making a copy for Luke.

"Also locations," Becca informed me. "We're big on adventure. And we love taking risks. We're members of the Mile High Club."

Aha.

"Several times over," Sid assured me.

"Let's Remember the Ladies," I said to my U.S. History class, "as Abigail Adams once wrote to her husband John during the American Revolution. Specifically, our first two First Ladies—Martha Washington and Abigail Adams. How did their marriages impact the new United States? Who wants to start with some background?"

"The Washingtons were plantation owning Virginians," Ed began. "They were American gentry with huge tracts of land and an expensive lifestyle. They liked their European luxuries."

"They also had over a hundred slaves," Jon added. "Martha was a wealthy widow with two children when she married George."

"But here on the east coast, Abigail and John lived the simple life," Maddie said. "Both were from the Boston area—her father was a minister, his was a farmer. Their farm in Braintree was tiny in comparison to Mount Vernon."

"The Adamses were in the thick of it in Boston," Cassie remarked. "Right from the beginning of the bickering with the British. The Stamp Act, the Boston Massacre, the Tea Party, the Coercive Acts imposed on Boston and its harbor. Abigail and their son John Quincy—our sixth President—watched the Battle of Bunker Hill from a high point near their house."

"From 1774 on, while John was in Philadelphia, representing Massachusetts in the Continental Congress—and later on during his diplomatic stint in Europe—Abigail stayed behind to run the farm and educate their four children," Heather added. "They were apart for most of the next ten years. So they wrote lots of letters to each other, and kept them. Which is why we know so much about their marriage."

"Meanwhile, Martha burned all *their* personal letters," Adam said, helpfully. "After the General died."

"You've all read your history books," I laughed. "Well done. But let's talk about them as men and women, and their relationships to each other. How did these two power couples help lay the foundation of this country? Who was Martha Washington, for example, and what was her contribution?"

"We tend to think of Martha as the gray haired old lady in the white cap," Piper answered. "Chubby and sweet looking. But Martha as a young widow was a hot ticket with a passionate nature and a lot of money. She had her choice of second husbands—and she wanted George. They were married early in 1759, and were happy together for forty years."

"Known as Patsy in her youth, Martha was born into the plantation elite—a prestigious tobacco growing family, and she married wealthy Daniel Parke Custis while she was still a teenager," Suzie added. "Seven years later he was dead, and Martha was a very independent woman. There were no trustees named in Daniel's will—Martha was free to make her own decisions regarding her property."

"Lucky lady," I remarked. "And very unusual for the period. But what was Martha like? What was it about her that attracted George—beyond her big bucks?"

"Charm," Henry said. "Martha was the perfect hostess. Gentle, kind, and motherly. She knew how to run a comfortable, yet efficient home."

"Intelligent, but not an intellectual," Ed continued. "Martha was a good listener, and very composed. She could soothe anyone."

"She was brought up to follow the British aristocracy's ideal of lady-like deportment," Megan announced. "Stylish dress, ultra sociable and gracious—she could sing, dance, and ride beautifully. She was great at needlepoint and embroidery."

"Nothing wrong with any of that," Rob commented, and we all laughed. "She could read and write, couldn't she? Do the accounts? Express an opinion?"

"She was a tough lady," Suzie countered. "Mrs. Washington spent every winter with her husband and the encamped army during the Revolution—and the conditions were ghastly, especially during the season at Valley Forge. She and the other officers' wives helped hold the men together until the fighting resumed in the spring."

"They didn't have central heating, remember," Henry added. "No electricity, or washing machines, or bathrooms—not even running water. There was a constant shortage of food and supplies. Everyone jammed together in small houses—and it was much worse for the soldiers."

"Martha was reportedly terrified by the sound of the guns," I prodded them, "so why was she there? Why not remain in relative comfort at Mount Vernon?"

"It wasn't necessarily safe for her at home either," Ted answered. "As wife of the Commander in Chief, she would be in big trouble if the Brits decided to sail up the Potomac River and grab her."

"She wanted to please George," Kim retorted, "and George needed Martha with him when the fighting was suspended. She created the happy household feeling that he craved during the war—to stay focused, I suppose."

"The confidence between them was said to be unconditional," Heather told us. "They were full partners in their marriage, and apparently discussed everything—and anything."

"I guess George couldn't trust anyone else," Matt commented, thoughtfully. "It's lonely at the top, and as the new American icon George had to appear to be perfect to everybody—except Martha."

"She humanized him," Henry remarked. "Washington must have appeared pretty unapproachable, otherwise."

"Martha made her own decisions," Rob said. "Washington never played the General card when it came to his wife. She did as she pleased. And he genuinely enjoyed her company. Their mutual love and support kept him going, which kept the Revolution going. The Washingtons were together for more than half of the war."

"Nice," Suzie said, wistfully.

"Martha was a quietly confident woman," Maddie mused, "with tremendous dignity—but her very powerful husband was never fazed by her independence."

"He relied on it," Piper added. "Which is why the Washingtons were such a formidable team."

I referred to my notes. "Martha Washington once wrote that whether one experiences happiness or misery is wholly dependent upon one's approach to life—rather than one's circumstances. She worked hard at maintaining a calm and optimistic outlook at all times, and was determined to be cheerful and happy. Mrs. Washington's presence inspired hope and courage for all of the men." I looked up. "Comments?"

"It's all about the so-called Still Center," Cassie said, wisely. "That quiet place deep inside that we all have—well, most of us," she made a face at Matt, and he grinned, "where there is only humor, peace, and serenity. We create our own realities."

"Excellent Cassie," I replied. "Quite possibly it was this Still Center that sustained Martha through eight years of war, and then through another eight years while her husband served as our first president. Washington was committed to the public good, and his wife was committed to him."

"But they were only really happy at home farming, in Virginia," Jon noted. "Martha found political life tedious, and was exasperated when the General was elected President—especially the second time."

"I think it's interesting that George was repeatedly sick during his presidency," Kim remarked, "but healthy throughout the war."

"Outdoor living," Heather replied. "He didn't like being stuck in an office, placating everybody, and being manipulated by Jefferson. He preferred riding and planting."

"Martha was afraid that the stress would kill him before he could retire," I said. "But let's get back to the women. As wife of the Vice President, Abigail Adams always stood with Martha at formal gatherings. Abigail was famous for her blunt opinions. What was her assessment of Martha?"

"Easy and polite," Suzie answered.

"Modest," Kim added. "An object of respect."

"Unaffected and feminine," Ed concluded. "Sounds like the perfect First Lady."

"Washington published his farewell statement in the fall of 1796," Piper said, "and John Adams was sworn in as the second U.S. President in March of 1797. George and Martha arrived home in Mount Vernon later that month."

"And there they stayed," Cassie concluded. "Entertaining visitors and improving the estate. Until George's death in December of 1799."

"He really wasn't meant to make it to the next century, was he?" Matt queried.

"New era for the country," Heather pointed out.

"Final points about the Washingtons?"

"Their very real partnership was the foundation of the General's success," Suzie replied, sighing. "Which affects all of us, even in this century."

"George always put Martha's comfort and safety before everything else," Henry commented. "Even in his will."

"Martha's combination of warmth and bravery enabled her husband—the top patriot—to remain buoyed up," Jon concluded. "Despite the amazing pressure he was under to win the war and then hold a new government together."

"Well done!" I said. "Now let's examine an entirely different sort of marriage—and partnership. The two 'Dearest Friends,' Abigail and John Adams. What was Abigail like?"

"She was an early feminist," Ted answered. "Abigail Smith Adams was a self taught intellectual. She was brilliant with language, keen on research and historical analysis, and one of the best journalists that we have regarding the American Revolution."

"Abigail was fiercely independent, grounded, and sane," Kim said. "She served as John's rock—he was an explosive guy. Insecure and volatile. Impatient. Vain. His wife provided the stability he needed to reduce his stress and keep him calm. She exhibited stoic acceptance—most of the time."

"John was an early activist against the British in Boston," Adam continued. "He was a member of the radical groups the Sons of Liberty and the Committees of Correspondence. He reported everything that he heard to his wife, and his involvement from the beginning transformed Abigail from colonial farmer's spouse to visionary patriot. He read drafts of his essays to her and asked her advice—she was his political confidante throughout their marriage. John recognized Abigail as his equal."

"They were married in October of 1764," Heather said. "Even before the problems with the Brits began, Abigail spent much of their early marriage alone. John's law practice dragged him all over Massachusetts on horseback."

"You always knew when he was home," Henry laughed, "because Abigail would have another baby."

"They were constantly moving back and forth between the farm in Braintree, now Quincy—and the house in Boston," Kim said. "The redcoats arrived in Boston in 1768, and life became increasingly scary. John sacrificed his law practice and working on his farm for public service. Their marriage was a joint endeavor. He and Abigail were committed to the American cause as partners and colleagues."

"Abigail once wrote to John—'I long impatiently to have you upon the Stage of Action.' She honored her husband's abilities and integrity, and put her faith in Providence," I told them, "as John took off first for Philadelphia and the Continental Congress, and then later for France and Holland. All right. The Revolution is over. Abigail and their daughter Nabby join John and John Quincy in Europe as Ambassadors for the new United States—her first public role. The Constitution is ratified. The Adamses return home, and John becomes our first Vice President. At that time our capital is briefly New York, and then Philadelphia.

"Abigail was an ambitious woman, with a sharp mind and tongue. She was a product of the Age of Reason, and prized learning and morality—and their importance in public service. She was acutely aware of the social inequalities of her time—her claim was that women inherited intelligence and curiosity that were equal to that of men." I paused. "Let's talk about the period of Enlightenment for a bit. What did that word mean in the eighteenth century?"

"It meant science," Suzie said, pulling out her notes, "and skepticism. Which is odd, when you consider how we use it today. The movement began in Europe with men like Locke, Voltaire, and Newton, and it was about challenging any idea that was founded in tradition or faith—so no more superstition."

"The ideals of the Age of Reason also opposed religious intolerance, and abuse of power by the church and government," Piper added. "Liberty and democracy were key concepts."

"Enlightenment definitely had an important impact on the American colonists," Henry said, "especially Benjamin Franklin and Thomas Jefferson—who were both big on scientific analysis. They each introduced new perspectives on nature, and the human relationship to our environment."

"What was Deism?"

"The belief that Observation of Nature proved the existence of God," Ed quoted. "It was a religion for intellectuals, who liked Reason. They rejected the authority of the church, but still believed in one god."

"The Enlightenment period continued until the early nineteenth century," I said, "and then Romanticism took over, which later produced our emotional friends Emerson and Thoreau, and the Transcendentalists."

There was the collective sound of groaning.

"So now we have a good background for what drove Abigail, and the rest of the patriots, to toss everything they knew from European customs, and create a brand new society. Along with the Washingtons, Abigail and John hosted a 'republican court;' a balance of formality and simplicity, and Abigail, like Martha, became an asset to her husband in the all important government social circle. After Washington's two terms were over, the U.S. experienced its first peaceful transfer of power, and John became our second President. What was that administration like?"

"With only four more years of life in public service to go," Megan grimaced, "John's one term was pretty tough. He and Abigail took it on together; and conflict after conflict occurred. The tension between Jefferson and Hamilton; Jefferson's break with John and Abigail over anti Federalism; dealing with Napoleon and the French. John had no executive experience, and he didn't have Washington's presence—or Jefferson's charm. Abigail was his one trusted advisor."

"Why is there no memorial to John Adams anywhere?" Piper queried. "No building in DC; no face on our money—he's not even on

Mount Rushmore! And Adams had his hand in everything, from the beginning."

"He wasn't likeable?" Matt wondered.

"People thought he wanted another king, so they didn't trust him?" Maddie volunteered.

"Jefferson stole John's thunder," Ed concluded. We all laughed.

"After a particularly nasty election, Jefferson beats John Adams in 1800, and serves two terms," Suzie said. "John finally returns to Massachusetts and his farm."

"Abigail and John eventually renew their friendship with Jefferson—once he's out of office," I continued. "The U.S. wins the War of 1812—we've been at peace with the Brits ever since—and with the exception of some varied family crises, all is relatively calm for the Adams family."

"Abigail passes in 1818," Suzie said. "John, who is roughly ten years older, continues on, until his famous double death with Jefferson, on July 4, 1826—exactly fifty years after the signing of the Declaration of Independence."

"Spooky," Megan shivered. "How did the Age of Reason explain that one?"

"Look at it as the Universe sending a powerful message," I told them. "These men and women had set the stage to begin the world over again. Remember what Abigail Adams once wrote—'It is not rank or titles, but character alone, which interests posterity.' Integrity was paramount in her mind. For now, think about this question— what is liberty? The inalienable right to own property? Or, the birthright of every individual—regardless of government?"

CHAPTER ELEVEN

Opening Night

The Bar Association Meeting was being held in the new auditorium at University of Connecticut Fairfield. A panel of administrative judges was slated to talk to us about changes that had been proposed for the Practice Book in civil and family litigation. More than five hundred lawyers from all points in Connecticut were filing in and taking their seats.

"Hope they have adequate ventilation in this room," Tina joked.

"All the puffery?" Denise grinned.

"Reminds me of the Jersey Turnpike in August," Tina replied.

I located three chairs together and moved in quickly to claim them. To my left was an elegant blond woman dressed in a beautifully cut gray suit. I smiled at her as I sat down, and she extended her hand.

"Schuyler Jamison," she said. "I'm in Litchfield County."

"So am I," I responded, surprised. "In Bridge Hollow. Our satellite office is, anyway," I added, and introduced Denise and Tina. "They run the Westport part of the practice," I explained. "But I still make the drive down here to Fairfield County on occasion."

"I used to work in Bridge Hollow," Schuyler began. "For about eight months. Then I moved to a firm up in Salisbury a year ago."

I suddenly realized why she looked familiar. I lowered my voice.

"You used to work for Esther MacInerney. I know Lacy Basdin quite well."

"How is Lacy doing?" She asked quickly. "We lost touch after I left. Frankly...."

"You just wanted to cut and run? I know the feeling. Lacy is not doing as well as she should be."

Schuyler nodded. "Lacy's a good lawyer, and with some experience, she'll be just fine. She is not going to get anywhere if she stays with Esther, however." She paused. "Let me guess. Has Esther begun the shut-out on Lacy?"

"If you mean blocking calls and emails, keeping her out of the loop with clients, and pitting the rest of the staff against her, then the answer is yes. I take it that this is a pattern of behavior with Esther?"

"Oh Lacy and I are the most recent in a long line of the used and abused at that office," Schuyler said grimly. "Esther does it to the clients too, by the way. Very few people are aware of how often she's been reprimanded by Statewide Grievance for forcing a client into an impossible position, and then filing a motion to withdraw at the last minute. But she always schmoozed her way out of those complaints," Schuyler added, a bitter tone in her voice. "I'm forty-five years old, Emma. Been in the practice over twenty years, with a lot of court time—including Appellate arguments and jury trials—under my belt. And that woman treated me as if I was a first year associate. Then I found out that she does the same to every lawyer who works for her." She swallowed, and then looked embarrassed. "Sorry. I thought that I had recovered long ago from my time served in that office."

"I've told Lacy that I think Esther suffers from Narcissistic Personality Disorder," I informed her, in a whisper. "I've had some personal experience with NPD, and it is brutal. The key to dealing with these people is constantly reminding yourself that you are not the problem."

"Thanks. But knowing that I wasn't the crazy one didn't help alleviate the stress when there were no other jobs to be had, and Esther was signing my paychecks. At first she acted as though we were best friends. She took me out to lunch—offered to help me move—even gave me several cash advances when money was tight. Then the abuse began. She'd send me to court at the last minute; shadow me at depositions and berate me about my performance afterward; constantly make changes to my schedule with little notice. In just a few months she gave me two substantial raises, offered me a partnership, and then terminated me."

"That *is* nuts."

"But the funny thing was," Schuyler continued, "as I packed up my books and certificates, all I could feel was relief. Imagine being legally bound to that woman! I used to have nightmares about it."

"Like marriage," I said, shuddering.

"She actually told me that she wanted a 'marriage'!" Schuyler exclaimed. "And all I could think of was 'Yeah, right'. So you can sashay off to Hartford, while I do all the work, and you make all the money." She shook her head. "And that's exactly what happened. Once Esther was elected to the State Senate, everyone kept telling me that I should be happy—that it meant job security. But the money was nothing compared to the hours that I was putting in, and I knew how unstable she was. I never felt comfortable with the fact that so many of our male clients could manage to pay our huge retainers, but not child support or daycare expenses. In the end, I cared more about my reputation with the judges." She paused. "Is Jeff still there?"

"Yes."

"Sweet guy, and very helpful whenever I had a question. But odd. He knew exactly what Esther wanted to hear, and exactly what she wanted done—and he always did it. Regardless of what he thought; even ethically. It was like working with a Stepford Lawyer."

"Ethically?"

"Well—morally. We'd represent the husband in a divorce. Esther would tell Jeff to lowball the numbers, or inflate the wife's earning capacity, and he would, even when he knew that it wouldn't fly with Family Services, or with a judge. Of course, I was the poor soul who had to go in and make the lame arguments; and get the blast from her back at the office when we lost. And the land use cases!" Schuyler leaned in. "Do you know how connected Esther is in Bridge Hollow? With the town leaders, I mean?"

"She sits on a number of boards, doesn't she?"

"She sits on way more than that Emma. Ask around."

At the lunch break I told Denise and Tina about my conversation with Schuyler Jamison.

"How weird is that, Em!" Denise exclaimed.

"What do you mean?" Tina asked.

"We're in a crowd of hundreds of people, and Emma ends up sitting next to Lacy's predecessor at Esther's office. Talk about synchronicity!"

"That kind of thing happens to me all the time," I announced. "I'm so used to it that I just expect it now. It means that I was supposed to get some answers today, and not only about Lacy."

"Like the hot topic in Bridge Hollow?" Denise asked. "The historical parcel behind the theater? I know that you've been approached by several of the abutting landowners. What's happening with that?"

"There's a town meeting scheduled for January. Luke and I are going. They're trying to sell it to a company that wants to put in a commercial marina and dockside tavern."

"But I thought that it was a public park? How can they do that?"

"Good question."

That night I turned the volume up on the classical music station, and rode Joy alone in the indoor. I had set up ground poles in lieu of fences, so we could work on judging our distances at the canter.

I knew from my research that everything is energy—positive

or negative. People use the terms dark and evil to describe various behaviors, but essentially the common denominator is negative energy. There are individuals whose sole recreation is the domination and torment of good souls. The weapon employed is emotional pain—a much more difficult method of cruelty to inflict. It involves a love of tyranny that resembles a cat releasing and then recapturing its prey.

This type of twisted behavior usually begins with a show of extreme kindness and generosity. The victim is goaded into believing that s/he has found an understanding friend, even a savior. Dependence on the person in power is encouraged, and the controller insinuates herself into every avenue of the target's life. Then the so-called mentor turns, and her victim is left helpless in confusion and fear. The petty tyrant feels a quiet enjoyment in the victory, and feeds off the energy generated.

But dark beings are easily bored. As each victim succumbs, rebellion is smothered, and the emotional prisoner responds dully like a wounded beast who is merely enduring life. The triumph becomes stale, and the mental sadist searches for fresh quarry to conquer.

Psychotherapists have labels for the insanity of such persons, and varied explanations for the origins of their perversions.

After two decades of working with clients, I preferred the simplest analysis. If one's desire to be appreciated is thwarted, the only outlet may be cruelty—to be felt, to matter at some level—and the habit of cruelty may evolve into a desire for power over other human beings. It becomes pleasurable to cause suffering. There is complete absence of conscience, and zero remorse. Regarding the ancient argument of Nature vs. Nurture, as far as I was concerned, Nature took precedence—almost every time.

Esther MacInerney used her position as a lawyer and political leader to sustain her hunger for domination. She delighted in controlling the lives of her staff and her clients—particularly terrified women in the throes of divorce—and the elderly and intellectually challenged clients for whom she served as conservator. When that pleasure was diminished, she ran for public office.

I had experienced more than my share of bullies in this life-time—I had even done some bullying of my own. But that ship had sailed. Compassion and understanding aside, Esther's behavior was intolerable.

Thus far, Esther had done nothing obviously illegal. But if I was able to prove her involvement with town land deals—especially if it resulted in any personal enrichment—then her carefully constructed illusion of public servant would explode.

Jerome Forester called me at the office a week before opening night of *My Girlfriend's Deceased*.

"Emma! I hear that you're doing splendidly as the comical doctor's wife."

"Thanks Jerry, I hope so. It's a good group of people, and I'm enjoying myself."

"I was wondering if I could get your viewpoint on something," he lowered his voice. "Off the record, if you don't mind."

"Of course."

"Esther MacInerney. We hired her as counsel for the theater, purely on reputation. What's your opinion of her work?"

I took a deep breath. "OK Jerry, you're a friend of Luke's, so I'm going to break a personal rule regarding another member of the Bar. The woman is a monster. She knows family law, definitely, but not much civil. She's smart, and can learn fast. But her methods are the problem—they're a deadly combination of noise without substance, and a total lack of integrity or compassion. Most of what she says, or does, is a calculated fake, generated purely for PR effect. Frankly I was horrified when I saw the announcement of her new position with the theater."

There was a momentary silence.

"Jerry?"

"I really appreciate your honesty, Emma. And so will my partners."

"Has anything happened?"

"More to the point, nothing has happened. MacInerney never shows up for Board Meetings. If we call her, we talk to her associate, some young guy barely out of school. Then we'll get a placating email, always from the road. My understanding is that the third lawyer is gone now?"

Lacy had been offered a much better position with Joel Newman's office. She had danced out of that office, and never looked back.

I sighed. "Jeff's on his own, poor man."

"Well, between you and me, we are less than impressed with the Senator's lack of commitment to her position with us. I doubt that this association will last long. If it doesn't, I've been instructed to inquire—would you be interested in taking over?"

"Definitely. I'm flattered, in fact."

"Please don't be. I'm well acquainted with the folks at Tallmadge Academy, and I've heard good things. I promise to keep you posted."

I hung up, remembering something Sophie had once said to me about the return of the sacred feminine to this planet.

"Anything that isn't here to promote kindness and support the growth of community will die quickly Emma—one way or another. Depend on this. It, or they, will not be able to survive in this new energy."

I had been skeptical at first. But global events had proven Sophie correct. I wondered what this meant for individuals like Esther MacInerney, who spouted devotion to public service, but who were really only about promoting self. They trampled good people and considered them weak and valueless. The only real goal was to inspire fear and then feed on it. Their negative energy was like poison to the true hearted. However, for every poison there must eventually be an antidote.

Opening night of *My Girlfriend's Deceased.* I shared a dressing room with two of the other minor female characters. Luke and Angela had both sent bouquets, and Carlie and Julie had painted a Good Luck banner that we draped over our mirror.

"Anyone taking bets for tonight?" Erin asked. She played one of the med students.

"The odds are good for at least two major unexplained disturbances," Philomena, cast as a medical professor, replied. "I heard that anti-ghost charms were being distributed in the greenroom."

I considered running out to get one.

Sophie appeared at that moment with little bags of herbs for each of us.

"Put them in your pockets now," she said. "And wrap yourselves in white light as you leave this room."

The show was sold out. I tiptoed onstage and peaked from behind the curtain. I saw Luke sitting with Sophie and Angela, and the women from my office, six rows back. Toward the rear of the house, Carlie and Max were in a group with Julie and several students from my U.S. History class.

I did some deep breathing to dissolve the boulder in my stomach, and returned to the dressing room, where Philomena was taking impressive gulps from her hip flask.

"My opening night ritual," she grinned.

The Stage Manager, Bill Wheeler, looked in. "All set ladies?"

Twenty minutes later the curtain went up.

The play opens with a very funny number called *Anatomy Lab.* Fifteen med students dance around three cadavers on tables. There is cavorting amongst the men and women, various references to outstanding body parts—live and dead—and general merriment, until one of the professors walks in, outraged, and the students scramble to feign adult level decorum.

The next scene takes place in the Dean's office. As Professor Fox's wife, Rosalie—I was on.

Rosalie is a woman who wants every man around her to sit up and take notice. As her husband is clearly uninterested in fulfilling her connubial expectations, Rosalie is open to alternative avenues of satisfaction.

I undulated onstage in my tight red cocktail dress and fuck-me heels, and earned a few wolf whistles from the audience—my history students expressing respectful support, no doubt. I wiggled on to Fox's desk and displayed my abundant bounty, but to no avail.

Then Jonah Corrigan—the hero—strolls into the Dean's sanctum. Professor Fox is Jonah's landlord, and Jonah has come to register several complaints about the house. Rosalie's inner cougar is awakened, and the chase is on.

In the next scene Jonah is alone in his bedroom, or so he thinks.

As he sings a song called *Solitude*, extolling the virtues of soothing quiet after a stressful day, Loretta Whitcomb—the ghost in residence—glides through the doorway. She sits on his bed, ruffles his hair, and finally follows him into the bathroom for his shower. There is the sound of running water, and then a horrified shout, and the audience perceives that Jonah is aware of Loretta's presence at last.

Jonah then attempts to convince his two housemates—Clark and Ray, of Loretta's existence. They ignore the signs at first, but Loretta also likes attention from men. She smashes dishes in the kitchen, pulls down window curtains, plays with remotes, and closes the fireplace damper while a fire is burning. Fake smoke rolls across the stage, Jonah's housemates realize that they are not alone, and the lights fade on Act One.

"How are we doing folks?" I heard Jerry Forester's voice backstage.

"Little stuff," Rory, who played Jonah announced. "Someone grabbed me during the shower scene, just as Loretta came off."

"I thought that shout sounded better than just your acting!" Sharon, cast as Loretta, teased. "I smelled lavender on the stage earlier. Really strong. Is anyone wearing it?"

No response.

"Well stay alert," Jerry said, nervous. "I don't want any accidents. Good job people. Looks great from out front."

Act Two opens back at the medical school. Jonah is in the library, where he meets Elaine, a fellow student. Jonah is finally in the driver's seat with a woman, as Elaine is a shy personality, and inclined to be a loner. He sings *Experts in Biology* to Elaine, but she remains ambivalent.

Enter Rosalie Fox, who has her own methods of haunting her prey, and no interest in allowing Elaine to usurp her power over Jonah.

At the end of the second Act Rosalie is chasing Jonah through his rented house, while they engage in singing their duet, *The Benefit of Experience*. Loretta floats in midway through the song, and proceeds to attack Rosalie while Rosalie is in hot pursuit of Jonah. Rosalie can't see Loretta, and waves off the various attempts to trip her, and the moving furniture that blocks her, as mere incidentals in her quest.

Sharon and I had agreed to be as careful and deliberate as possible throughout these maneuvers. Sharon was in flat slippers under her nineteenth century gown, but the director had insisted that I wear spike heels as I hurled myself across the set after Rory, and the danger of turning an ankle—or worse—was obvious.

I was tearing around the sofa, belting out my part in our musical ode to cougaring, when the drinks cart suddenly rolled right in front of me. I caught a strong aroma of lavender, and the flash of a human shape as I started to topple over. In an impressive athletic twist Rory caught me, and engaged in some pretty serious groping as we both winged our next few moves, still singing, and then quickly returned to the script.

There had been a loud *OH!* from the audience.

"Was that what it looked like?" Jerry asked, when we were all safely offstage. "Are you all right Emma?"

I felt for Sophie's herb charm in my pocket and nodded.

"How was it from out there?" Sharon asked anxiously. "I think we covered up pretty well."

"Really good choreography, that's all," Jerry replied. "I don't think they realized that something was wrong. Well done, all three of you. That could have been a disaster."

The Stage Manager called us for the first scene of Act Three.

Jonah and his housemates attempt various methods of sending Loretta into the light on their own, to the tune of *Please Go Home,* and then finally engage professional help.

Meanwhile, Jonah is doubling his efforts to win Elaine's favor, while fending off the determined Rosalie, who is becoming more and more frustrated with his lack of interest.

In the big finale, Loretta wavers about leaving her family home after a century and a half, but finally sees her parents waiting for her on the Other Side and departs, stage right, singing *Be Brave, Make the Big Change.*

Rosalie—in a hot pink negligée—appears the same night in a bedroom that she thinks is Jonah's, but turns out to be Clark's, and is finally sated.

Professor Fox considers retirement, and selling the house.

Various other sub plots achieve conclusion, including some amusing antics in the gyn-ob department.

Jonah and Elaine get together, and both realize that perhaps the medical profession is not for them. There is a reprisal of *Solitude* as a duet, and then the entire ensemble returns to sing *The Benefit of Experience,* highlighted by Rosalie and Clark smoking their morning-after cigarettes.

"Only thirteen more performances to go," I murmured to Philomena, as the curtain came down.

The cast party was held at Bostwick Tavern, in one of the big rooms upstairs, overlooking the lake.

"The running gag about body parts is hilarious," Julie remarked.

"Yeah," Max agreed. "You're never really sure what they're talking about."

"Med students have to be pretty ghoulish, I guess," Suzie said.

"Sets them up for being doctors later," Carlie replied.

"You and Rory Miller seem to be hitting it off, Ms. Carbury," Megan giggled.

"Did it seem like that?" I asked, self conscious. "I'm just grateful not to be encased in plaster at this moment."

"Lucky he's so quick on his feet," Henry noted, laughing.

"And so good with his hands," Matt added.

Had they brought binoculars?

Luke said nothing, but I caught him smiling.

"Well?" I asked him, once the youthful contingent had moved off.

"Interesting performance, Emma," he said. "Very convincing."

"Maybe she was tapping into a part of herself that hasn't come out in a while," Sophie responded.

It was always impossible to hide anything from Sophie.

Denise, Tina, and Annie from the Westport office arrived, and I endured a second round of ribbing.

"I particularly enjoyed the scene where Rosalie has Jonah trapped in the supply closet," Annie remarked.

"How about when she leaves the big box of condoms in his backpack?" Tina grinned.

"She's like a runaway train in loud cocktail dresses!" Annie smirked.

"Beyond pushy," Tina agreed, laughing into her champagne. "Reminded me of a woman I knew in law school. She thought that hip checking men into the wall was the way to their hearts. Guys always ran screaming in the other direction."

"I never knew that you could act—or sing, Emma," Denise said, thoughtfully. "Quite illuminating. Especially when your character switched so effortlessly from chasing Jonah to snagging Clark. You were just *so* believable. You really *nailed* Rosalie."

"Didn't she?" Annie chortled.

I felt my face grow hot. "Are you all right Em?" Angela asked.

"There's a reason for everything, Emma," Sophie said quietly, when we were alone. "Even performing in this show. You are meant to learn something from playing Rosalie. Go deep and work it out. Only you will know if the answer is important or not."

That night I dreamed that I am in a swimming pool with my next door neighbor from high school. Mark wants me to help him with his French homework, but I have other plans. I pull off his bathing suit and try to kiss him, but he paddles away, crying. As I tread water I realize in horror that while Mark is still fifteen, I am an adult in my forties.

CHAPTER TWELVE

Hawthorne and the Transcendentalists

My cousin Leslie called me at the office.

"Em, we're going to Vail the week after Christmas!"

"Well done! Do you ski?"

"God no. I can barely handle an escalator. Greg's half sister is getting married. To some Austrian with a lot of money. He's putting the whole family up in a posh hotel by one of the lifts." She laughed. "I have to lose ten pounds in two weeks."

"Good luck with that."

"Thanks! I'll call you when we get back."

My next call was from Stan Mullins—the client whose noisy neighbors were scaring the horses.

"Nothing's changed since you wrote those letters, Emma," he reported. "If anything, it's worse. My wife says that Mrs. Grudberg watches to see when she and my daughter are riding in the ring, and then seconds later—the boy is out there roaring around, blasting their eardrums. Now my wife will only get on her horse if the kid is in school, which means my daughter is too. Why did I bother building this place if they can't enjoy it together?"

"I'll make an appointment with the Chief of Police, Stan," I replied. "This isn't just a nuisance case any longer. It's harassment."

"I'd appreciate it," Stan said, sounding exhausted. "I guess the whole honor-thy-neighbor thing doesn't work so great in Bridge Hollow."

My Book Club held its November meeting at Angela's big house in Ridgefield.

Tina explored the enormous wrap around porch with its views of the best sites of colonial Ridgefield. "This place is amazing, Angela. How old is it?"

"1754," Angela grinned. "It was here for the Battle of Ridgefield, anyway, although I don't have a cannonball sticking out of my foundation, like the Inn does. My family has owned the property for three generations. The upkeep is staggering, but I admit that I've never wanted to live anywhere else."

"Any ghosts?" Eliot asked.

Angela glanced at me quickly. "I've heard that the Rector of the original Episcopalian Church is still here, preparing his sermons in a small room on the third floor. I've never seen him, but I occasionally hear the scrape of a chair, or footsteps walking back and forth."

"As though he's practicing his speeches," Dottie concluded.

"Exactly. He doesn't bother me—I'm used to the noise. And my dogs keep me company when Leo isn't here. They refuse to go up to the third floor, though." We digested this information in silence. "OK!" Angela was suddenly brisk. "Who wants what to drink?"

After dinner Denise called the group to order.

"We're beginning our study of the Transcendentalists," she reminded us.

Eliot sighed. "God, I hated this stuff in high school," she complained. "And it sure isn't any easier to get through now."

"That's why we agreed to start with Hawthorne's short stories," Dottie said.

"Transcendentalism is Idealism," Denise continued. "A belief that the physical world is also spiritual, and faith in the inalienable worth of every creative individual. According to Emerson, transcendentalism is 'not new, but the very oldest of thoughts cast into the mould of these new times.'

"In this nation the movement took place mostly within fifty miles of Boston, from the 1830's to the 1850's—although arguably the era ended with Emerson's death in 1882. The important point to remember is that in the early nineteenth century, the United States was a brand new country. America had yet to make its imprint on Western culture. Everyone was still looking to Europe for art and literature.

"Writers such as Emerson, Thoreau, Emily Dickinson, Margaret Fuller, Hawthorne, and Alcott...."

"Bronson Alcott," Dottie put in. "Not his much more famous daughter Louisa May."

"Correct. They lectured and wrote in a variety of venues that encompassed philosophy, theology, social activism, literature and poetry. These people formed the first literary community in the U.S., and started what might be called an American Renaissance. Transcendentalism was a uniquely American philosophy—one of individuality and idealism—and irrevocably tied to the spirit of New England."

Eliot made a face. "I vaguely remember my English teacher babbling on about Materialists versus Idealists. I regurgitated it all for the exam, not having a clue what it really meant."

"Materialists, like John Locke, were rationalists," Denise continued. "They required external proof for everything. Idealists, on the other hand, worked from intuition, rather than the senses. They didn't look for evidence—they just knew."

"Knew what?"

"That most of what we need can be learned by observing the natural world," I replied. "Hence Emerson's 1836 work, *Nature,* which many historians view as the founding document of Transcendentalism in the United States. 'The foregoing generations beheld God and nature face to face....Why should not we also enjoy an original relation to the universe?' Emerson, a minister, argued that people didn't need intermediaries in robes to connect themselves with spirituality. Transcendentalism was not a religion, but a common ground for everyone," I concluded, thinking of Shamanism.

"Consider the Hudson River painters," Dottie said. "The landscape artists in New York. It was the first native school of American art. From about 1835 to 1870 they produced glorious paintings filled with light and color—and they drew their inspiration from the spiritual unity that they found in nature. Americans were fascinated by the untamed wilderness in the west."

"They studied British Romantic poets like Wordsworth," Tina added, "who looked to the creative and imaginative power in nature, especially in water imagery, for illumination."

"And to the spark of divinity in all of us." Denise said. "This was our beloved New England of nearly two hundred years ago—casting off its hellfire religious beliefs in a punishing God. You can imagine how Transcendentalism went down with the church and the Calvinist orthodox leaders of the period.

"Recall that the American Revolution erupted in the Boston area— Emerson's 'shot heard round the world' and the battles at Lexington and Concord. Sixty or so years later, a group of free thinkers—many were Harvard educated—began an entirely different kind of revolution. One that advocated the value of the creative individual, and a more organic, free flowing way of life."

"The Commonwealth of Massachusetts has a lot to answer for," Eliot muttered.

"Concord in particular attracted the Transcendentalist group with the beauty of its surroundings. The members deified nature, morality, liberalism, independence, and leisure."

"I think it helps to consider a broad overview of New England at that time," Tina suggested. "The people were hardworking and practical. They were passionate about education, and their ideals regarding freedom. They were wary of any form of political authority, yet they adhered to quite severe religious practices. Add to that a rugged, often hostile landscape that was very difficult to farm. The area was a perfect stage for big change."

"The decades between the War of 1812 and the Civil War produced a time of economic prosperity for New England," Denise continued. "And with that prosperity came a new social and cultural awareness—especially regarding liberal causes such as the abolition of slavery, women's suffrage, and educational reform. Transcendentalism valued each individual as equal to, and connected with everyone else. It is therefore understandable that this group of Idealists would abhor slavery, or sexual discrimination.

"In 1836 the Massachusetts Supreme Court ruled that any slave brought over the state line would automatically become free. The United States was being split apart because of slavery. The Alcotts and the Thoreau family were active in the Underground Railroad, which ran through Concord on its path to Canada.

"In summation," Denise said, "before we move on to Mr. Hawthorne; Transcendentalism, so named by German philosopher Immanuel Kant as a 'class of ideas that transcends experience'...."

"What the hell does that mean?" Eliot barked.

Tina shrugged. "It's all about our journey to understand our relationship to the universe—taken by staying still and paying attention—and transforming from each experience."

"...and was in essence an awareness of the creative power of nature, with an emphasis on individual expression, and a breaking away from the form and tradition of the past. Humanity and nature are inextricably connected. There was a mystical acceptance of intuition. As Thoreau once wrote—'Surely joy is the condition of life.' The Transcendentalist movement broke away from the traditions of the past, and looked toward a bright future—a new way of thinking and living."

"Well done Denise!" Angela said. "OK, Dorothy. You're up. Nathaniel Hawthorne."

Dottie pulled out her notes. "Hawthorne was born in Salem, Massachusetts on July 4th, 1804 of local seafaring, Puritan stock. He was educated at Bowdoin College in Maine, where his classmates included Longfellow, and future President of the United States Franklin Pierce. Between 1828 and his death in 1864, Hawthorne produced nearly a dozen novels, two volumes for children, a considerable amount of nonfiction, and roughly one hundred short stories. During his lifetime he and his family lived in various parts of Massachusetts, including Concord, and Lenox—later of Edith Wharton fame—Salem, and Boston.

"Hawthorne's fiction signaled the emergence of truly American literature. He was considered an unappreciated genius by his contemporaries.

"Hawthorne was not a humorous author, but there is a certain satirical irony to his writing style. It is famous for its atmosphere. Henry James once commented on the 'haunted world of Hawthorne's imagination,' and Anthony Trollope said that 'in no American writer is there to be found the same predominance of weird imagination as in Hawthorne.' He was fascinated by the supernatural; his stories were usually allegorical, often mysterious, and always fanciful and imaginative.

"Nathaniel Hawthorne was a descendant of witch hunters, a fact that surfaces again and again in his stories. Much of his work was based on the cultural heritage and romance of New England. He was intimate with American history, and his devotion to the use of history in his stories lends a powerful stamp of truth to his fiction.

"*The Scarlet Letter*, considered his masterpiece, was published in 1850. This novel, as well as *The House of the Seven Gables,* is representative of Hawthorne's view of the profound impact that the past has on the present. He was reportedly a shy man, who preferred solitude and observation to participation. He had a deep understanding of human nature and made extensive notes of his observations in his journals—many were used later as descriptive snapshots of realism throughout his stories.

"Hawthorne was particularly concerned with evil, and the effects of hypocrisy and sin on the conscience. His stories are dark and brooding for the most part—pretty grim. They focus on the conflicted morality and sham falseness of society. He was a master storyteller of the secretly broken law, the double life, the skeleton hidden in the closet—and the consequences thereof."

"Weird," Eliot concluded.

"In essence," Dottie said, "Hawthorne wrote parables. He was a contemplative moralist, and his stories are filled with symbolism."

"Thanks Dottie. Who wants to go first with a short story?" Angela asked.

"I want to start with *The Haunted Quack*," I replied, "which is hilarious. Hawthorne is so sarcastic about the practice of medicine that I laughed out loud in several places."

"You *would* find that story funny," Denise remarked, grinning. "It's kind of a summary judgment of your attitude toward doctors."

"Most doctors, anyway. As the story opens, the narrator is traveling on a canal boat bound for Utica, in New York State. Amongst his fellow passengers he notes a tall, thin, shabbily dressed young man with a pale and cadaverous face. This particular gentleman is restless, and is disinclined to mingle with the other folks on the trip. He mutters in his sleep, dropping words such as 'murder' and 'poison,' and bidding an unseen 'bloody old hag' to be gone. The narrator assumes that this poor man is a conscience-smitten criminal.

"Eventually they converse. The name of this guilt-ridden individual is Hippocrates Jenkins, who was born on Nantucket, and relocated to New York as a boy. At first he is apprenticed to a boot and shoe maker, but later moves in with a local physician and his wife to learn to 'cobble up people's bodies' instead. He describes this Doctor Ramshorne...."

Eliot frowned. "As in fleecing his patients?"

"Presumably. Ramshorne is described as a successful practitioner, because all of his fellow medicos have left the area, and he is therefore raking in the fees. Ramshorne has combined the offices of apothecary and physician—he makes his own drugs, and bullies his patients into buying them. Hippocrates points out that many of the doctor's former patients are now sleeping peacefully in the churchyard nearby.

"Apparently there is some question as to Doctor Ramshorne's credentials. As the local lawyer—a rival in popularity—puts it, Ramshorne's diploma is a fake, his thesis was written by a Hessian veterinarian, and Ramshorne is no more a doctor than is his jackass.

"Hippocrates spends the bulk of his medical education manufacturing Ramshorne's concoctions. The doctor is well paid for his compounds, and when he suddenly departs this life—apparently none of his recipes worked on himself—Hippocrates takes over Ramshorne's practice of quackery.

"At first all goes well. Hippocrates makes money, creates new nostrums, and assuages his conscience with the rationalization that even if his inventions do no good, at least they can do no harm."

"The real theory behind the Hippocratic oath," Tina grinned.

"But then he meets his Waterloo in Granny Gordon, for whom he prescribes his Antidote to Death, otherwise known as the Eternal Elixir of Longevity—a mixture comprised of forty-nine separate ingredients. Mrs. Gordon ingests the entire bottle and proceeds to Death's door. Granny's husband the blacksmith swears to kill Hippocrates. The old lady threatens to revenge herself upon him by haunting him day and night—and then expires.

"Knowing that he has little time before the entire town is informed of his malpractice, our hero dumps the remainder of his concoction into the canal, and makes a run for it. He hides in New York City for a time, all the while terrorized by the ghost of Granny Gordon. Hippocrates reports to the narrator that the old lady's apparition taunts him every midnight, wrapped in a red cloak, waving the empty bottle of his bogus Elixir in his face—accusing him of poisoning her.

"Hippocrates, finding this torment insupportable, resolves to return to Utica and give himself up to justice. Hanging, he concludes, is better than dealing with this dead harpy every night."

"What the narrator says to comfort him is the best line in the story," Tina laughed. "He tells Hippocrates—'if he had killed fifty old women, they could do nothing to him, if he had done it professionally.' Sure, if the accepted medical standard of the time was pouring gallons of garbage down people's throats."

"The boat docks," I continued, "and waiting on the wharf is the sheriff, the lawyer, and the old lady's husband. Hippocrates, in horror, falls into the canal. They fish him out, and we learn the ironic twist—Granny Gordon has recovered from her swoon, the town has supposed Hippocrates forcibly abducted, and had he not returned, Mr. Gordon would have been hanged for Hippocrates' murder."

"So he had been haunted by his conscience," Dottie said, "and not by an actual ghost."

"Yes," Angela agreed. "But not enough, it seems. As the story ends, Hippocrates is happily announcing his intention of returning to the practice of quackery."

"Some people just refuse to learn a lesson," Denise concluded. "Which is why we lawyers have jobs."

"Too true," I laughed. "Who's next?"

"I'll take *The Gray Champion*," Tina announced. "It's nice and short."

"Oh good," Eliot said.

"Did you read *any* of Hawthorne's stories, Eliot?" Angela asked.

"I read *The Ghost of Doctor Harris*," she replied, "thinking that it would be interesting. But basically it's four pages about an old clergyman who dies, but continues to return to his favorite chair in some library reading room in Boston. I didn't really see the point."

"The story isn't so much about the ghost, as the narrator," Dottie informed her. "He's the only one who can see the Reverend Doctor Harris after Harris' demise, but because the ghost doesn't speak to him, never does anything about it."

"People don't," I said, glancing at Angela. "It's easier."

"Well, *The Gray Champion* certainly has a point," Tina remarked. "It's chock full of American historical symbolism, which is Hawthorne's favorite thing. He explains that New England once suffered from heavier wrongs committed by the British than those that later precipitated the Revolution."

Dottie looked puzzled. "Hawthorne says in the first paragraph that James II was 'the bigoted successor of Charles the Voluptuous.' What time period is this?"

"I looked it up," Tina replied. "James II succeeded his brother Charles II, known as the Merry Monarch, in 1685. James didn't last long. He tried to push Catholicism on the Brits, was formally deposed by Parliament in 1688, and eventually fled to France in 1689. His Protestant daughter Mary II, and her husband—and cousin—William III of Orange, jointly acceded to the throne. Apparently this marked the beginning for a new kind of royal government for the Brits—constitutional monarchy. The House of Lords and the House of Commons agreed to a Bill of Rights that made the monarchy subject to Parliament.

"According to Hawthorne, James II manages to infuriate the colonies during his short reign. His Governor annuls their colonial charters, destroys their liberties, and threatens their religion. Until that time, the colonists have enjoyed perfect freedom.

"Once the rumor that James II is about to be sent packing reaches New England, the people become hopeful. The Brits respond with a display of power. The story takes place in April of 1689. The

Governor, Sir Edmund Andros—Hawthorne calls him a tyrant—assembles his redcoats and has them march through Boston accompanied by an ominous drum roll. Behind the soldiers rides a party of gentlemen—the Governor and his council. With them is the clergyman of the King's Chapel, 'riding haughtily among the magistrates in his priestly vestments, the fitting representative of prelacy and persecution, the union of church and state, and all those abominations which had driven the Puritans to the wilderness.' Another double rank of soldiers brings up the rear."

"Intimidation tactic," Eliot said.

Tina nodded. "The people in the streets are descendents of the original pilgrims, who had settled these shores in pursuit of religious freedom sixty years previously. Hawthorne describes them as having sad visages and dark attire, like their Puritan forebears. 'The whole scene was a picture of the condition of New England, and its moral, the deformity of any government that does not grow out of the nature of things and the character of the people.' One of the colonists loudly begs Heaven for a Champion to save them."

"Incoming!" Dottie remarked, grinning.

"Of course," Tina continued. "Suddenly an ancient man attired in the old Puritan dress—dark cloak, steeple hat, long gray beard, with a heavy sword at his side and a staff in his hand—appears from the crowd and advances toward the Brits. With about twenty yards between them, the old Puritan stops the army with his upraised staff and a command. The drum is immediately quiet, and the soldiers halt.

"The Governor and his men mock the old man, yet he remains firm. He warns the Governor that the cry of the oppressed people of New England has disturbed his rest. Then he prophesies that the King has lost his throne, and the Governor himself will soon be in prison. This announcement stirs the people in the street, and they prepare to fight. The Governor is shaken, and orders a retreat, and the old Pilgrim fades into the twilight. By the end of the following day, The Gray Champion's prediction has come true."

"So who was this apparition?" Angela asked.

"Hawthorne tells us that he is seen eighty years later, once more in Boston for the so-called Massacre, then in two more years on the green in Lexington," Denise answered. "And subsequently on Bunker Hill."

"The Gray Champion is the spirit of New England," Eliot volunteered.

"He is the symbol of personal freedom," I concluded. "An allegory for the energy of the original colonists. They defied an oppressive authority that they did not recognize, and dared to live their lives on their own terms."

"*Howe's Masquerade* has a similar theme," Dottie told us. "It is one of four stories that takes place in the Old Province House in Boston—the mansion of the royal governors of Massachusetts. Built in 1679, in the narrator's day—pre Civil War—it is a tavern. He describes the grand staircase, the venerable fireplace, and the octagonal cupola—with its far off views of Bunker Hill. An old gentleman in the bar tells him the story of Howe's masked ball.

"The time is the American Revolution, during the last days of the British siege of Boston. Sir William Howe, with a collection of redcoat officers and loyalist gentry, has decided to ignore the advancement of Washington's troops, and throw a party. Many of the guests are dressed as historical figures, and one group decides to lampoon the American officers, including the 'ragamuffin General of the rebels,' wearing tattered uniforms and rusty swords. Many taunts are aimed at New England, with much mirth and buffoonery, but one of the older guests is not amused. Colonel Joliffe is a stern old figure, 'representing the antique spirit of his native land.' Joliffe is a famous former soldier, and a person of known Whig principles.

"Suddenly, music is heard from outside the house—it sounds like a slow funeral march. A man in an old fashioned black suit appears from the throng, throws open the front door of the mansion, and steps back, staring upward at the grand staircase.

"The party guests watch in amazement as a line of historic authority figures in costumes descend. All are of a dignified, commanding presence, and each man waves in triumph to an unseen crowd as he crosses the threshold and vanishes."

"The old Puritan governors," Denise noted.

"Yes," Dottie continued. "Colonel Joliffe explains to the crowd that these men were the 'rulers of the old original Democracy of Massachusetts.' Several more groups of characters come down the stairs. These figures, however, appear to dread passing through the doorway. Joliffe's granddaughter gives us her explanation: 'Now were I a rebel, I might fancy that the ghosts of these ancient governors had been summoned to form the funeral procession of royal authority in New England.' Hawthorne uses a gradual diminution of lighting to create atmosphere—the figures are becoming mere shadows. The spectators are speechless with emotion—a combination of contempt, fear, and curiosity.

"The last figure makes his descent. To everyone's surprise, he is a shrouded replica of Sir William Howe himself. Their host, furious, advances on his twin."

"He thinks that this man is an actor, poking fun at him," Eliot suggested.

"Not for long," Dottie replied. "Howe is horrified by what he sees, and recoils. The specter stamps his foot, shakes his clenched hands in the air, and passes into the night. The funereal music fades as the bell tolls midnight in the steeple of the Old South, and a deep boom of cannon from Washington's army is heard, closer than before."

"Whoa!" Eliot cried.

"Pretty intense," Tina agreed.

"Colonel Joliffe takes pleasure in having the last word. 'The empire of Britain in this ancient province is at its last gasp to-night; almost while I speak it is a dead corpse; and methinks the shadows of the old governors are fit mourners at its funeral!' The narrator tells us that this masquerade party is the last festival that the British ever hold in the old province of Massachusetts Bay."

"Hawthorne certainly knew how to engage an audience," Angela said.

"And his commentary regarding the abuse of political authority is certainly timely," I added.

"What do you mean?"

"It's not over, is it?" I answered. "Oppression comes in many forms. Often we don't even understand that it's happening, or who's really running the show."

"Don't tell me that you believe in all this conspiracy stuff that's on the Web!" Eliot scoffed.

"I don't know that I *believe* in anything in particular," I replied. "But I know what I feel."

"I agree with Emma," Denise said. "It's all smoke and mirrors out there. It's as though we're being distracted with nonsense about the economy and the price of oil—sports scores and fashion and celebrity antics—everything but what's really happening."

"Which is?"

Angela jumped in. "We're still fighting for freedom."

"Interesting perspective," Eliot said, amused, "coming from a journalist."

"Listen to Emerson's view of the transcendental era," Denise continued, reading from her notes.

> There was new consciousness. The former generations acted under the belief that a shining social prosperity was the beatitude of man, and sacrificed uniformly the citizen to the State. The modern mind believed that the nation existed for the individual, for the guardianship and education of every man. This idea, roughly written in revolutions and national movements, in the mind of the philosopher had far more precision; the individual is the world.

"Historically, when people have looked to government to solve problems, the problems have only escalated," I reminded them. "Government is permitted authority. Freedom comes from the *individual*, making his or her own decisions."

"Exactly," Dottie said. "We need a modern Hawthorne to remind us of what we *won't* tolerate."

Tina nodded emphatically. "Before the enraged spirit of George Washington makes an appearance on Capitol Hill," she said.

CHAPTER THIRTEEN

Christmas

Margaret Brady and I had met years earlier at a fancy hunter/jumper show barn, before I had seen the light of reason and pulled Joy out of that world. Peggy was in her late thirties, small with long reddish blond hair and a fierce competitive spirit. Like so many dedicated amateur show riders, she spent a good portion of her life on the road and in hotels.

Email from Peggy at the big Florida show in Wellington, entitled: "Booked that flight yet?"

Hi Emma,

I am so sick of pink stucco and palm trees! There aren't a huge number of restaurants in this blessed town, and every night they are all jammed with horse people—talking about horses. Don't they have lives? Don't they ever watch the news, or read a book, or go to a movie, for god's sake?

And my barn! My trainer Brad has announced that his board fee is going to be higher when we get back to Connecticut. His wife Cindy, who'd much rather be at the beach (and whines about it daily) is so busy showing their sale horses that she missed my first class this morning. I had to ask another trainer to help me. Then, Jackson spooked at a billboard that he's seen a hundred times, so I didn't get a ribbon.

Van arrived yesterday. The creep broke my heart, but still

assumes that I'll be perfectly happy to lend him one of my horses to show. He followed me around all day yesterday, and was there today for Jackson's performance. So now, on top of being rejected by him, I've been humiliated in front of him as well. It just doesn't get better than this.

Oh wait. Yes it does.

Whitney (the barn manager) and Chris (the assistant trainer), who are normally best friends (or so they tell us repeatedly) got into a horrible fight two days ago, and still aren't speaking to each other. They appear, stony faced, by the side of the ring, clapping for all the clients who are showing. Then they both sprint for the farm golf cart, one inevitably leaving the other one stranded, so that the clients are forced to play taxi back to the barn with the woman left behind. It's like being back in the second grade, but a lot more expensive.

I saw on the Web that there are some great deals with low airfares to West Palm right now.

Lots of love, Peggy

The Bridge Hollow Garden Club had been founded in 1947, and incorporated as a nonprofit organization in 1981. As a general rule I shied away from the activities of any group that involved attending formal tea parties and wearing big hats. However, the BHGC was comprised of dedicated environmentalists, who took the preservation of Lake Washington and the Hunterbury River seriously. I showed support at their public events as often as I could.

To open the holiday season the town had been invited to a Christmas tree lighting ceremony in Playhouse Park. The Garden Club Chair climbed to the top of a large mounting block and waved her bullhorn. The crowd gathered around the enormous live spruce and drank hot mulled cider in near darkness.

Luke slipped his hand into my left pocket.

"I *warned* you to bring gloves tonight," I whispered.

"I did," he whispered back.

"As many of you know," the chairperson began, "as a member of the Garden Club of America, our chapter's mission here in Bridge Hollow is to promote the enjoyment and appreciation of gardening, the conservation of our natural resources, and to advance the study of horticulture. Tonight marks the end of our year long celebration of the tree.

"Trees are the oldest living beings on this planet. They provide us with food and shelter. They clean our air of the pollutants that we create, they protect our soil from erosion, and they sustain immense webs of life in forest habitats. In addition, trees also nurture us with soul-satisfying beauty.

"We are very proud of our colonial and Revolutionary history in Bridge Hollow. One of our more famous landmarks lives here in Playhouse Park. Tonight I would like to draw your attention to the large White Oak behind me—a *Quercus alba*. It is a first generation Charter Oak—the product of an acorn from the original Charter Oak that stood in Hartford until 1856, when it fell in a storm. At the time its age was estimated to be between eight hundred and one thousand years. Bridge Hollow's stately specimen is nearly one hundred and seventy years old and over eighty feet tall.

"In 1662 King Charles II of England granted Connecticut a colonial charter, allowing for a form of self-government. Twenty years later King James II decided to consolidate the colonies and put them under closer supervision. The King annulled Connecticut's charter, and on October 31, 1687, the newly designated Governor of the Dominion of New England, Sir Edmund Andros, marched his troops into Hartford to claim the colony's charter. According to legend, the colonists waited until Andros had seen the document, and then extinguished all the candles in the room. The Charter was taken in the dark and hidden in a huge hollow oak tree which stood on the nearby Wyllys estate. The people of Connecticut refused to submit to the King's representative in the colonies...."

"Hurrah!" One of the teenagers shouted.

"And the charter was saved. It served as Connecticut's Constitution during and after the American Revolution. The Charter Oak has been famous ever since. Many people considered it to be a symbol of the spirit of American independence and of the colonists' quest for freedom from oppression and unjust government. So—in honor of that event—whether or not it actually happened—and in celebration of Bridge Hollow's two hundred and fiftieth anniversary this year, we will light the town Christmas tree."

The colors erupted in a glorious rainbow of red, gold, blue, and green—which illuminated the large lawn behind the theater, and threw the town's version of the Charter Oak in the spotlight. Everyone clapped.

Then someone screamed.

Flashlights were shone on one of the lower heavy branches of the old tree, where a full sized human figure was hanging by the neck.

Carlie had covered the event for Bridge Hollow's weekly paper. "I got to see it up close," she announced. "It was an effigy of Esther MacInerney—a really good likeness. Down to that sparkly star pin she always wears, and her bleached hair, green contacts, and big fake teeth. Someone was making a political statement."

"You think?" Julie exclaimed.

"There was a sign stuck to her chest," Carlie continued. "A quotation from the Declaration of Independence. Here—I have it in my notes. 'But when a long train of abuses and usurpations, pursuing invariably the same Object evinces a design to reduce them under absolute Despotism, it is their right, it is their duty, to throw off such Government, and to provide new Guards for their future security.' I'm guessing that people in Bridge Hollow aren't thrilled with the job that Esther's doing in Hartford."

"Sounds rather personal to me," Sophie remarked. "When you consider what happened to Esther on Halloween."

"I'd be purchasing a trained Doberman at this point," I agreed.

We were having a Saturday lunch at the Tavern, in preparation for some focused Christmas planning.

"I'm kind of sorry that I'm going back to Vermont for the holidays," Carlie admitted. "Things are heating up here. I'm worried that I'll miss something good."

"I promise to text you the second that spaceships land on the green," I replied, passing her the cheese fries.

"So Luke wants us to come to the farm this year?" Sophie asked. "Is he sure about this? Didn't you say that he's invited his family as well?"

"His sister sounds like a real sweetheart," Carlie volunteered sarcastically.

"Great," Julie sighed.

"Franny is—well—an exacting personality," I began. "Not overly warm, I admit."

"What about presents? Are we abstaining like last year?"

"Yes," I said firmly.

Sophie looked at me. "Even Luke?"

"We've agreed that my new study at his farm will be my gift," I said. "More of his aunt's furniture is coming in this week—and that Luke's present from me will be season tickets for the theater."

"No jewelry?" Carlie asked, dismayed.

"None."

"But you and I are exchanging gifts, right?"

"Let's order dessert girls," Sophie announced, passing the menu to her daughter.

Email from Peggy in Florida, entitled: "You're still coming, right?"
Hi Emma,

I spent all day Monday in the Wellington ER. They said it was the worst ear infection they'd ever seen. I must have caught something from the grooms, who have been coughing like crazy for a week. I had a really cute male nurse though. I was just wondering if he could possibly be straight, when he got a call that his wife was in labor on the next floor, and cantered off. Oh well. They gave me some heavy duty cough syrup so I can sleep.

We went on a trail ride yesterday. Whitney's horse was spooked by a bobcat and almost jumped into one of the canals.

Jill was champion in the amateur owners again. Now she'll be even more insufferable.

Geraldine is out of control with the shopping. She's determined to get a Hermès saddle now. Her CWD is what? Six months old? But what's another few grand? And she admitted to me yesterday that she has nine custom show jackets. The woman hasn't won a ribbon since June. Her husband was down here last week, dropping off her new BMW convertible. Nice guy. Too bad she's too busy chasing her gay trainer to notice. Their barn is across the street from ours, and their show stalls are in the same tent. It's like being an extra for an episode of a really bad sitcom.

That Italian place you like is still serving their terrific gnocchi with pesto sauce. But no pressure.

It's been over eighty degrees every day this week.

Love, Peggy

My meeting with Chief Ernie Marino was not productive.

"I really don't see the problem, Ms. Carbury," he growled. "Rick Grudberg has the right to ride his motorcycle on his parents' property with their permission. You should be talking to them, not me. This isn't my concern."

"I *have* spoken to them—and written to them. My client Stan Mullins tells me that the situation has escalated, if anything."

"What do you mean?" Marino snapped.

"Mrs. Grudberg is now watching the Mullins barn. On several occasions Mrs. Mullins has seen Bonnie Grudberg hustle her son out to his bike as soon as the horses come into the ring. Rick then proceeds to roar around—up and down the various piles of refuse—as close to the women riding as he can get. This terrifies the horses, and both riders have been thrown numerous times as a result. According to Stan Mullins, the engine on Rick's motorcycle is unusually loud. The boy's behavior is dangerous, it is calculated as such, and it is curtailing the Mullins family's ability to enjoy their property. This *is* potentially a criminal matter, Chief Marino."

"What are you going to do?" He sneered. "Have some geek with a noise level monitor come out and test the kid's bike? Give me a break." Marino rolled back in his chair and stood up, his big arms crossed on his chest.

I also stood. "I have filed a formal complaint with the First Selectman, with the Town Attorney, and with the State. Liability insurance doesn't cover intentional behavior—are you aware of that? If someone gets hurt on the Mullins' farm as a result of Rick Grudberg's motorcycle, I will sue Julian Grudberg, take his land, and put them all out on the street. I will also disseminate the fact that you were aware of the problem, and did nothing to prevent it. Do I make myself clear?"

Marino's stormy eyes glared at me.

I sat in my car for ten minutes, clearing negative energy. As I pulled out of the police station lot, I suddenly felt tremendous empathy for Suzie Marino. I now understood the source of the defiance that she often displayed in class.

Josie and Stephen had been married for two years. Josie, ten years junior to her husband, wanted to work out the issues that she had with Stephen's teenage daughter Beth, who lived with them. Stephen had refused counseling, but had agreed to meet with an attorney mediator. I took a deep breath and let it out slowly, centering myself. This matter was a minefield of emotional triggers for me.

"I don't see that there's an issue for discussion," Stephen was saying. "Beth is polite to Josie, and helpful around the house. She gets good grades, and is no trouble. Why are we even here?" He shouted at his wife.

Josie looked stricken. "We're living in the house that Stephen and his former wife built together, and raised their daughter. I feel that I'm the guest, while Beth is the mistress of the home, and completely in charge."

"You *knew* that I had custody of Beth when you signed on for this gig," Stephen barked. I watched Josie pull back in her chair.

I addressed Josie's concerns first. "You're saying that you are feeling powerless in the home?" Josie nodded. "Can you give us some examples of this?"

"A few weeks ago Stephen and I took a long weekend off to visit some friends in Maine. When we returned, I found that Beth had asked her cousins to stay with her, and they were still in residence. Stephen had known of her plans and hadn't bothered to mention them to me. He said that since it wasn't my house, it wasn't my place to worry about it."

"That is *not* what I said," her husband protested. "I merely said that since Beth had my permission, I didn't see that any further conversation was necessary."

"But I feel inundated with Stephen's family, and I have no say in anything! I'm his wife. *I'm* the mistress of the house! Shouldn't I be consulted about guests, *before* they arrive?" She looked to me for confirmation.

"Perhaps I can help you both come to an agreement regarding house rules."

Josie appeared to be gathering strength. "Beth's always moving things around. Pots in the kitchen, sheets and towels in the linen closet. Even furniture. One day I came home to find her painting the laundry room."

"It was very thoughtful of her," Stephen said.

Josie threw up her hands. "She's constantly reminding me that she was there first, Stephen. That's the whole point. It's a control game. Why don't you see that?"

"Let's brainstorm on some ideas. Josie—what is an example of a house rule that you'd like to see in place from now on?"

"The kitchen is my exclusive domain," Josie said. "Neither one of them do any cooking, although Stephen mans the grill in good weather."

"What about you, Stephen?"

"Holidays," he replied. "Josie has relatives scattered across western Connecticut, and I'm beyond tired of spending every blessed Thanksgiving, Easter, and Christmas on the road, visiting three or more towns a day."

"And I'm tired of spending every weekend with your daughter," Josie retorted.

"What amount of time does Beth spend with her mother?" I asked.

"Almost zero," her father said. "They're not close."

"They would be, if you'd let Beth have a car," Josie said. "I think you keep her with us on purpose. If she had more freedom she'd be out of the house more often, and I could relax."

"Now you're calling *me* controlling?"

Josie laughed. "The acorn is still *attached* to the tree in this case, dear."

The following Saturday I borrowed Luke's truck and trailer, and Joy and I went for a hack in Playhouse Park. I pulled into the lot designated for horses, backed Joy off the trailer, removed her cooler, and swung into the saddle. The extensive bridle paths on the property had recently been restored and widened. Joy picked up a leisurely trot and we circled around the formal gardens and down to the lake.

The dock had been removed from the water and stored in pieces on the shore. Joy stepped sideways and gave them one of her special looks, but I nudged her with my short spurs and she moved on. We paused to take in the stillness of the lake, not yet frozen, but with an icy film over the shallow areas. Cattails grew in drifts on the bank. I pulled my cell phone out of my pocket and took several photos. Joy stood quietly; her ears twitching in every direction to the calls of the birds.

Past the boat launch area was a grove of trees—maples, dogwoods, and evergreens—which had been planted for the town's two hundredth year anniversary, and had been thriving for the last fifty years. With the leaves gone their wonderful shapes were distinct, and beautiful. Tall conical greens were set against the rounded outlines of the deciduous trees—spidery branches tapering gradually as they reached to the sky. I slowed Joy to a walk to appreciate the composition of the landscaping, working out a new painting in my mind.

Then I noticed the orange plastic ties encircling many of the trees. They were marked to be cut down.

"Trees have powerful energy," Sophie had explained at one of her talks, "and are actually aware when they are designated for sacrifice. Their life force will immediately withdraw as a result. Trees clean the atmosphere of the toxic gasses we create—like carbon dioxide—and they release oxygen into the air, which we need to breathe. More humans and less trees equals eventual disaster for every human on this planet."

Without thinking, I jumped out of the saddle and ripped every piece of neon plastic off the trees. I stuffed the evidence into my pocket, led Joy to the nearest bench, mounted, and cantered off, breathing hard.

Abby and I were spending all of Christmas week at Luke's farm. Christmas Eve morning I packed my suitcases, and filled Abby's L.L. Bean tote with necessaries, including a new bag of food, and a fleece sweater. I watered the plants, checked the kitchen, and then sat on an ottoman in my library, looking around. Abby jumped into my lap and licked my face.

"A whole new adventure begins today, Abs," I said, hugging her. "And a new family. It's not just the three of us any longer."

Luke's bull terrier Rufus was waiting for us at the front door. He and Abby engaged in their sniffing ritual, followed by some friendly tail wagging. Luke helped carry my luggage upstairs to his room.

The last of Aunt Beatrice's antique furniture had arrived. I now had my own chest of drawers, and a dressing table with bench in the corner.

"I've been burning sage all over the property for a few days," Luke announced, "so we should be fine. Come and see your study. The chaise came back from the upholsterers last night."

A small round cherry tea table with four chairs was placed to the right of the fireplace. The chaise longue, newly covered with a floral print in deep blues and greens, was angled from the opposite wall. There were several landscapes hung between the windows—"I left space for your paintings," Luke said—and a tall bookcase by the door. My easel had been set up next to it, and a bouquet of pink roses sat on the writing surface of the secretary desk. Logs had already been laid in the fireplace.

"Let's have dinner in here tonight," I said, and Luke laughed.

"Proof that you're pleased," he noted. "Wait 'til you see Beatrice's silver."

Angela and Leo arrived later that afternoon. We put their bags in the big guestroom.

Ryan and Patty Hubbard—Luke's farm managers—were visiting relatives in New Jersey, so Luke and I went out at sunset to bring the horses and goats in from the pastures and feed them their grain. Leo deposited two flakes of hay in each stall while Angela checked their water.

"Looks like you got your wish, Em," Angela whispered, as I collected the buckets and brought them back to the feed room. "You wanted a house on the water, and a horse farm. Remember? That day we were kayaking on Lake Washington—nearly two years ago."

I walked into Hamish's stall and brushed his legs while he ate. Across the aisle Joy nickered for attention. Angela slid open the door and offered her an apple.

"I do remember. In fact, I was just thinking about that this morning."

"You never said anything about a man though," Angela teased. "Nice bonus."

"Very."

Angela raised her voice. "How's the ghost situation Luke? I hear that Sophie has conducted several clearings here."

Luke grinned. "All quiet. She got the last of them to move on, finally. A lot less creaking and banging at night."

"I can relate."

"How many horses does this make with the new boarders?" Leo asked.

"Twelve right now, including our four."

"And the stall count?"

"Fifteen here in the barn, and another six at the end of the indoor. Plus the goats in the other barn."

"A lot of work," Leo observed.

"Too much for just Patty and Ryan," Luke said. "With my travel schedule, what I really need is a full time barn manager to take up some of the chores, like dragging the rings—ordering hay, shavings, and feed—and looking after the boarders. Would be great if he or she could work the horses. There's a two bedroom apartment upstairs—the challenge is finding the right person."

"Get Emma to cast a spell," Angela suggested. "She can manifest anything."

Abby and Rufus appeared at the big front doors, looking expectant.

"Cocktail hour!" Angela announced.

Journal entry for Christmas Day. Loarn Farm. 9 p.m.

Today didn't produce quite the drama of holidays past with my mother, step children etc, but still impossible to survive without the consumption of many glasses of good champagne.

Franny, her husband Scott, and their three offspring arrived at ten— two hours early—bringing all of their own wrapped gifts, so we were forced to watch their ritual of opening packages for the first thirty min- utes that they were here. Franny then completely took over in the kitchen. Angela and I disappeared to my study with a pot of tea (Aunt Beatrice's china is amazing—Royal Crown Derby and very fragile) and a plate of cranberry scones, while the men collected the dogs and took off for the barn. The kids are well behaved (suppressed, according to Angela) and spent most of the day in Luke's library in front of the big TV.

Since I am not the mistress in this house, I have no responsibilities. It's very freeing.

Sophie and Julie got here at one, as arranged, with more champagne, bless them, and a huge Christmas log for dessert.

Dinner was served at three. The ladies and I offered to help but were waved off by Franny, so we looked on with glee as Luke attempted to remind his sister that she was a guest in his home. Leo and Scott found sanctuary in sports-speak, and the children were managed (dominated, according to Angela) by their mother at the kitchen table.

Sophie asked me if I was having any flashbacks to Christmas dinners with Nick's kids and my family. Astonishing how she knows these things. I feel like I handled it well. That is to say—I stayed neutral and let Luke handle it. The fact that he is even aware of the problem is a big step forward.

By six Franny had packed them all up and left, and I'm still not clear why they came in the first place. Was she staking a claim on the farm and its contents? Hardly worth the two hour drive from Manhattan, although it was fun to watch the children with the goats. Angela thinks that Franny is merely taking over for Aunt Beatrice as the family matriarch, who if present in spirit, was not visible. Franny very obviously made a tour of the house, checking on the inventory of antiques. She even asked Luke about B's jewelry. "It's in the bank, Fran," he replied, sharply. I don't blame him.

This farm needed to be cleared of more than just ghosts, and it feels as though Luke is finally able to set some healthy boundaries with his siblings. I can't even imagine how difficult it was for him as a child, living in this isolated area, constantly retreating from their hard-edged, bottom line nastiness. It explains his strong emotional connection with the land and animals. I wonder what the parents were like.

Franny came in to this room several times during the day, and is clearly furious that this desk is mine. She reminded me that it's worth at least twelve thousand dollars—twice.

Makes it even more enjoyable to sit here in comfort, now that she's gone—hopefully for years.

Luke apologized to us after Franny's entourage had headed south. Sophie and Julie left shortly thereafter, and the four of us had a second, cheerful meal here in my study at 7:30. At this moment, Abby and Rufus are passed out together on my chaise. Luke and Angela are doing night check in the barns, and Leo is watching a war movie. I've got Tchaikovsky's Nutcracker *playing in the background, and the peace is blissful.*

9:40 pm. Luke just came in to tell me that he loves having Abby and me here—for the first time he feels as though he has a real family.

CHAPTER FOURTEEN

Town Meeting

Email from my cousin Leslie entitled: "Nuptials by the slopes."
Howdy Emma,

We're back from Colorado! Lest I forget, thanks for the sperm whale cutting board. Greg thought it was something to hang on the wall, but I rescued it just as he was plugging in the drill.

OK, general observations first. On a positive note, Vail is the ultimate in frozen resorts, and the hotel was fabulous. Built to resemble a Victorian mansion, it was full of antiques, with outdoor hot tubs and a huge second floor balcony looking over the town. Several old fashioned bars. Greg and I had a suite done in Camp in the Rockies décor. Headboard out of twigs, armchairs in buffalo check upholstery. Gargantuan fireplace. One of those footed bathtubs for two, and heated towel racks. Trish, Sara, and Gaby had two adjoining rooms down the hall. Gaby was terrified of the stuffed grizzly in hers, and slept every night with her sisters, and the connecting door locked. Ben was assigned a small room next to the balcony. He said that the bridal party spent their evenings lobbing appetizers at passersby, so he never got any sleep.

Did you ever meet Greg's delightful half sister? She wasn't at our wedding. Recall that Kari is the daughter of Greg's father from his first marriage. A kind of Alice

Roosevelt Longworth, only not as well behaved. (Didn't Teddy Roosevelt once say that he could be President of the United States, or manage Alice—but not both?) Kari took her mother's side in the divorce and has behaved disgracefully to her father ever since. Greg's dad is perhaps not the most considerate of people, but Kari goes above and beyond the norm for nastiness. The groom is Hans from Vienna, heir to one of the crystal dynasties over there. Major money. They put on quite an event. The food was exquisite, and they bought three day ski passes for everyone.

But I digress.

Greg and the kids, upon arriving at the hotel, deposited their belongings and disappeared in the direction of the ski lift, which was literally out our back door. I had a massage in our suite. I was still wrapped in my towel when Kari showed up at the door. Her usual phony, trying to be all things to all people—and surreptitiously stabbing them in the back—self. "So glad you could come... blah blah blah." I looked right at her and said "Really?" This stopped her cold.

I had two frozen margaritas with lunch and prepared myself for the ordeal of the rehearsal dinner.

In a determined effort to publically harpoon her dad, Kari had decreed that he would be double walking her down the aisle with one of her maternal uncles, a man who hasn't made a family appearance in decades. I did not attend the rehearsal, but Greg—as one of the ushers—reported later that the dual daddy thing with Uncle Whosis was extremely cumbersome, and the aisle wasn't wide enough for the three of them at one time.

The rehearsal dinner took place at a restaurant across the street. This was the part of the festivities that I was looking forward to the least. It was a smallish party, and we knew almost no one there. Our kids were not invited. We were literally stalked by the Maid of Honor. She and her boyfriend sat at our table; there was plenty of room elsewhere, and the seats were not assigned. I was as animated as possible, with a little help from three glasses of chardonnay. I knew that everything we said was going straight back to Kari and her mother anyway, so I might as well make it good. Still, very uncomfortable.

I've just heard that Comet escaped out the back door and has had a slight tiff with our neighbor's Airedale, so I'm sending this much now. Stay tuned for Part Two.

Kisses and hugs, Leslie

The She Lions practiced at the Bridge Hollow School rink two nights a week.

"Emma!" Prue exclaimed. "So you've finally decided to skate with us!"

I waved my helmet at her, feeling a little ridiculous. "I dug all my old gear out of the basement and got my Bauers sharpened. I hope these ladies are patient with rusty new members."

"Infinitely! You'll get good fast. Don't worry—it'll be fun."

Prue introduced me to the captain of the team. Gretchen Hartley was about forty-five, tall and thin, with a wide smile and short red hair plastered to her face. She handed me a jersey—moss green with gold lettering. My last name and the number 12 were on the back, and on the front, a roaring lioness with a small crown on her head.

"We're pretty flexible, Emma! You play as much as you like, whenever you can. It's a good group of women and we enjoy ourselves. The rink also has time slots for adult open stick, if you want to practice on your own."

Half an hour later I was suited up and seated with the rest of the team, waiting for the BHS Varsity boys to finish their ice time. I noticed Max Armstrong and Jim Stoddard—the star center—and the other wing, skating in a center rush formation toward the blue line of the attacking zone. Stoddard had the puck, and then suddenly, he didn't. It bounced off the middle of his blade and flew hard into the left wing's leg. He fell over, breaking his stick. The coach blew the whistle, and demanded to know what Stoddard thought he was doing.

But the coach couldn't see what I could. The ghost of a hockey player, wearing the number 7 on his back, and a leather helmet circa 1950, had skated straight for Stoddard, and whipped the puck away from him. He had then jumped over the boards to the bench area, and disappeared.

The boys regrouped, and ten minutes later we were on the ice, doing agility drills, and then practicing stops and starts, and figure eights. Crossovers were an effort for me, especially to the right, and my legs began screaming at me early into the warm-up. Gretchen watched me carefully, and then put me in the left wing position for the rest of the practice.

"Good job Emma!" Prue said, back on the bench.

"You need to work on skating backwards," Gretchen announced to me, "and practice with your stick as much as you can—I use a weighted ball on the driveway. Otherwise, damn good after so many years out of playing. I'm putting you on Prue's line for next time. Email me if you can't make it. Our next tournament is in six weeks, and I'd like you to be up for it, if possible."

Prue and I stopped at the Tavern for dinner in the Tap Room. We spent the first thirty minutes catching up, and then I cautiously introduced the subject of BHS hockey team history.

"As far as I know, they've had a team here for a good seventy years or so—they played on the lake before the rink was built. The Tallmadge Academy girls came on board in the eighties."

"Any horror stories?" I picked up my wine glass and attempted to look nonchalant.

"Not that I'm aware of, but I'll ask my dad. He played for BHS." Prue ordered another beer. "So what made you come out for the She Lions Emma? I thought you OD'd on hockey during your marriage."

I laughed. "Nope! Just got sick of attendance being a prerequisite for being Mrs. Bennington. Once I was free of the coercion, I realized that I missed the action. So Luke and I have been showing up for the home games—mostly BHS, but some of the TA events

as well. He's talking about going to a few Yale games this winter—
Yale's his alma mater."

"Did Luke skate? I thought he was a rower."

"He played hockey, but never well enough for the Varsity team—
or so he says. He rowed for Yale."

Email from my cousin Leslie, entitled: "Part Two coming up."

Hi again Emma,

The morning of the wedding I took my first ski lesson.
Perhaps subconsciously I was hoping to break a bone,
thereby avoiding having to attend. But, to no avail. There
were five of us in the class, all over forty, and we spent three
hours snowplowing down a little hill near the lodge. We also
learned the fine art of getting up from a fall (falling down
was the easy part) and sidestepping. We all kept tripping
on each other's skis. My butt resembled a snow cone. Of
course, Greg and the kids flew by us on their way to lunch.
My feet hurt so much from the rental boots that I barely
made it to the door of our suite. Greg found me on the floor
in the hall, twisted in half, trying to undo that damn back
buckle, screaming Get Them Off, Get Them Off, with lots
of bad words in between. I then proceeded to the spa for a
manicure/pedicure and a hot stone massage.

I got rave reviews for my nuptial attire, by the way. Ankle
length, plum silk, sleeveless with square neck. Matching
wrap. Black heels and sequin bag. Gown very fitted to the
old figure. I wore one of those body smoother things for the
extra hourglass effect.

Greg and I were dressing when we got the call that Greg
was wanted on the balcony for pictures with the bridal party.
He came trotting back a moment later with a wrist corsage for
me. I had a flashback to our junior prom (and narrowly avoiding teen pregnancy that night) as Greg cheerfully snapped
the thing on my arm and returned to the photo shoot.

All the guests were bundled into horse drawn carriages
and transported to the church. Huge beasts. The kind with
hairy legs. Feet the size of frying pans.

We had reading material while we were waiting for the bride. Ever been to the theater and actually read the play-bill? That's what this was like. A bio on everyone: the bride, the groom, all four parents, the bridesmaids and the ushers (we were written up as "Greg practices law in Maryland. He has a wife, four teenagers, and a dog"). Six attendants on each side. Plus, the minister, organist, and the trumpet section (yes, there actually was one). A whole treatise on the bridal gown. How Kari designed it and had one of her fashion people make it up. Lots of extras on the material, and the jewelry. So pretentious and self promoting. So Kari.

The processional came down the aisle. When Kari's mother finally made her appearance, she was wearing a near duplicate of the navy blue dress that Greg's mother was wearing. Gaby pointed this out to everyone. Loudly.

The Bride, sandwiched between Greg's dad and the Uncle, looked like a portrait of Eleanor Roosevelt on her wedding day. Buck teeth and complete absence of chin. Her father seemed angry and hurt, not to mention crowded. After all, the Uncle (who resembles a hound dog) never did anything for Kari. The entire spectacle was meant as a gesture of solidarity with her mother, but instead came off as a sophomoric display of mean spirited behavior. Can't *wait* to see those pictures.

The reception, mercifully, was at our hotel. The third (and final, I promise) installment will be along shortly.

Much love, Leslie

The Bridge Hollow Town Meeting took place at 4 pm on Saturday. Luke, Sophie, and I found seats near the front of the BHS auditorium. Town Hall officials appeared from both sides of the stage and took their places in a row of chairs facing the crowd.

Esther MacInerney was the last to arrive. She gave a nod to her constituents, accompanied by her usual cold toothy grin, and took a seat next to Leonard Abel, who was Chair of the Conservation Commission.

"What's she doing up there?" I heard a man behind me grumble. "I thought we sent her to Hartford?"

"Likes to have her finger in everything," another voice replied.

I scanned the room and located Lacy Basdin and her parents. Jeff and the two paralegals were seated on the opposite side of the auditorium. A command attendance, even on a Saturday.

Then I noticed Suzie Marino and her father, sitting two rows back. Chief Marino's face froze as he saw me, but Suzie smiled and waved.

The First Selectman, Chester Shea, stood at the podium; his bald pink head shining with perspiration.

"Good afternoon. The only item on the agenda today is the proposed changes to the property known as Playhouse Park—the details of which were outlined in *The Bridge Hollow News*. The land located behind the theater and abutting Lake Washington was given to the town as a public park in 1821, by the Gilmore family. Nearly two hundred years later, the cost of maintaining the property has opened the question of selling the parcel to a private entity for development. We are here today to address your questions."

A sea of hands appeared. "Have there been any offers?"

Shea nodded. "Several. The most attractive proposal thus far has come from Lavandula, LLC, a Connecticut based company."

"That's the marina and restaurant?"

"Correct." The audience registered dismay in loud whispers.

"Are we voting on anything today?"

Shea patted his forehead with a handkerchief. "No, this is merely an open forum for discussion. The Conservation Commission will be meeting in a few weeks to consider the various proposals." He nodded to Leonard Abel. Esther beamed.

"What else is on the table?" An elderly man in the front row asked.

"A corporate retreat compound, a summer camp, and a nature center."

An angry buzzing emanated from those assembled. I had a vision of men and women in dark suits carrying kayaks down to the dock, briefcase straps slung over their shoulders.

"What about the legal issue?" A woman from the back of the room bellowed. "How does Town Hall have the right to sell our park? Doesn't the land have historical significance?"

"There is a provision in the trust document," Town Attorney Norman Daley replied, "which will be addressed at the formal hearing. The parcel may be sold if the cost becomes burdensome to the town. I will be reading my opinion into the record at that time."

The murmuring escalated.

"What the hell does burdensome mean?" Someone shouted.

"Who decides that?" Another woman demanded. "And what will happen to our Charter Oak?"

Esther stood up. "Think about the benefits folks! More commercial taxes being generated means more money for the town, and more business coming in for all of us. We've done the numbers, and we'll present that report at the hearing as well. It's time that Bridge Hollow began attracting a younger crowd."

"She's already assuming that the marina will get the vote," the man next to Luke growled to his wife.

"If it hasn't already," she replied.

"I guess all that ice tea mix that got dumped in her pool in September didn't send her a strong enough message."

An hour later the meeting was adjourned. As we rose and began retrieving our personal items I overheard a conversation two rows back.

"Just like the debates before the election."

"Feels fixed, you mean?"

"Like reading from a script. Did you know that Esther had her staff write dozens of questions on index cards—all in different handwritings and pens—to be handed to the moderator before the debate began?"

"So she already knew the questions?"

"And the answers. Ellen Basdin told me. Her daughter used to work for MacInerney."

"Who is this Lavandula, LLC, Emma?" Sophie asked. "I'm not familiar with it. Interesting. That's the Latin name for lavender."

"Yes," said Luke, holding Sophie's coat up for her. "I wondered that too. I've done business with most of the development companies around, but I've never heard of this one. Know anything about them?"

"No. But I think I have a new assignment for Carlie on Monday."

Email from my cousin Leslie, entitled: "Where was I? Oh yeah, the reception."

Hey Em,

The hotel had cut itself off from the outside world for this clambake, and I must say that with all the funky décor, the many comfy rooms, and the flowers in the dining room (which were lovely), it really was a festive evening.

However.

You know how normally when you arrive for a wedding reception, there is a table with all the place cards arranged alphabetically? You grab your card, proceed to Table X, and park your purse at the best available chair.

Not at this weenie roast. Our names were already tagged at each seat, waiting for us. It took everyone ages to find their allotted space. My family was assigned to the farthest table, and I was placed facing the band, with my back to the entire room. Greg was stationed at the head table with the rest of the bridal party, but Greg's parents received similar treatment. So, in keeping with the junior high level of cattiness, I refused to turn around for anything. Not the first dance, not the cake cutting, not the bride dancing with her father (and I kept waiting for her to insist on a threesome with Uncle Hound Dog). Nothing. When she and Hans made a brief appearance at our table later on, I complemented her on the menu.

I danced a total of two dances with Greg; the rest with

various members of the combined families, including Greg's lesbian cousin Harriet (who seemed very enthusiastic about this). Greg was all over the place and I was frankly a little annoyed—we were doing this at his entreaty, when I'd have preferred to spend the week in traction. The kids had a good time though. Trish met the younger brother of somebody and danced with him most of the night. Gaby, Sara, and Ben amused themselves by joining an impromptu game of strip poker in the library.

The heat had been cranked up in the dining room, so the dancing became a tad sweaty. After a good three hours of serious boogie, Kari announced that she'd like a photo with Greg and me. My hair was sticking to my face at this point, but at least I had time to refresh my lipstick. I dutifully stood with my arm around her and the men on either side for a couple of shots, feeling somehow that this was all part of the plan.

Fairly soon after this the band closed up, and I escaped to our suite. This was at about eleven. Greg finally climbed into bed at one thirty. He had looked particularly stud-like in his tux, and I had been feeling amorous. But at that hour he was SOL.

We had all been invited (via huge hostess baskets in our rooms) to "join Kari and Hans for breakfast" in the hotel café the morning after. (Everything that woman does annoys me). I took off for a coffee shop down the block, leaving Greg with the kids. Greg came by later to inform me that the party was breaking up.

We took another ski lesson that afternoon. Ever been on a rope tow? You straddle a bar, and sit on a makeshift seat as it hauls you up the mountain. I only got dumped once, but that was enough. People do this sport to relax?

What are your plans for Easter?

Love, Leslie

CHAPTER FIFTEEN

Florida

The explosion came just after eight on Thursday night. Luke and I were finishing up in my kitchen when the boom blew through the house. It rattled the windows and shook the china in the cabinets.

Abby ran to the windows that overlooked the lake and began barking furiously, leaping from the couch to the ottoman, and back again. We could see the red glow of fire at the top of the hill in town, and a few moments later heard the sirens of emergency vehicles as they converged at the sight.

"Where is that?" I gasped.

"Wentworth Hill," Luke replied, picking up my binoculars. "The highest spot in Bridge Hollow, or we wouldn't have this clear view."

And suddenly I knew—in an intuitive flash that was based on nothing that I could rationally explain—that Esther MacInerney's Cameron Manor had been obliterated.

"Esther's husband is dead, Emma," Luke reported the next morning. "He was in his office late—alone. Most of the mansion is gone, and the rest of the block is damaged pretty badly. Walls were forced back from the pressure—plenty of structural issues, but no other injuries. The source of the explosion appears to be a leak in the propane tank, but it may be months before it is determined whether or not this was an accident—or a crime. The State has stepped in to take over the investigation."

Lawsuits. If the explosion was determined to be the result of negligence—Esther and her husband's estate would be in for some long and very expensive battles.

But the explosion was not an accident, I could feel it. Gilbert MacInerney had been murdered.

"This is what happens when I go home to the sticks," Carlie howled, a week later. "Huge stories! And someone else gets to cover them for the paper."

"OK, so you missed the blow up and the death," I began, in soothing tones, "but you may nail the underlying scandal instead."

Carlie perked up. "Really? Like what?"

"Start with the Connecticut Secretary of the State's office in Hartford. Find out everything you can on Lavandula, LLC. Call Angela if you need help—she has contacts all over through her television station. We need to find out who's behind what's going on in this town. The energy's been like pea soup around here for months."

"OK. When are you leaving for Florida?"

"In a few days, so you have plenty of time to do research while I'm gone."

Sylvia and Todd had been divorced for eighteen months, and the parenting plan regarding their small son and daughter had been working smoothly—until Sylvia's job had transferred her to another part of the state.

"He wanted to drag me back to court with motions for modification," she told me, tearfully, "but I told him that our money would be much better spent figuring this out on our own."

"So I agreed," Todd said. "I admit that I've had enough of lawyers and hearings—and wasting thousands of dollars on nothing."

"That's a sensible position to take," I replied. "Frankly, I'd love to give up trial work entirely and just do this. It's so much better to make decisions regarding your own life, rather than have a total stranger do it."

"Litigation doesn't impress me as a compassionate—or terribly efficient process," Sylvia remarked.

"No," Todd agreed.

"Good. In the mediation world, we call this a buy-in. So, let's get started. What is your situation now, how is it about to change, and what can we do to alleviate the stress for both of you?"

I wheeled my baggage through the automatic door and was immediately suffocated by ninety-two degree heat. Time to change the turtleneck.

Peggy had pulled her car up to the curb. She was dressed in shorts and flip flops, and her suntan was well advanced.

"It's so great to see you!" She exclaimed. "This show seems longer every year."

I settled back in the leather seat and watched the palm trees go by. Peggy laughed at me. "They're predicting a big snowstorm in the Northeast tonight," she said. "Six to eight inches in Litchfield County."

The winter was already beginning to leave my body. "I could use a margarita," I said.

"Let's drop your things at the apartment first. The Backyard still has the best frozen drinks."

Peggy had rented a condo in a gated cluster of buildings near the show grounds. Typical of South Florida, the color scheme was beige and white, with mocha furniture and bad lighting. The only window in the living room was a sliding glass door onto a small stucco patio. I walked outside—she had a pretty view of a pond and some interesting landscaping. A large sign warned: 'Absolutely no swimming!' Alligators?

"The gang may be at the restaurant when we get there," Peggy announced. "They like the big square bar."

Jill and Geraldine were drinking Cosmopolitans. I ordered some spinach and artichoke dip with chips, and gratefully partook of my first margarita.

"Ken should be here any minute," Geraldine announced, with one eye on the door.

Ken was Geraldine's trainer. He was gay, but had come out late in life. Geraldine clearly wanted to be the woman who would change him back again.

"There he is!" Geraldine exclaimed. She immediately shoved her chair over to make room, compressing Jill into the large man on her left.

"We won the high prelims!" Ken informed us. He ordered a dirty martini.

"You were marvelous, Ken!" Geraldine gushed.

"Did you see that combination in the jump-off? Winsome was perfect!" Ken gloated. "We have a shot at circuit champion!"

"You remember my friend Emma, don't you Ken?"

"It's been a while, hasn't it? How's Joy doing?"

"Good," I replied, truthfully. "We're learning to be a team."

"You should have brought her down. She's a cute mare."

"Thanks. I'm pretty proud of her."

"Let me know if you ever want to change barns. She's got what it takes."

Geraldine was obviously tired of the attention that I was receiving from Ken. "Are we looking at any jumpers for me tomorrow?" She was practically in his lap.

"I have one or two lined up. It all depends."

"On what?"

"On how much you want to spend."

Peggy kicked my ankle.

"I completely rely on your judgment, Ken," Geraldine purred. "You know that."

Ken glowed with the promise of big commissions.

Jill waved at the door. "Martie! Over here!"

Martie eased her way through the masses.

"Haven't seen you people all winter. Whoa Geraldine! Are those yours?"

Martie pointed her finger, and we all gaped at Geraldine's chest. Her striped shirt was definitely stretched tighter than I recalled from our previous encounters.

"Why, what do you mean?"

"There's more to you than when last we spoke! Who's your surgeon?"

Geraldine's red face hardened. "I don't understand what you're trying to imply."

"Imply nothing. You can't go from B cup to D cup without a little help from God. Or, in this case, from Doctor Slice and Stuff."

Geraldine's face reddened even more. Ken grinned. Peggy grabbed a potato skin. I checked my watch.

"You must be hungry, Emma. We're heading out for dinner, folks," Peggy announced. "See you at the barn tomorrow." As we were leaving, I saw Geraldine twist her arm around Ken's, and take a sip from his martini glass.

Seated at our table at Anthony's I asked: "Is Geraldine selling her hunter? I thought she loved him."

"She loved him because Ken found him in Holland and brought him back. But Ken's tired of doing the hunters and is currently into jumpers. Now Geraldine wants a jumper."

"What does her husband think of all this? He must be fed up with supporting Ken. Especially when Geraldine is so hot to return Ken to the Straight Life."

"Good question. I think Fitz likes Geraldine to be happy. Maybe he doesn't see Ken as a real threat."

177

"Well, not emotionally, anyway. The guy's definitely anti-vagina. But financially?"

"If Fitz is worried about money, he isn't going public about it." Peggy scanned my face. "No offense, Emma, but you look a little off. What's happening in *your* life?"

I shifted in my chair. "Bags under the eyes, hair not shiny, nose dripping—what?"

"Not that bad. You're just lacking your usual enthusiasm, I guess. No sparkle. Has something changed? How's Luke?"

I dunked my bread in some olive oil. "Luke is as wonderful as ever. It's me. I've been having mini anxiety attacks lately—which hasn't happened since the divorce. I don't know why."

Peggy put down her fork. "I do."

I stared at her in surprise.

"Come on, Em. You and Luke are serious, and you're obviously headed toward some kind of commitment. Which is bringing up old stuff from your marriage."

"You mean that I'm confusing Luke with Nick?"

"I don't see how anyone could do that," Peggy said drily. "Nick is an arrogant jerk, and a total phony. He playacted the role of husband your entire marriage. I honestly don't know how you stood him as long as you did. In fact, no one does. But Luke—god Emma, he's pretty close to perfect."

"I know."

"Look, I've never been married. But I've dated too many losers to even count without a shrink in the room. Luke's terrific. He's kind, and he's a gentleman. It would never occur to him to hurt anyone, and he's obviously crazy about you."

"I know."

"Stop saying that! What do you *feel?*"

"I'm terrified that if I don't figure this out soon, I'll lose him."

"Has Luke said anything to you along those lines?"

"Of course not," I replied, quickly. "But I keep having dreams.

Nick again—just like I did before we split up. Sometimes he turns into Luke, but more often the opposite happens. I can intellectualize what this means—I've done the research. It's all about current emotional situations bringing up old garbage. I'm being warned that I'm mixing apples and oranges—that was then, this is now."

"So, follow that excellent advice!"

I shook my head. "It's just not that simple Peggy. I've spent the last few years building up my independence, getting myself back, better than ever. I'm worried that a formal commitment with Luke will change all that—and I'll be returned to where I was before. In the shadows again. Less than who I am, somehow."

Peggy gaped at me. "Oh good grief. That lovely man? Trust me, honey—hooking up with Luke is the best thing that you've ever done for yourself. Most of the women on this planet would kill to be in your shoes. Enough of this! Eat your gnocchi. Have more wine. I'll find something for you to ride tomorrow. Did you bring your hat?"

"And my tall boots," I replied, grinning. "Thanks Peggy."

"No worries. Here comes more bread."

We were both up at six the next morning so that Peggy could meet her trainer at their barn before her class was due to start. The barn was an easy driving distance to the show grounds. However, hacking a horse back and forth was a long haul, so the farm had rented stalls at the show as well, and trucked the horses in.

We drove by show barn after show barn. We slowed by grooms riding their charges on the side of the road. Many nationally renowned trainers were working horses in rings as we passed. Several golf carts buzzed by us, some with horses in tow; all with small terriers perched on the front seat.

It was a wonderfully balmy day. My old Baker backpack was slung over one shoulder; I had sunscreen, antibacterial hand-wipes, and my wallet. I was looking forward to tack shop row.

While Peggy had her lesson, I lounged at the umbrella table with some of the boarders. Most were familiar from years past. Jill offered me some ice tea.

Peggy and Jackson were working on the flat, saving the jumping practice for the schooling ring on the show grounds. The humidity was already a problem, and her show shirt was glued to her back. Riding in this weather was not appealing to me.

"Geraldine took Ken out to dinner last night," Jill giggled. "They went to some fancy restaurant in Palm Beach. I was not invited."

"I know she's supposed to be a brilliant vet," Olive replied, "but she's an idiot about men."

"She *is* wonderful with the animals, I admit. But no common sense! Ken has her completely befuddled. Last week, we were all supposed to meet at the fondue place in West Palm, and at the last minute Geraldine cancelled because Ken wasn't feeling well. She announced that she was spending the night at his house, to nurse him."

"Shhh! Here she comes."

Geraldine, astride her hunter, had crossed the road from Ken's barn and was walking over for a visit.

"Showing today Geraldine?"

"I'm doing the adults. The braider forgot to come this morning, so Maestro's groom had to do it. Does his tail look OK?"

"I never would have known," Jill replied. "Nice jacket."

"Custom, from Gilder's. Twelve hundred dollars. They ordered the fabric from London. Did you see my new Hermès girth?"

"Aha. Well, good luck today."

I moved over to the ring. Peggy was walking Jackson to cool him out.

"Why don't you meet me at the tent Em? Take my golf cart. Would you mind hauling my backpack and my water bottle? Brad and I are bringing the horses over in the rig."

"I thought Cindy was coming to do that."

Peggy frowned. "Brad doesn't know where Cindy is. She is supposed to be showing the pre-green horses this morning."

"Do you mean that Brad hasn't seen Cindy since last night?"

"Exactly."

Someone must have revved up the motor in Peggy's golf cart. I roared by Ken on a bay gelding. He appeared to be having a delightful chat with one of his female clients. I wondered if Geraldine had seen them.

The guard at the gate waved me in. I scanned the tents, looking for number eight. Overlook Farm's colors were royal blue and yellow, so it was easy to spot their set-up. All the boarders had their matching tack trunks (royal with yellow monograms) lined up near the entrance. The farm drapes (royal with yellow trim) displayed two rows of show ribbons fluttering over a seating arrangement of outdoor furniture (upholstery in royal with yellow piping). The landscapers had done an excellent job with potted azaleas, ornamental grasses, salvia, and coreopsis. The ground was meticulously mulched with cedar chips. I said *Hola!* to Peggy's groom and sat down on the love seat. Brad's terrier leaped into my lap.

"Bruno! You're looking good!"

Bruno wagged his stubby tail.

Brad's rig pulled up, an amazing vision in royal blue with yellow lettering. Peggy emerged from the cab, and they unloaded Peggy's jumper and three additional horses. The grooms scurried to get their legs unwrapped.

"Peggy, it's ninety in the shade. Why don't you just wear a polo shirt? It's perfectly acceptable in the jumper ring."

"Never!" Peggy replied, wiping her forehead. "But I do think that I'll forgo the jacket today." She yanked on her long sleeves and started to fuss with her hair net. I left her in front of the mirror in the tack stall.

I heard loud voices outside and went to investigate. Cindy and

Brad were standing by the truck, earnestly engaged in a shouting match.

"Do you know how LATE it is? You were supposed to help load the horses this morning."

"It's only seven-thirty, dammit! My class doesn't start for half an hour. What the hell is your problem?"

"MY problem? Where WERE you all night?"

"OUT! That's all you need to know."

Cindy marched over to her tack trunk. Brad slammed the cab door and pulled out. I told Peggy that I was going for a bottle of water and made a quiet exit on foot. I dodged golf carts, horses and bicycles. Several photographers had displays set up along the way. I glanced at one beautiful eight-by-ten and realized that it was of Peggy on Jackson in the amateurs. I made a mental note to tell her.

All the vendors seemed to be in exactly the same spots as my last visit. I made a beeline for the Baker tent; they had hung the new vests in the front. I eyed the price tag and pulled out a medium. Its collar was done in the signature Baker tartan. The coats were attractive as well.

"That's the last of them!" The saleswoman appeared on my right. "We had a few cold days last month, and the vests just flew out of here. Try on the coat. They're very warm."

"They're beautiful, but we have a heated indoor. I'll get more use out of a vest."

"Where do you live?"

"Northwest Connecticut. Near Litchfield."

"Oh sure. You've had some cold weather this year."

"Too much. I definitely needed a break."

"Well, the vest is perfect for the winter season up there. And you can wear it into the spring months when you're back outside. Will that be cash or charge?"

The announcer encouraged the adult jumpers to hustle over to ring number five. I got my water and walked to the schooling area.

Peggy and Rebel were sailing over a three-six oxer—a big double jump. She motioned to me; I kissed Rebel's pink and gray nose.

"Your old trainer is here, Emma. Hal. I just saw him. He's coaching a girl in the equitation ring."

"Did he see you?"

"I don't think so. He's wearing a blue polo. His hair has gotten really gray."

I meandered over to the next ring, with one ear tuned in on Peggy's gatekeeper. I didn't want to miss her trip. I spotted Hal almost immediately. Peggy was right—he was definitely looking older. I watched him help a teenage female. I could hear the familiar pep talk. The girl seemed nervous.

"Emma! I didn't know you were coming down this year!" Kitty. Wife of Hal.

"Just visiting Margaret for the week."

"So Joy's not here?"

"No."

"Not regretting your decision to leave us, are you?" Big smirk.

"On the contrary."

"Shopping?" She looked at my Baker bag.

"Yes."

"Remember, all the fancy gear in the world won't make you a better rider."

"Thanks for the tip."

I watched her scurry over to Hal and whisper in his ear. He looked toward me and smiled. Kitty started whispering again. He turned away.

Peggy was on deck when I got back to the jumper ring.

"What happened?"

"The pit bull headed me off. Nothing ever changes at Green Gates. Which is why I left."

Peggy and Rebel were magnificent. They finished the jump-off with no faults. We all clapped vigorously.

"Excellent!" Brad said. "I'll stick around to see if you got a ribbon. Go have fun with Emma."

Peggy and I met Whitney, who was Brad's barn manager, for dinner that night. We had agreed to let Whitney bring up the Cindy question, which was difficult, as we were both panting for information. Whitney did not disappoint.

"Did you hear them this morning? In front of everybody!"

"Seems rather par for the course at this show," Peggy remarked.

"True, but it must be galling for Brad; the whole community knows that she's cheating."

"Are we aware of the identity of the miscreant?" I asked.

"Some skiing buddy from New York State. He's down here to see her. Chris says that they've been at it, on and off, for years."

"What is Brad going to do?"

"Probably nothing. She owns half the business. It makes more sense to stick with the marriage."

"There are probably a lot of horseshow couples in the same boat," I mused, thinking of Hal.

"I saw you talking to Kitty Woods," Whitney said. "What's their situation?"

"They still have their farm in Redding. Joy was with them for a little over a year. Hal is basically a good guy, but he prefers working with nice quiet geldings that give no trouble. Joy, as you know, is a mare with a definite opinion. She tortured that poor man. As does his wife." I laughed. "Kitty! Her name should be 'Tigress'!"

"Or 'Cheetah'?" Peggy grinned. Whitney choked on her Coors Light.

"So why did you leave their barn?" Whitney asked me.

"Kitty was just brutal to work with," I replied. "Total Queen Bee. She'd do as little as possible around the farm, spending most of her time on various leisure activities. Then she'd waltz into the barn, snapping at every person in her way, expecting her horse tacked up or her trailer hitched to her brand new truck. She was famous for interrupting lessons. Hal had to focus his attention on her when she was in the ring. To hell with paying customers. She is supposedly a professional, but none of the mothers could stand her, so she does the books and the ordering and the scheduling."

"She's not particularly talented," Peggy added. "Built like a short pear. No balance. She'd get on all the push-button horses and parade around. I never once saw her show. Hal is good with most horses, but he and Joy never got it together. Maybe he can't handle tough women."

I grinned. "Like me, you mean?"

"Did you have a falling out with Kitty?"

"Did she ever!" Peggy exclaimed.

"Kitty asked me to meet her for a drink in Danbury a few months before I left. She had three very quick cabernets and starting shooting off her mouth. I heard all about her latest conquest. He was a real estate broker in Roxbury. His wife didn't have the same interests—the kids took up all her time. Kitty was very loud and many of our fellow drinkers were definitely entertained. She clearly expected me to be supportive of her behavior. It made me sick. I marched back to the farm and told Hal's daughter everything that her stepmother had said." I paused. "I don't know what I was thinking."

"I do," Peggy said.

"Hal has a daughter?" Whitney said.

"Alex. She's probably about twenty-five now. Sweet young woman and extremely competent with horses. Joy loved her. Kitty broke up Hal's first marriage. She has done everything she can to keep Alex from having a relationship with her father."

"So what did Alex do?"

"Nothing at first. Then Kitty pulled one of her nasty maneuvers, and Alex let her stepmother have it about the affair—right in front of Hal."

"And guess what happened!" Peggy broke in. "Hal believed *Kitty!*"

"You can't be serious!"

"Kitty convinced him that I was spreading this terrible story because I wanted him for myself. She told the other boarders that I was some kind of pathological liar. Alex was forbidden to speak to me again. I had no choice. I had to move my horse. If for no other reason, how could I possibly work with a man who was *so* ball-less? I had lost all respect for my trainer."

"So why did you go over there today?"

"I don't know. Curiosity, mainly. He's just as spineless as ever. The Shrew still runs his life. It's pathetic."

Peggy and Whitney both looked at me, but said nothing.

CHAPTER SIXTEEN

Past Flames

The day after I returned from Florida I took Sophie to dinner at the Tavern.

"Emma," she said, registering concern. "What's up? I've never seen you this tense."

"Men from my past," I replied, barely taking a breath. "They're coming out of the woodwork. I hear about them, I dream about them, or I run into them! What is going on?"

"Love interests?"

I shuddered. "Mostly. A few were just flirtations."

"Give me examples."

I steadied myself. "Mark. We went out, or made out, really, for most of my freshman year of high school. Then he broke up with me and started dating one of my friends. Later, he announced that he was gay. Then there was Kevin. We were together my entire junior year—I even wore his class ring. Then just before the prom he dumped me to go out with my sister. I had to hand the ring back to him so he could give it to her. Tim. He was going steady with one of my closest friends, and I stole him away from her. He took me to the junior prom. Next is Phil. He was practically engaged to another close friend, and we ended up having sex just before the senior prom—but he still went to the dance with her. I was there with someone else. We sat together at the same table."

Sophie whistled. "This is still high school? You sure were busy!"

"I'm just warming up. I really believe that I went to Vanderbilt to get away from the army of guys that I'd be leaving behind in Connecticut. But guess what?"

"Episode Two—The College Years?"

"Exactly. I got my first taste of Southern men—the phony charm and gentleman-like behavior, and I bought in to it. All nonsense, of course. It started at the beginning of freshman year with Hank from New Orleans. I got rid of him via a note—pretty lame, I know—to then take up with Rich, from Houston, who thought my family had a lot more money than we did. When he realized his mistake—just before finals...."

"Great timing."

"Oh it was. He claimed that he couldn't date me any longer because an old girlfriend of his had just been killed in a car accident—Nichelle, her name was. Don't ask me why I remember that. Anyway, within two weeks I saw him out with a new female—a sophomore with lots of social connections. Rich was quite the climber."

"Then what?" Sophie asked, waving at the waitress for another glass of wine.

"Sophomore and junior years for me were frankly a blur of one night stands—guys I took to sorority parties. The multitude was a real joke with my sorority sisters," I laughed, thinking of the award that I had received just before graduation: *God's Gift to Men.* "At least half were blind dates. Senior year I started up with Neil, from South Carolina, who *was* a perfect gentleman. We spent a lot of time together—mostly going at it in my room at the sorority house. He had money, and a car, and he was very generous. He took me to nice dinners, out and about in Nashville." I paused, musing for a bit. "Neil was a year behind me, and when I graduated, I broke up with him. Can't remember why.

Distance probably—I was going back to Connecticut for law school and was not interested in keeping in touch."

"Hmm," Sophie replied. "Any dreams about Neil?"

"No."

"I thought not. Pray continue."

"First year of law school I dated an older guy—not a classmate—who was getting divorced and had two kids. He ended up going back to his wife. After that, I met my first husband, Shawn—you know all about him."

"Lawyer. Cheated on you and hid money. Recently got divorced for the third time."

"After Shawn, there were a couple more lawyers and one judge before I started dating Nick. The one that keeps coming up is Rob. He had a girlfriend in Rhode Island, and I knew it. But we spent so much time together that I just assumed that she would conveniently disappear from his life. Then she caught us together, and he felt so guilty that he married her."

"Ouch! How has Rob reappeared?"

"He lives near here. I didn't know it until I attended a Bar Association function a few weeks ago, and there was Rob. Still married. Still kind of goofy—just a little heavier than I remembered." I took a big swallow of ice tea. "That's it. After Nick, there were a few dates with yet another judge—nothing happened there, thank goodness."

"And now it's Luke. That's quite a story, Emma. And quite the pattern."

"Emotionally unavailable men?"

"That's issue number one," Sophie nodded. "Seduction energy. Sounds like you threw yourself at guys you knew couldn't give you what you thought you wanted. And the few pearls that *were* available, you threw back. I grant you—there weren't many."

"What's issue number two?" I asked, suddenly nervous.

"Betrayal by women who are supposed to love and support you—

189

and conversely—betrayal *by you* of women who expect your loyalty. Mostly the former."

"My sister—Kate—going out with Kevin, knowing that I was so into him?

"That's one example, yes. But I think that it goes deeper than that. Is this also a recurrent theme with you? Female friends who let you down?"

"Definitely. But the irony is that I've always held women to a much higher standard. Women should know better. Men—well— one expects men to stray.'

"One does if one still needs to heal, certainly. Tell me, of this— uh—variety pack of man-flesh, which of them are coming up the most?"

"I've been having repeated dreams about two of them: Kevin, and Rich—the social climbing Texan who used his dead ex as an excuse to unload me. Nick has been a regular for years. I must be still healing from the divorce."

"OK, so men who arguably have betrayed you. Probably old childhood stuff coming up."

"But I thought I cleared that energy months ago!" I exclaimed, astonished. "While the divorce was going on."

Sophie sighed. "There are layers, apparently. Like an onion. We are constantly shedding old energy. It all has to come up for you to clear it. You'll get there eventually, I promise. OK, that covers the dreams. What about the real life stuff? You told me about Rob. Who else?"

"Mostly guys from high school. The seriously old flames. Phil is now getting divorced—someone he met in college, and wants me to represent him. I haven't seen him in twenty years. Tim is running for the state legislature—I just got a flyer about him. And then there's Hal."

"Hal?"

"Joy's first trainer. I ran into him, and his wife, just recently during my trip to Florida. That was never anything more than a flirtation, but his wife was jealous and made a big deal about it at the time."

"Fine. I've got the picture." Sophie said. "Here's what I think, Emma. Recall from my witchcraft classes that everything is energy. Each experience that we have, the emotions that we feel—good or bad—they're all sitting there, in and around us, until we do something to clear them. Like psychic imprints on our hearts. A Shamanic healer I know refers to this phenomenon as 'energetic shrapnel.' In your case, something has triggered deeper layers of your past gunk, and it's rising to the surface, attracting more of same—begging for healing. Can you think what that trigger might be?"

"Luke?"

"It seems to me that your last, and perhaps only, healthy relationship was with a man in college, and that ended in a crash and burn because of distance. Every guy before, or since, pretty much, has been an utter disaster. Would you agree with that assessment?"

"Definitely."

"Enter Luke, who is about as ideal a man for you as it gets. All the old emotions have rushed forward, and you've gone into romantic red alert."

"So this isn't all about warnings? Same nightmare, different gent?"

"I don't think so. You're being warned, if anything, that you're approaching the situation with Luke as though he's Nick, or Rich, or whoever. Does that make sense?"

"It sounds so obvious when you break it down, Sophie, and I'm very grateful. Logically, I see your points exactly."

"But anxiety is a terrible thing—I know. Try raising a daughter by yourself," Sophie grinned. "You worry about everything. Looking back, it wasn't all that horrifying."

I relaxed a little. "But why now, Sophie? Luke and I have been together for over a year."

"My guess is that you feel a shift—and it's scaring you. I'm not asking—and it's none of my business. But it's important, and as I said after opening night of the play, it's something that you must work out for yourself." She hesitated. "When we first met, you told me that you'd had some less than satisfying encounters with Shamanic healers, and that you'd given up on the practice entirely."

I nodded. "I had sessions with four different practitioners in the course of a year and a half. I found them all to be very cold, and completely lacking in compassion."

"I want you to trust me on this Emma," Sophie said. "The woman I just mentioned—her name is Kezia Brennan. She lives up in Salisbury—works out of a converted barn on her property near the lake. I want you to go see her. I guarantee you that she's kind, and funny, and she'll detach you quickly from all of these men, so you can move on with your life. What do you say?"

"I trust your judgment Sophie," I replied, laughing. "And I'd really like to unload these guys."

"Good. Here's Kezia's card. Tell Luke that he's welcome."

"The Federalists and the Anti-Federalists in the late eighteenth century," I announced, and the teenage babble in class subsided. "Who were they, and what were their respective agendas?"

"They were originally political factions," Adam explained, "that emerged between the signing of the Declaration of Independence in 1776, and the ratification of the Constitution in 1788. By the time Washington left office in March of 1797 they had evolved into political parties."

"Whose battles got seriously nasty," Suzie added.

"The Anti-Federalists took some pretty bad bites out of President Washington," Jon volunteered, "which was probably considered sacrilege back then. He was determined to remain neutral politically."

"Good. Let's start with the Federalists. What did they stand for?"

Heather raised her hand. "They believed that a powerful federal government was necessary to build a strong, unified nation. They supported the Constitution, and favored the formation of a national bank and the growth of cities and manufacturing."

"The Federalists were elitists," Henry continued. "They believed that the well educated and the wealthy should lead the nation."

"So they preferred to stay on the right side of the Brits," Maddie said, "and put a tax on foreign goods. They were horrified by what was happening in France with their Revolution."

"Who were their leaders?"

"John Adams. Alexander Hamilton," Megan replied.

"Excellent. Now, tell me about the Anti-Federalists."

"Jefferson and Madison were the biggest guns," Kim said. "Although Madison was the Father of the Constitution—which confuses me."

"The Anti-Federalists feared that the Constitution made the President too powerful," Ed remarked. "They didn't want another king controlling their lives, and felt that a strong central government left the states too weak."

"So they opposed the creation of a national bank," Rob added, "which was Hamilton's pet project."

"The Anti-Federalists promoted agriculture as the core of the economy," Cassie said. "Like the French, they believed in the power of the common people."

"Eventually they evolved into what was known first as the Democratic-Republican Party," Suzie explained, "and then, around the time that Andrew Jackson was elected the seventh President in 1828, as the Democratic Party."

"Wonderful. And as we know, by the 1850's these parties were focused on one issue in particular."

"Slavery. The Democratic Party," Adam began, "promoting states' rights and an agrarian culture, supported it."

"And the abolitionists from all factions regrouped to form the Republican Party. Who was the most famous Republican of that era?"

"Abraham Lincoln!" The chorus shouted.

"So we now have a loosely painted background for our landscape. Remember that in the 1790's the U.S. was in essence an experiment. Our leaders were the ultimate mediators—actors in a brand new play that would become a very important world stage—and they knew it."

"So the Founders were aware that they were writing history as they went along?" Jon remarked. "That explains why so many of their letters are still in existence! They were setting themselves up as icons." He smirked. "Isn't that a little pompous?"

"Definitely. Good actors generally are," I said, grinning. "Back in the eighteenth century it all came down to personal honor. Character and integrity. Eventually our laws would take over, and politicians could be replaced. Not in the beginning though—the people *had* to be able to trust their elected officials. The new nation would not survive otherwise. Recall what the Revolution ultimately stood for—a dread of corrupt politicians in distant places sucking the common people dry.

"Now, let's look at the lead players in this particular American comedy-drama," I continued. "Who were they?"

"George Washington," Adam began.

"And Martha Washington," Megan added.

"John and Abigail Adams," Henry continued. "Jefferson. And the Madisons—Dolley and James."

"That covers the first four Presidents. Who else?"

"Benjamin Franklin," Heather said. "Tom Paine was extremely influential, but probably doesn't qualify as a leader."

"Alexander Hamilton," Maddie remarked, "although he got a little strange in the end there."

"They all knew each other, right? It was a pretty tight group. Friendships formed, broke up, and sometimes reformed. Why is that particular point important?"

Suzie raised her hand. "They knew who they could trust—sometimes to their detriment." She grimaced. "But politics was all about in your face debates back then."

"Good. And ultimately?"

"It meant they could make concessions and bring about compromises," Ed replied.

"Mediation, my friends. Balancing interests. Compromise. No one was really a winner, or a loser. It's what kept this country together in the beginning. And in my opinion, it is still the basis of all productive lawyering today—although too many of my brethren in the litigation sections would probably disagree.

"What, if anything, have we learned from the genesis of political parties in the United States?"

"Never burn your bridges?" Piper asked.

"Keep your enemies close?" Rob volunteered.

"You have to give to get?" Cassie added.

"It all boils down to character," Matt concluded. "You have to walk the talk."

"Otherwise it is just an illusion that we have a choice—correct? What do I mean?"

"That we're just voting for the same product in different wrappings," Jon replied. "We're tricked into believing that we're actually getting the government that we want—and even if the other side wins, that it's still good for us, because it was created by people who know better than we do."

"So really, our only choice has to do with the particular wrapping," Suzie said, grimly. "The rest is just words."

"The mistake that most people make—believing that words equal action," Megan said.

"That's an excellent point," I said. "George Washington was not a big talker. When he did speak, his comments were carefully chosen to create a precise impact on his audience."

"He was revered as an honorable leader," Piper nodded.

"Yeah," Henry added. "It's the gabbers that you have to watch out for. They're the ones who are twisting the truth and distracting everyone."

"It's all designed to keep us from thinking," Cassie replied.

Matt waved his hand violently. "OK, so today we know this. We get that the real power lurks in the shadows—invisible—while figureheads who talk much and say little are in the news—all over the planet. We've accepted that organized bad is still trying to run the show. What can we do to fix it?"

Sophie's angry voice suddenly popped into my head. "The battle on this earth is between high and low frequency people," she had said. "Individuals must learn that they affect everyone else with their energy. If we want peace and abundance on this planet, we have to stop playing villains and victims. It starts with disciplining ourselves, and taking responsibility for ourselves. Evolution isn't measured by the level of one's education—it's the amount of fear that one has overcome."

"We acknowledge our personal fears," I began, "which takes courage."

"And then we look around to see who else needs our help," Maddie added.

"So, if we see injustice, what do we do?"

"We oppose it," Suzie shouted. The whole class stared at her. "We face the instigators and we make it clear. We say 'you are toxic for all of us and you must be stopped. We *will* stop you. Your behavior is not going to be tolerated any more.' And then we take them down."

CHAPTER SEVENTEEN

Hockey Ghost

My cousin Leslie called.

"I'm going to be in your area for most of next week Em."

"That's great. Why?"

"Joan." Younger sister of Leslie. Not one of my favorite relatives. "She's having a child care crisis, and I said that I would help out. My two oldest can cover for me at home. What's your schedule next week?"

"Nothing out of the ordinary. Let me know when you're in Danbury."

Kezia Brennan was a short woman in her late thirties, with dark hair and eyes, and a rosy complexion. She radiated a grounded peacefulness that I found soothing. I liked her immediately.

"Sophie said that you have quite a crowd to dispose of," she laughed. "I've got the perfect ceremony for such situations. I call it the 'Group Disconnect.' The results are always fast and satisfying."

"Excellent," I replied, feeling the thrill of pounds already lost. "Let the clearing begin."

"You've had some experience with Soul Retrieval, correct?"

"Several. But they all had to do with my marriage, and my family. No boyfriends."

"Well, with this journey, we're going to cut the cord on anyone who still has a piece of you. Remember that with relationships at any level, bits of our energy are lost, but at the same time we are taking on shrapnel from other people, and it needs to be removed. So you'll be enjoying a combination of Soul Retrieval and energetic spring cleaning today. This journey will also differ in that it will be interactive. You're coming with me."

I frowned. "So I'll be seeing what you see?"

"Absolutely—the healing is more powerful this way, trust me. No one likes some stranger barging in cold and telling them about their life. It's obnoxious. Much better that you experience the journey first hand."

I took a deep breath and let it out slowly. "OK. I'm open to this."

"Good. Let's move over here." She led me to a comfortable sitting area with chairs and sofas covered with blankets of various Southwestern patterns. "You can sit, or lie down. Your choice. I'll be on the couch with my drum."

I sat up straight in a club chair with my feet flat on the floor, closed my eyes, and began the breathing.

"Here we go," Kezia announced. She started the slow beat of her drum. One two three four. One two three four.

We are in the woods, near a lake. In an open area a group of men is waiting in a circle. Kezia and I walk to the center. The sun is setting over the water. I hear animals moving amongst the trees, and occasionally a bird calls out. Suddenly, I see the black bear. She saunters over to me and stands up on her back legs. She's enormous.

"The bear is here to protect you," Kezia says, gently. "She's your power animal and she represents strength and courage."

Oh good.

"Tell me who you see," Kezia prompts. The beat of the drum becomes faster.

I glance around the assembly. "Past boyfriends," I reply. Wow, are there really this many of them?

"Look down at your body. Where do you see the cords?"

"Everywhere," I report. "The thickest are attached to my stomach area."

"The solar plexus. Who's at the other end?"

"One is Mark. The other is Rich."

"Time to let go, gentlemen," Kezia announces, her voice firm. "Emma wants her energy back."

"OK," Mark replies. "No problem." He turns and walks away.

"Later babe," Rich grins, waving. He disappears.

I watch the two cords dissolve and vanish.

"Now who do you see attached to you?" Kezia asks me.

"My first husband," I tell her. "Shawn."

"Where is the cord?"

"It's wrapped around my neck."

"Do you have anything to say to Emma, Shawn?"

Shawn shrugs. "Nope."

"Then off you go."

One by one we disconnect my old flames, and send them into the woods. Finally, only Rob is left.

"I'm sorry Emma," he says. "I never should have led you on. I always knew that I intended to marry Jen."

I thank him, and he is gone.

The bear puts her huge paw on my shoulder for a moment. I express my gratitude, and she lumbers off toward the water.

"Time to return," Kezia says. The drum booms loudly for seven beats, there is a pause, then seven beats again.

I opened my eyes. We were back in Kezia's barn.

"Emma," Carlie's voice on the intercom was tense. "Lieutenant Alsworth from the Bridge Hollow Police is holding for you."

"We have a situation over at the cemetery," Eva Alsworth said, "and since it indirectly involves your client, I thought I'd give you a call."

"Indirectly?" That sounded hopeful.

"This is regarding Myra Nathanson's new gravesite. For the big golfing monument."

"They're moving her entire family to an unpopulated area of the property. That was our agreement. So potential new residents will be forewarned of the—uh—circumstances."

"Right," Eva agreed. "Great compromise, Emma. Only the backhoe turned up something unforeseen this morning. Literally."

"A body!" Carlie exclaimed, fifteen minutes later.

"I believe the proper term is unidentified remains," I replied.

"And it's definitely female?"

"Or a guy in a dress and long brown hair. The forensics people are working on it now."

We received the news the following week.

"The body is Claudia Marino, Emma," Lieutenant Alsworth informed me. "Chief Marino's wife."

"They're sure?" I gasped.

"Oh yes. Dental records made it fairly easy. Also a broken ankle from her cheerleading days."

"But I thought that she took off with a boyfriend last year," I stammered. "I never met the woman, but everyone was talking about it."

"Well, everyone was misinformed," Eva said grimly. "The Chief has been suspended, while we investigate this case. It was definitely murder. Claudia's neck was snapped."

I suddenly thought of Suzie, and felt worse.

I now knew the identity of the female ghost who never left her side.

Email from Peggy, finally back from Florida, entitled: "Sex and the Show Barn."

Dear Emma,

It's *so* great to be back in sunny Connecticut. At least the snow is shoveled off my deck. I still haven't unpacked, but hey, it's not as though my social life is banging on the door, dragging me out every night.

While we're on the subject.

The big news is that Whitney has been having an affair with Geraldine's husband. For more than a year. Remember Fitz's trip down to Wellington to bring Geraldine her new car? Geraldine wasn't in Florida that weekend. But Whitney was. Geraldine got copies of Fitz's calls and texts, and went into orbit. She's telling everyone on the circuit that she was betrayed by Whitney, who was one of her confidants regarding Ken (and making him straight again). According to Whitney, Fitz is now waffling between love of a good woman (Whitney) and appreciation of a well paid spouse (Geraldine). Geraldine says that she's willing to take him back. What an imbecile. Looks like those fake boobs were a complete waste of cash.

Updates as we get them. Love to you and Joy.

Peggy

The BHS Varsity Boys Hockey Team was playing Harcourt Academy at home on Saturday afternoon. Luke and I bundled up the dogs and brought them along.

We found a spot in the stands high above the red line. Abby sat quietly in my lap with Rufus on the other side of Luke. I scanned the populace for known faces and noted many of my students, as well as some of their parents, scattered on the BHS side. Carlie, with Julie and their group, had planted herself just behind the team bench, hands already full with popcorn and hot chocolate. I waved for Sophie to join us.

"Ready?" I asked her.

"Armed and dangerous," she replied.

Luke shook his head and grinned. "It's never dull around the two of you."

Prue had gotten the information that we needed from her father.

Austin Bailey had been the star center of the undefeated BHS team in 1959. A senior, he had been accepted to Cornell and was slated for hockey greatness when he was killed during a play-off game.

"It happened at the BHS rink," Prue had explained. "Dad was

watching. He was pretty young at the time—a sophomore, but he remembers Austin being slammed into the boards, and just lying there. The boy died in the hospital a few days later. Dad said Austin had a reputation—he was a real jerk. Kissed up to the coaches, and liked to bully his teammates. He was not what you'd call a gentleman with the girls, either. There were complaints from the Tallmadge administration, as well as from parents in town."

"Any idea what his number was?" I had asked.

"Lucky number seven," Prue had replied. "He was famous for hat tricks. Couldn't do anything wrong—on the ice."

The first lines faced off, and the game began.

Prep school hockey wasn't as glitzy as the Division One college games that I was used to, but the action was terrific. Jim Stoddard with Max Armstrong as his right wing, and Charles Hanson on his left were blurs of navy blue and gray as they flew around their opponents, battling for possession of the puck. At the end of the first period BHS was leading, four to two, and the level of playing was impressive.

"Anything?" Luke asked Sophie.

"No sign of Austin yet," she replied.

I watched Carlie wave to Max through the heavy plastic in front of her.

Halfway through the second period we had a sighting.

Austin Bailey appeared from the opposite end of the rink, moving fast. He streaked through the other players and made a beeline for Jim Stoddard.

"Head's up," I said to Luke. Sophie grabbed my arm, and Abby barked once in response.

Harcourt Academy had the puck. Their right wing passed to the center who skated around the BHS net. It looked like an easy shot—until Jim Stoddard charged into him from behind, knocking them both into the goalie.

The whistle blew.

"That was calculated," Luke said.

Apparently the ref agreed. Stoddard was in the penalty box, and BHS set up their defensive formation in front of their goaltender, a player down.

Sophie began her descent toward the bench.

"Is this what you've been waiting for?" Luke asked.

I nodded. "Sophie's got to be where she can communicate with Bailey."

"Can she talk through the plastic and all this noise?"

"Doesn't need to. She'll use telepathy. She just has to get his attention."

There wasn't much time. Jim Stoddard was in the box for two minutes while his teammates attempted to kill the penalty, or Harcourt scored.

But Austin Bailey didn't hang around in the penalty box.

"He's going for Max!" I shouted. Several people turned and stared at me. Carlie winced, her eyes glued on her boyfriend.

The Harcourt team was passing the puck in textbook power play moves. Austin Bailey skated across the blue line and appeared at Max's left. Suddenly Max roared up to the Harcourt player who had control of the puck, raised his stick, and hooked the boy's arm. The puck flew into the boards, and the whistle blew again.

"Two players down!" A girl next to me moaned.

Max joined Jim in the penalty box. It would be a miracle if Harcourt didn't get a goal with five on three.

But the BHS defense was excellent—they iced the puck twice, managing to kill Jim Stoddard's penalty without allowing the other side to score.

Max was still in the box, fuming. Carlie wisely stayed in her seat.

Sophie also remained in position. We both scanned the rink for Bailey, but the second period ended without further incident. The Zamboni rolled out to resurface the ice.

Carlie texted me: Was that Austin?

Sophie texted me: Ready for round three.

"You and Sophie need a quicker way of communicating!" Luke said, laughing.

"We're working on it," I replied. "She's better at telepathy than I am, but I'm learning."

"Oh," Luke answered, taken aback. "I was thinking more along the lines of walkie-talkies."

The third period began. BHS was still leading, seven to four.

Jim Stoddard resumed his star player technique, his ghost attachment skating closely alongside. Stoddard passed crisply to Hanson. I admired their seamless teamwork and control—skates barely leaving the ice, executing each maneuver without breaking their smooth stride. It all looked so effortless.

But I knew better. Ice hockey is the fastest, most difficult team sport in existence. It's a defensive game of position—each member of the team has a particular territory to patrol and protect. A player has to be able to trust the other people on his or her line.

The Harcourt left wing had the puck and skated ahead across the blue line into the BHS zone. He drop passed it to their center, who moved in on the goal. We all watched, aghast, as Jim Stoddard revved forward and then rammed the blade of his stick into the boy's abdomen.

"Spearing," Luke said. "Serious penalty."

Five minutes in the box. Stoddard pulled off his helmet and bashed it into seat next to him. Seconds later Harcourt Academy scored.

"Austin Bailey's ghost is still with Jim," I reported to Luke.

"Sucking Stoddard's rage, no doubt," Luke replied.

"Big power surge for him," I agreed.

Sophie moved in on her target. She pulled her ammunition out of her coat pocket and waved it at the ghost. He went rigid, and I knew that she was communicating with him.

"What is that?" Luke asked, squinting.

"School paper from the time that he died," I replied, ignoring frantic texts from Carlie and Julie. "She's telling him that she knows who he was, and encouraging him to move on."

"Is he?"

"Not yet. Wait, now he's looking center ice. He's skating out there—wow, I think the white light may be the big face-off. Yep." I smiled at Luke in triumph. "The Universe has a sense of humor. I can't see Austin Bailey anymore, so that's a good sign."

Sophie climbed back up the bleachers, looking pleased.

"I've lied to ghosts before," she said, laughing, "but I feel that today was my all time personal best."

Luke and I registered interest.

"I told Bailey that he was wasting his time with high school hockey—that the Cornell team was waiting for him on the Other Side. So, he grabbed his stick and skated off," she chuckled.

"How will this departure affect Jim Stoddard?" Luke asked.

"He may feel shaky for a few days, then he'll recover his energy, and return to normal," Sophie said. "Whatever normal is for him."

"Good," Luke remarked, practically. "Because BHS is headed for the play-offs, and we can't win if he keeps pulling these stunts. Thanks, Sophie."

Angela called Wednesday morning. "I had lunch with Leslie today," she reported. "It's bad over there."

"Anything that I should know about?"

"Apparently Ashley's teacher pulled Leslie aside this morning for a little chat."

"Oh really?"

"The teacher had tried to reach Joan at work, but the person who answered the phone had no idea who 'Mrs. Lewis' was."

"She probably goes by her maiden name at the office."

"She does. But the teacher didn't know that."

"What was the nature of the discussion?"

"Ashley's got some bathroom issues. As in, lack of attendance."

Yet another reason that I never had kids. Dogs don't require underwear.

"Leslie told the teacher about the divorce."

"The teacher didn't know? They've been separated for months!"

"And then apparently Joan lambasted Leslie for telling family secrets without permission."

"While she's there on an errand of mercy?" I yipped.

"You're having dinner with Leslie soon right? I'm sure she'll fill you in."

My cell phone rang that evening. Leslie.

"I'm sorry Em, but I think that I'm losing my mind."

"What's wrong? Are your nieces OK?"

"If you mean, are they breathing, then yes, they're alright. It's my sister."

"Are you at her place right now?"

"I'm sitting in my car in Joan's driveway. She thinks I'm talking to Greg. God, Emma, this house!"

"What do you mean?"

"It looks like a bomb site. I couldn't get out of the back door, the mound of laundry is so high. Every dish she owns is in the sink. And there are *bugs*."

"No!"

"Yes. They have taken up residence in the dishwasher."

"How are the kids?"

"Strange. Ashley has retreated into a bubble world of her own. She jumps when you speak to her. Kellie is a terror. She's already ransacked my luggage and my wallet. Joan calls it 'undisciplined'."

"How long are you staying?"

"Until Sunday. I was lucky to get this much time off from the hospital. The goal is to get the girls through the school week—and Kellie's birthday is on Friday. There's the party at school and another on Saturday morning at the house."

I heard her take a deep breath.

"In the last forty-eight hours, I have done approximately ten loads of laundry. I have gone food shopping twice. I have driven the girls to school and picked them up again twice. I have fed and walked the dogs. I have fed the girls. I have had dinner waiting for Joan when she came in from the train station. Both nights."

"With you so far."

"On Monday nights, the big rubber garbage tubs are hauled to the curb for pick-up on Tuesday mornings. This past Monday, however, the dogs got into the trash and dragged it all over the driveway. We awoke the next morning to discover this. And there the garbage remained until I cleared it up and put the cans back in the garage. There are three bays. All three have electronic doors. I must have pulled one of the releases by mistake while I was wrestling with the refuse. Last night my sister marched into the house in a fury because her remote wouldn't work."

"With dinner sitting on the table, et cetera?"

"You've got the picture. I allowed her to rant for a while, and then I let her have it."

"And her response?"

"This is a quote—'I *live* to be able to open my garage door from the car and drive in.' Have I mentioned that there is no furniture in the living room, and they've been here for five years?"

We arranged to meet in Kent for dinner the following evening.

I had suggested a restaurant in the center of town. Our features were so similar that we looked like sisters, although Leslie, two years older, was slightly shorter, and had lighter hair and finer features.

The waiter brought us Grey Goose martinis, up with a twist. I watched while Leslie put an impressive dent in her cocktail.

"OK. Tell me."

"Kellie's eleventh birthday is tomorrow. I took her to get the party supplies. I ordered the necessary for the school party, and the cake for the celebration at the house on Saturday. I helped Kellie to send

out the email invitations on Monday night. I have to assist at the school party in the cafeteria after class tomorrow, and no doubt tomorrow night I will be decorating the house. Joan told me that she has yet to go look for Kellie's birthday present. This is apparently a huge imposition, as she is very busy in the office right now. Did Angela tell you about the bathroom issue?"

"Yes. Has Joan said anything about it?"

"She doesn't seem to notice. But then she never does the laundry, so why would she? Ashley is another story. She is utterly withdrawn. When she does speak, it's in a whisper. She reads in a corner or she parks herself in front of the television. Kellie tells me that her sister spends hours on her bike, riding around the neighborhood. I'm having a terrible time getting either one of them to eat anything but fast food. I think that they are both very worried about their father."

"Has Art been around at all?"

"No, but the girls are constantly calling or texting him."

"Is the babysitter due back any time soon?"

"Supposedly, on Monday, which is fortunate. I couldn't take much more of this, even if I had the time off. My sister should never have had children. She's either capitulating, or screaming, every night."

I felt a trigger pull in my gut, and a motion picture of my childhood attempted to manifest in my head. I exhaled slowly, transmuting the energy.

Leslie started her second martini. "Oh, and here's the best part, Em. Joan announced that she and the girls are coming with us to Nantucket in July."

CHAPTER EIGHTEEN

Dolley and James

Email from Peggy entitled: "Have you seen this week's *Hoof Gossip?*"

Dear Emma,

Well, have you? I nearly lost my lunch. A full page spread from Geraldine's trainer, Ken, congratulating everyone in his barn for a successful Florida season. He's the only one who won anything! On his own sale horses! And those were bought by his rich boyfriend, who spent the winter alone in Greenwich. What a load of phony baloney. But I can hear you right now. You're thinking 'what else would you expect from a group of crazy people who spend thousands of dollars every year for a handful of dollar-ninety-eight ribbons?' OK, but at least I won a wool cooler for Jackson last week. That's something.

Geraldine has been bad-mouthing Whitney all over Fairfield County. So, Brad and Cindy have fired her on principle. Please recall the fact that Cindy has been cheating on Brad for years, and Brad knows it. Also bear in mind that if Ken, the newly gay trainer, had so much as crooked his little finger in Geraldine's direction, she would have come running. It's been the joke at their farm for months.

Know anyone who could use a good barn manager?

Give Joy a big slobbery wet kiss for me, won't you?

Love, Peggy

I met Carlie and Julie in the Tallmadge Academy library after class. Carlie had booked one of the private study rooms for our discussion.

"Here's the information you wanted on Lavandula, LLC," she said, pulling a file out of her backpack. "Sorry it's been so long—the State takes forever to get back to you, and then I had more digging to do once they did."

"What do you mean?"

Carlie frowned. "The officers of Lavandula aren't who they claim to be. They all live in Connecticut, but they're actually relatives of the people who are really running the company, and don't want their identities made public."

I waited.

"It's all name games, Emma. The President of Lavandula is listed as Glen Hollister. He lives on the other side of Connecticut, near the Rhode Island border. He's a real estate lawyer, and he's Gilbert MacInerney's nephew."

I remained calm. "And the others?"

"Elise Dreyer is Leonard Abel's married sister. He's the Chairman of the Bridge Hollow Conservation Commission. Althea Lathrop is Norman Daley's daughter."

The Town Attorney.

"I saved the best for last. Judith Allis is—or was—Claudia Marino. Her maiden name was Judith Claudia Allis."

Julie was outraged. "You're telling us that half of Bridge Hollow's government runs the company that is trying to buy our historical park for development?"

Carlie nodded. "And a big profit—if they pull it off. The Playhouse Park isn't the first parcel that they've targeted. I have one other bit of interesting information. You know your noise case Emma? The one with the garbage guy's kid on the noisy motorcycle, harassing the horses? I did some checking on the Grudbergs. Guess who Bonnie Grudberg was in high school?"

Julie snapped her fingers. "Bonnie Marino. I went to grade school with their son. She's the sister of our Chief of Police."

Carlie looked at me. "What do you want me to do, Emma?"

I smiled. "Do what you do best, honey. Write an article."

Moira and Alan were regularly flying back and forth between their homes in Connecticut and London.

"We just want to lay down some ground rules," Moira explained, "because our lives are often quite chaotic—especially for the children. The nanny comes with us when we travel with the family. We also have dogs."

"It's a bit much," Alan agreed.

"What kind of ground rules?" I asked.

"Expectations," Moira said. "Regarding social functions. Obligatory business events. Extended family vacations and holidays."

"Our life together is one big juggling act, and we feel that we'd like to formalize our understanding of how it all works—if it does."

"Where would you like to begin?"

"We should explain our careers to you," Moira replied. "I buy art for people. My clients have decorators and landscape designers, and they need someone to advise them on acquiring paintings, sculptures, tapestries—whatever they like. I work all over the United States and Western Europe, so I'm constantly in the air for business."

"I'm a management consultant," Alan said. "I work primarily in North America, but I'm beginning to expand into Great Britain, Ireland, and France."

"We have two daughters—twins. They're twelve. They attend school here, but they also have taken summer classes in London. The girls are approaching the age that makes it difficult for us to just shove them on a plane and go."

Alan nodded. "They want more continuity with activities, friends—and boyfriends, I suppose."

"So the question is," Moira continued. "How do we accommodate their needs, and maintain our businesses? My family is primarily in England—Alan's is here. We're willing to compromise, but neither of us is much into sacrifice. We'd like some help creating a meeting of the minds—for all four of us."

Admirable. And I thought my commute to Westport had been difficult.

"Let's throw some ideas around," I suggested, pulling out my legal pad and uncapping my fountain pen. "Just start brainstorming. We can analyze your options later."

"We understand that there is no perfect solution," Moira said, practically. "And that whatever we decide has to be flexible."

"As long as we remain a family," Alan replied, "we'll be happy."

The next meeting of the Book Club was to take place at Tina's home in Fairfield. Angela and I arrived early, and we agreed to a walk on the beach.

"This is pretty close to where you lived during your divorce, isn't it Em?" Angela asked.

"I was just a mile or so west of here—off Southport beach."

"Is it difficult to be back? Are old feelings coming up?"

"I thought they would be, but no. If anything, I feel completely detached from life in Fairfield County. It helps that I rarely have to drive down to the Westport office these days."

Angela regarded the homes crowded together above the sand. "This is a busy place. The noise from 95 and the Post Road, the trains, even ships blowing their horns on the Sound. Not much serenity."

I paused to point out some litter that had washed up. "What astonishes me is how expensive this area is, when look—we're staring at Long Island. New York City is an easy train ride. As far as we can see the land is flat and unvaried. And the architecture is almost completely lacking in character. It's hardly what you'd call idyllic."

"You're spoiled by the country," Angela laughed. "Most of the people here would be bored out of their minds where you live."

"I'm sure you're right about that. Now that I've been up in the Northwest corner for almost two years, I can't imagine being around so much craziness all the time. I couldn't handle it. The energy seems insane to me. I have to have silence—and solitude—every day."

We assembled in Tina's living room.

"We're continuing with our study of powerful First Ladies," Angela said. "We've covered Abigail Adams and her partnership with our second President—John Adams. Today we are discussing *A Perfect Union, Dolley Madison and the Creation of the American Nation* by Catherine Allgor. All right Tina. You have the floor."

"Dolley Payne Todd Madison was the wife of our fourth President, James Madison," Tina began, "who was the father of the U.S. Constitution. But what's interesting is that Dolley unofficially stepped into the role of First Lady earlier in her husband's career—during Jefferson's administration, when James was Secretary of State.

"As we know, Jefferson was a widower, with an unusual family life. He was not inclined to consider women as equals, and did not include political wives in his all male partisan dinners at the White House. The task fell to Dolley, wife of Jefferson's protégé and successor to the Presidency. According to Professor Allgor, Dolley was the architect for modern social politics in Washington—and one of the most famous women of her time.

"Dolley was born in 1768 and raised as a member of the Society of Friends, or Quakers. A culture that valued pacifism, simplicity, and equality, Allgor writes that it was her religious background that Dolley later used as a powerful tool to build cooperation and manipulate politics in Washington.

"She was reportedly tall and curvaceous, with a sparkling confidence and a warm demeanor that was immediately engaging. But her childhood was difficult. Her father, a rigid Quaker, was not financially successful. He died leaving Dolley's mother to provide for the family by opening her home in Philadelphia—then the nation's capital—to political boarders.

"Dolley married her first husband, John Todd—a Quaker and a lawyer—in 1790. They had two sons, Payne and William, and the new family lived happily until John and William died from the yellow fever epidemic that killed one fifth of the population of Philadelphia in 1793.

"As a beautiful and wealthy widow, Dolley was admired by many men, including the awkward and reserved hypochondriac James Madison, seventeen years her senior. The congressman was the eldest son of a prosperous Virginia landowner. He was already famous for his collaboration with Thomas Jefferson regarding the new American republic, and his close advisory position to President Washington.

"Dolley married James in September 1794, after less than a year of widowhood. As James was Anglican, Dolley lost her membership with the Society of Friends, but nevertheless the match was a good one. Dolley's vivacity was a perfect foil for James's shyness and lack of social prowess. Apparently James was that rarity among men—he was considerate, easy going, and devoted to his wife."

Eliot giggled. "He was also about two inches shorter."

"Everything has its compensations," Angela retorted, and we all laughed.

"Professor Allgor tells us that the 'potential for change was in the air' after the Revolution," Tina continued. "She reminds us that the war had been fought for the liberty that is due to everyone as a natural right. Women had kept the economy going during the Revolution—running the farms and businesses, and boycotting British goods—so that the men could fight. Afterwards, the boundaries became blurred, and a new age of 'republican motherhood' emerged. White women utilized their gentle subtlety to influence men."

"They operated on the theory that *manners* create the foundation for civilized society," Dottie sighed. "What a lovely premise."

"Are you getting a visual of Congress debating over a series of elegant high teas, Dorothy?" Denise asked.

"I think the goal was stability of the Union," I said. "These people were creating an entirely new form of government, remember. Once the Revolution was over, there had to be a way to keep the new nation together. The leaders were making it up as they went along, all the while dealing with the country's ingrained distrust of power."

"They were terrified of even a glimmer of monarchy, which they had just escaped—and anarchy—which eventually saddled the French with Napoleon," Dottie added. "The early Americans were looking for that delicate balance between formal governing and oppression."

"After Washington stepped down, animosity grew as the two political parties emerged," Tina continued. "This was the beginning of our political party system. John Adams and the Federalists promoted strong centralized federal power over the states. They were elitists—honoring English tradition and opposing democratic reforms such as expanded suffrage—and were especially prominent here in New England.

"On the other side of the fence Jefferson, Madison, and the Republicans—later known as the Democratic-Republicans—hailed from the South and West. They espoused liberty and freedom of the people over power...."

"People meaning white men," Eliot snorted. "Not women or non-white males."

"...and states' rights. Professor Allgor says that the republican idealists could not accept any concept of governing but their own, which they presumed was for the common good. Hence the often vicious attacks that separated former good friends—like Adams and Jefferson."

"Jefferson," Angela reminded us, "as winner of the second largest number of electoral votes in 1796, was John Adams' Vice President."

"Ouch!" Denise exclaimed. "Is it any wonder that Adams wasn't reelected in 1800?"

I grinned. "That's the last time we had sworn enemies in the two top spots."

"From opposing parties, anyway," Tina remarked. "In what was later known as the Revolution of 1800, the United States experienced its first nonviolent transfer of power between parties. Jefferson, and the Republicans, had defeated the Federalists."

Eliot rolled her eyes. "Someone please explain to me the difference between 'democracy' and 'republican idealism.' We use them interchangeably in this country."

"Yes," Angela replied patiently, "but in theory they're very different. Democracy is basically 'majority rules.' Winner takes all, and the minority view misses out. Republicanism was supposedly about equality—as Eliot points out—for white men, undeterred by status of birth or wealth. Anyone with talent could go as far as he liked."

"Which is how a lawyer/farmer from Quincy, Massachusetts managed to become our second President," Tina explained.

"We have a foundation laid, then," Angela prompted. "Such was the political atmosphere when Dolley and James moved to D.C. at the start of Jefferson's administration."

"Washington D.C. was still being built," Tina went on. "There were terrible housing shortages, worse roads, a lack of shops and services, and very few women. As a result, the Madisons lived with the President for a while, before moving to their own home. It was at this time that Dolley began making social connections with the D.C. wives.

"Professor Allgor reports that Dolley and her feminine cohorts created an entirely new society of political women. They served at the same time to temper the behavior of the men, and to manufacture a very effective alternative to traditional government culture.

"Dolley was a steel magnolia, and an optimist. She began making the short, ceremonial visits known as 'calling,' to promote social relations between local gentry, political families, and foreign dignitaries. As Dolley's childbearing days were now over—she and James never did reproduce—she was free to develop her own interests. At the top of her list was generating a social network for the new federal government.

"Getting the men together was a bit tougher, apparently. Politics were taken personally, and debates often became violent. The problem wasn't just opposition—it was hatred. Eventually, members of Congress and various officials acknowledged the benefits of importing their female relatives to the capital to ease the strain of isolation, and Dolley began her reign as Queen of Washington society.

"First, in her home on F Street as the wife of the Secretary of State, and later in 1809 as the First Lady with her Wednesday night 'drawing rooms.' She created a simplified version of the European royal levée. Men from both parties, along with their female relatives, came together under her roof, ate and drank, and behaved with civility. She was cordial to everyone, and took the path of least resistance. Unlike the occasionally caustic Abigail Adams, Dolley Madison never expressed her political views publically. Allgor writes that above all, Dolley valued harmony.

"So—while Thomas Jefferson adhered to his governing style of control and separation of parties—the word reconciliation was not in his vocabulary—Dolley and James Madison were all about utilizing a lighter touch, and the rewards of meet and greet."

"Aha," Eliot exclaimed. "The sacred feminine rears its head yet again."

Tina nodded. "Allgor's title, *A Perfect Union,* is well chosen. The Madisons were a real team—a partnership which operated on a completely different level than say, that of Abigail and John Adams, or Eleanor and Franklin Roosevelt, as we will see later on."

"Dolley Madison was the ultimate Mediator," I agreed. "She never appeared to have an agenda—although in reality she always did—and she regularly used social means to promote diplomacy and heal rifts when official channels failed. She was brilliant at defusing animosity, and encouraging cooperation. And although she enjoyed playing the part of Washington's Queen for sixteen years, she never admitted that her purpose was anything beyond maintaining the unity of the American nation."

"She made the most of the softer side of politics," Dottie said, "which basically meant social schmoozing over the punch bowl. Dolley was a genius when it came to putting people at their ease."

"It's the best way to bring about conciliation," Denise remarked. "We use it in every mediation session."

"Don't forget that Dolley often took the brunt of attacks that would otherwise be aimed at James," Eliot said. "She was his stand-in. She could go where he couldn't as President—Congressional sessions and Supreme Court hearings to name a few—and she could write and speak to others in a social setting what he dared not, in case of interception. Madison took Dolley very seriously as his political partner."

"I found it astonishing that James Madison left the refurbishing of the White House entirely to Dolley," Angela noted. "He even turned all of his accounts over to her. Now that's trust—and respect."

"She was a very brave and devoted wife," Denise agreed. "She was instrumental in getting James reelected, and her courage during the War of 1812 is famous. But we all know that she enjoyed the game— or she wouldn't have played. Dolley packed a lot of powerful influence, considering the place of women in her time. She was at the center of government for years."

"I'm not a big fan of ritual," I admitted. "Too much of it from my sorority days. But apparently what Mrs. Madison created, with her good taste, her tolerance, and her general affability, was an identity with which Americans could connect. The White House, the social ceremonies—Dolley herself. She made the U.S. government personal, and put Americans on the map, so to speak."

"Symbolism brings people together," Angela said. "Whether it's a building, a flag, a song, or a personality."

"Dolley Madison was considered a celebrity," Tina concluded. "She was one of the new America's most valuable assets, and the most famous First Lady for decades."

CHAPTER NINETEEN

Easter

"Possible new civil case coming in half an hour, Emma," Carlie said. "I told her you were free."

"Do we know the nature of the dispute?"

"Siblings squabbling. I couldn't get any details out of her."

Barbara Gagnon arrived in due course. I invited Carlie to sit in on the interview, and take notes for me.

"Our family has been in Bridge Hollow for one hundred and fifty years," Mrs. Gagnon explained. "There was always a lot of money, and when my grandmother passed last year, my sisters and brothers and I all inherited."

"So this is a probate matter?" I asked.

"Not quite. The issue has to do with the family mausoleum."

I looked over at Carlie in dismay, and she stifled a smirk.

"Your grandmother is there? In the vault?"

"Yes, but the problem is, we're not sure where."

"Ah."

"Don't they put up name plates on those things—the cabinets, or whatever they're called?" Carlie asked.

"Normally, yes. But you see, we were never a close family, and as such, not terribly involved in the obsequies. Our mausoleum is almost full. Only two slots remain open, in fact. But nearly half of the—uh—residents, have not been identified as such."

"But surely the cemetery people keep a record?" I demanded.

"They're supposed to, but it's all wrong. They have my grandmother and her sister in spaces that are actually empty."

"So you want me to deal with the cemetery?"

"Only partly." Mrs. Gagnon pulled a document from her purse and handed it to me. "This is a letter from my brother's attorney. We can't seem to agree on who gets the remaining space in the vault."

I sighed. "Your grandmother's name?"

"Anastasia Randall."

Twenty minutes later Carlie escorted my new client to the front door, and came back into my office.

"Start a file on this one?"

"Sure. And take this retainer check to the bank when you have a chance, please."

"OK." Carlie glanced at her notes. "I don't get it. These people can't stand each other, but they still want to spend eternity crammed together in some body condo? Why don't they just buy graves or get cremated—like normal humans?"

"Excellent question. What is going on with the inhabitants of this town? Are they losing their minds? And more importantly—why are they all coming here? Is it me?"

Carlie shrugged. "Must be."

Leslie called at 8:30 am. "We're hitting the road now. Are you ready for the invasion?"

"Bring it on! Are you coming over the Tappan Zee?"

"Yes. I avoid New York City at all costs, but especially on holiday weekends."

"Well done. I don't want you taking any side trips to Long Island, like last time."

That morning I conveyed my watercolor field set, my easel, and my terrier over to the Playhouse Park and toured the property, searching for an interesting view of the lake. The grounds opened up in a large triangle with the theater at the apex, and wooded areas screened the entire parcel from the large homes on either side. Paths across the grass led down to the dock from various directions. Several perennial gardens, maintained by the Garden Club, outlined the terrace behind the theater, and a community vegetable garden, surrounded by an anti-deer fence, stood on the southeast side of the park.

I set up near one of the stone benches at the edge of the water. Abby stretched out on a tartan blanket that I had brought back from Scotland, her black nose twitching, sniffing wood smoke. I poured water into her bowl, and began mixing colors on my palette. I drew the shoreline at an angle, with reflections of the maples and birches in the water. In the middle ground I sketched one of the larger islands. As the leaves had yet to appear I decided on a cloudless blue sky, setting the composition so that the eye followed the land and then zigzagged along the surface of the lake.

Abby closed her eyes, front paws under her chin.

I had just dropped some sepia mixed with ultramarine onto the trunk of one of the background maples, when activity near the dock caught my attention.

A party of men and women was moving toward the water. Four of the men were carrying canoes between them; the women were laden with paddles, pillows, and lunch baskets. The age range was somewhere in the late twenties to early thirties.

And by the look of their clothing, the date was about 1870.

Abby opened her eyes and stared as this procession reached the dock, put the boats in the water, climbed aboard, and paddled toward the north end of the lake. There was no sound, and the canoes left no wake behind them.

Leslie's enormous Ford rumbled through the gate at three o'clock. The doors opened and four teenagers with their assorted gear erupted onto my driveway.

"The traffic wasn't bad," Greg announced. He hoisted a large green duffle bag over his shoulder and headed for the porch.

"A man of few words," Leslie remarked. "Ben! How about helping your sisters with the bags? Where'd Gaby get to already?"

Sara pointed toward the lake where Gabrielle was reclined on a steamer chair, frantically texting. Trish waved her portfolio. "I brought my latest masterpieces to show you, Emma."

"I baked a couple of pies, Em, and I thought I'd do my potatoes tonight."

"Terrific. Come have some wine."

The noise level inside my house was staggering. Luke poured drinks in the kitchen—his face a comedic study of shock. Greg grinned. "A bit loud, aren't they? A heartwarming combination of Super Bowl Sunday and Sherman's March to the Sea."

"Did everyone find their rooms all right?" I asked. "I thought that Ben and Gaby could sleep in the studio downstairs, and Trish and Sara upstairs in the twin guestroom."

There was a thunder of running feet overhead. Abby and Rufus came tearing down the stairs, barking with enthusiasm.

Ben burst into the kitchen. "When's dinner?"

Trish made an appearance. "Gaby and Sara are fighting again."

Gaby was next. "Mom! She's after me."

"What did you take this time?"

"These jeans fit me better than they fit her!"

"That hardly answers my question."

"Emma look!" Ben exclaimed, pointing. "Your dog is on the table."

Yes indeed. Lapping at the onion dip.

At six thirty we assembled on the porch and grabbed plates. It was an unusually mild, mid April evening. The lilac bushes in my garden were blooming, and there were two warblers in the birdbath. One executed a swan dive, preened, and shook itself vigorously.

"What's going on in this town lately?" Greg asked us, spearing asparagus. "Last time we spoke you had an exploding mansion—complete with the body of a State Senator's husband. Then the missing wife of the Chief of Police in an unmarked grave, a dubious land deal, and ghosts behaving badly at the theater. Anything new?"

"Carlie's articles," I said, walking into the library and retrieving them from my desk. I handed Greg copies of *Town Leaders Liable in Park Scam* and *Ghost Clearings by Sophie Sullivan*, both of which had appeared in recent issues of *The Bridge Hollow News*.

Greg whistled and began to read, with Leslie hovering behind him.

"So now the entire town knows that their State Senator and several local officials were connected—by blood ties—to the development company that was proposing to destroy the historic park?" Leslie exclaimed, incredulous.

"More importantly," Greg said, "two of those blood ties are now dead as a result of violence."

"You mean murder," I replied. "No proof yet though. Nothing to tie Chief Marino to Claudia's death, and the investigation is ongoing as to the gas explosion at Cameron Manor."

"What about the State Senator—this Esther MacInerney?"

"There's more than enough evidence that she had a huge pecuniary conflict of interest," Luke said. "She'll lose her seat in the Senate, and the two town officials—the Conservation Commissioner and the attorney—will be replaced as well."

"And the park? Is that safe now?" Leslie asked.

Luke nodded. "The Garden Club is taking over its maintenance, and I've promised to help out with their plans."

"Didn't you say that the Chief's daughter is one of your students, Emma?" Leslie asked. "How is she doing?"

"I haven't seen Suzie in class for a while. She sent me an email saying that she was living with her mother's relatives in town. Her teachers have been working with her through the internet for a few weeks, so she doesn't fall behind."

"Interesting that she didn't stay in the house with her dad," Greg mused.

"They don't get along well, or so I understand," I told him, determined to stay neutral.

"I want to hear about the ghosts!" Trish broke in.

I passed her Carlie's second article. "After the hockey ghost was sent packing, Sophie gave Carlie permission to write about it, and consented to an interview."

Luke laughed. "And I let her have a few quotes about Sophie's work at my farm."

"She'll be hounded by calls now!" Leslie said. "Everyone will want her services."

"It's already happening," I replied. "Sophie can clear negative energy from any space, person, or thing. Naturally that idea appeals to people. I'm helping her to form her new business."

"It's a lot quieter on my property now," Luke added, "and I'm grateful." He looked at me and grinned. "It's only a matter of time before Jerry Forester takes a leap of faith and hires Sophie to clean out the theater."

Saturday morning was sunny, with a light breeze. Greg and Ben unloaded the family's kayaks from the top of their SUV. Luke and Sara hauled my two boats from the garage down to the dock. Trish and I moved our painting equipment from the studio to the edge of the lawn.

"Do you want to go out on the water first, and then come in to paint, or what?" I asked her.

"This view is *amazing!*" Trish exclaimed, groping for her sketchbook.

"I guess that answers that," Leslie replied. "Ben! I need help with the blue tandem! Now where is Gaby? Gabrielle! Take those things out of your ears and focus. I said OUT! I want you to see to the paddles and the life vests."

Trish pulled out a brand new set of acrylic paints. We watched with amusement as the rest of the herd reassembled in their various vessels and departed. Luke and Leslie had paired up in one of the tandems. Greg was with Gaby, and Ben and Sara were in singles.

"Mom doesn't have great upper body strength, so she always has to paddle with someone strong."

"Wow, look at Sara go!"

"Yeah—she's super athletic. She rowed stroke in the four this year."

The gang came back in for lunch and we ate on the porch. Luke needed to return to the farm, so in the afternoon I got in the bow of the red tandem, and Greg took the stern. We set a leisurely paddling pace, hugging the shore.

"That's where Ben saw the snapping turtle," Greg said, pointing to a spot near the town beach.

"How's your new practice working out Greg?"

"Mostly good. The senior partner should have retired years ago, but the work is interesting, and my secretary is competent."

"That's so important, isn't it?"

"It's nice when you don't have to take an hour to proofread everything you sign."

"How's Joan doing? Any news on the divorce?"

"It's been confirmed that Art has a new amour in the city. Some marketing female, ten years younger than Joan."

"I know I shouldn't say this, but good for him."

"It was time," Greg agreed. "My sister-in-law can be a real challenge."

Email from my cousin Leslie, entitled: "Two down, two to go."
    Dear Emma,
        We have gotten Trish back to school after Easter break with only several minor calamities. The entire clan was

determined to come along, so we were more than cozy in the SUV with all of Trish's gear (including her new easel—I'll make sure that she sends you a thank you note), the other three kids, their overnight luggage, and the dog. Ben insisted that we bring Comet, and I was lucky to find a hotel that would put him up for the night. He only ate a couple of towels, which is a definite improvement on last time.

I'm already dreading May, when we'll have to bring Trish and all her stuff back home for the summer.

Some news on the Joan front, which I'm sure will amuse you. Joan forced a confrontation with Art's hot young babe girlfriend—Libby—of the mile long legs variety. I understand that hair pulling was involved.

Art has since announced that he's filing a motion for sole custody of the two girls, as he is now convinced that Joan is certifiable. I can't say that I find fault with his argument, having been aware of this fact for decades.

Sara has made her decision about her college acceptances, and she will be attending Georgetown in the fall. I'm trying not to imagine her in that tank of sharks in Washington, but you've always said that she's tougher than I give her credit for. I've pointed out that she'd only be an hour away from home all year—but unfortunately this did nothing to dissuade her.

Please let us know as soon as possible what we can do for our group trip to Nantucket in July. Are you sure that Luke is ready for this?

Love and thanks to you both, Leslie

CHAPTER TWENTY

Walk the Talk

Debbie looked embarrassed. "Will never liked kids, and I discovered that I was pregnant with Charlie after we broke up. Money wasn't a problem—my business does quite well. So I've been raising my son on my own."

"He's *our* son," Will snapped. "And you should have told me. I had a right to know."

Debbie shrugged. "I thought I was doing the right thing—for all of us."

"How can I help?" I asked.

Debbie handed me a file. "We've agreed to work out a parenting plan so that Charlie can get to know his dad, and I can have some time to myself."

"I want him to spend half of the week with me and my girlfriend," Will began.

"Which is out of the question," Debbie announced.

"Do you live in the same general area?"

"More or less," Will replied. "Charlie's in kindergarten near us in Woodbury. I'm a plumber, and I have my own shop, so I can pick him up after school on a pretty flexible schedule, and have him on overnights and weekends."

"What if you have to work late?" Debbie asked. "What if there's an emergency call? Does your girlfriend take him? How do I know if she'll be OK with him? This whole thing is making me really nervous."

"But daycare doesn't?" Will barked.

"Those people have all been investigated and certified. What do I know about Bridget? Just what you tell me."

"Bridget has no objection to a background check. You know that. She's a teacher dammit." Will punched the arm of his chair. "This is why we broke up in the first place, Deb. Your need to control everything. What's the problem? Afraid Bridget will take over with our kid?"

Time to intervene.

"I have various templates for parenting plans," I reported. "Perhaps one of them—with adjustments—will be acceptable. Shall we take a look?"

Kezia introduced me to the importance of clearing past life energy at our next shamanic session.

"We all come into each incarnation with energetic sludge from previous lives," she announced, "and it's imperative to heal it if we don't want old programs to repeat themselves. The goal is to advance with each go around that we have on this planet."

"But how do you know?" I asked.

"What needs clearing?" Kezia sighed. "It becomes pretty obvious, Emma. Your former tendency toward seduction—going after emotionally unavailable men—is an excellent example. People incarnate hoping to conquer past patterns with addictions, financial issues, and family challenges. What are some others? How about rescuing people who need fixing—and who then turn on you? You have some savior energy to address. Are you aware of that?"

"It explains my law practice," I said slowly. "Although we've pretty much weeded out the high conflict family litigation cases in our office."

"This is more than just career related energy," she replied. "It's a compulsion, and therefore something you must work through. I'm not judging you—we all have our lessons to learn.

"Let's keep this simple. I tend to be impatient with so-called spiritual teachers who get highfalutin with terminology and name dropping, and miss the big picture," Kezia admitted. "And I am *so* tired of being stuck in workshops comprised of lectures by other shamanic practitioners on gurus-I-have-known." She laughed. "Impatience is one of *my* tests in this life.

"The new earth is all about living in peace and harmony and cooperation. The fact that you and I are sitting here right now doing this work means that we are teachers. It also means that we have to nail down our personal issues first, before we can help other people. This is how we gain wisdom. We have to Walk the Talk.

"The key is to find peace within ourselves, before we can share that peace with others. So, we have to bring up our fears and release them. We need to stay grounded and calm. We must learn to have compassion for everyone, and to act with kindness, regardless of what is going on around us. This requires total absence of judgment. Does this mean that we're expected to make nice with abusers? Absolutely not. Nor are we expected to like everyone."

What a relief.

"As we progress with this work we grow more sensitive. People and situations that did not particularly bother us in the past will become intolerable. This is not a judgment call—it's more of an energetic reality. We need to avoid harsh relationships and environments as much as possible—and at the same time shield ourselves to stay in balance. We must pick our battles, stand up for what we believe, and master our feelings and thoughts. How you respond to the situations around you is *your* choice, so it's important to see the silver lining every day.

"Remember, everyone is operating on a different schedule with this transition. You can remain detached and still send your compassion and understanding their way. It all helps. What you send out to the Universe comes back to you—so be sure that it's good.

"The best defense against low vibrational folks is to raise your own frequency. When I use the term low vibrational, I'm referring to people who are still operating in 3D fear and scarcity mode. When you maintain a positive level of energy you become almost invisible to anyone who is not on the same level. They won't interact with you because there's no connect. It takes practice to do this—we've been programmed for centuries to wallow in negativity. But the result is a win-win situation for everyone. You've helped to raise the frequency of the planet, and you're safe from harm yourself."

"So theoretically, if we operate on a positive, high vibration every day," I began, thinking of Martha Washington, "then the low vibrations can't find us?"

"I know it sounds like airy-fairy Pollyanna talk, but it works. Learn to surround yourself with positive thoughts and feelings. Our homes, for example, are areas within our control. Keep a clean, orderly household. Eat healthy food. Decorating with plants and fresh flowers will raise the frequency immediately—so will pets. Light candles. Play soothing music. Forgive others, and forgive yourself. Above all, practice understanding and kindness."

Kezia grinned. "Now here's where it gets difficult, for you especially.

"Share what you've learned with others, but only when they ask. That's when they're receptive to what you have to offer. Otherwise—let people be! There's a big difference between helping, and enabling an individual. Notice when it's really an enmeshment going on—someone has unhealthy hooks in you, and is merely feeding off your energy. Families are particularly common breeding grounds for this sort of toxic behavior. So are unhappy marriages. No one has the right to suck your energy, or dump their garbage on you—and at the same time, people need to learn on their own.

"My mantra in this area is Discern and Detach. Assess the situation, trust your gut, and set clear boundaries. Put another way—practice the energetic equivalent of That's Mine, This is Yours.

Acceptance is a huge part of this work. You don't have to agree with their behavior—just don't try to fix it for them. Allow people to process on their own, but by all means offer assistance if they ask."

I thought of the long line of people in my life that I had tried to help—who had usually thrown a pie in my face as a response. Friends, boyfriends, colleagues, family members. Both spouses. My Acceptance skills obviously needed a lot of adjustment.

"The next piece of this important lesson is the fact that while we're all learning detachment from each other's energies," Kezia continued, "we are also advancing in Oneness—or Unity Consciousness—with the earth and all its inhabitants—thereby expanding our preconceived notions of family. We are all connected."

E Pluribus Unum. Out of many—One.

"I think I already know the answer to this question, Emma—but tell me. When you have to recharge your emotional batteries, do you get away from it all—or do you seek out the company of others?"

Henry David Thoreau had once written that 'to be in company, even with the best, is soon wearisome and dissipating.... We are for the most part more lonely when we go abroad among men than when we stay in our chambers.'

"I need to be alone. I need silence."

"Aha. I was right. You're an introvert."

I frowned. "Doesn't that mean that my attention is always inward—about myself? That's really not who I am."

"You're certainly not self centered—or shy. My point is that you are energized by being alone, and at the same time, drained by being around other people. Introverted individuals tend to be gratified with the inner world of the mind, rather than small talk in big crowds. When they do engage in conversation, it's about ideas, not trivial social matters. Extroverts, on the other hand, tend to think out loud. They recharge from outside of themselves—usually in social groups."

I suddenly understood the dynamic of my previous marriage.

"My ex husband drove me loopy with his everlasting need for cocktail mingling events—total strangers babbling for hours about nothing. And the verbal lists!" For years I shouted at Nick to write notes to himself, or to program reminders into his cell phone or computer. Anything but the mental diarrhea that I was exposed to every day.

I had another thought. "But doesn't that make every extrovert a psychic vampire? Draining energy from others to recharge?"

"Sure sounds that way, doesn't it?" Kezia replied. "Modern culture, especially here in the United States, values gregarious spotlight grabbers as the ideal—while intellectual, sensitive people are stigmatized as weak, or too emotional."

"But most of the world's great innovators were thinkers!"

"Exactly. They were able to find their quiet centers and manifest their dreams. As the mother of an introvert *and* an extrovert, I can attest to the agonies of keeping a contemplative, cerebral child from murdering his constant center of attention grabbing little brother. It was a relief to cart them both off to separate boarding schools."

"But how can a marriage like that survive?"

"In my opinion," Kezia said, "it can't. It's the old Space versus Smother conundrum. Neither party is getting what they need from the relationship. A no-win situation. A lot depends on the personalities of the people involved, of course."

"How does all of this tie in with Unity Consciousness?" I asked, confused.

"There is a difference between feeling connected with the planet—and the Universe—and having to take on everyone else's gunk. I find a simple meditation very helpful. Imagine yourself as a tree. Your roots are deep and firm in the earth, and your branches are flexible and reaching for the stars. Connection complete. You are supported, and loved—and you send that love out in return. It then circles back to you. Without all the unwanted sludge.

"Here's my advice on how to thrive in this new energy—spend as much time alone in nature as you can. Practice stillness and awareness. Live deliberately, and enjoy as many moments as you can. Trust in the flow of life. If you have a negative thought, you can immediately transmute the energy and remain unpolluted. Release your past and your fears—the same cycles will keep showing up in your life until you do.

"Most important—filter everything that you experience through unconditional acceptance and kindness. We all have feminine and masculine energies within us. The feminine teaches us to trust our intuition. It is the foundation for our ability to nurture and love. The masculine energy helps us to be brave and strong—how to keep our focus, and hold our vision for what we want to achieve. A healthy human is able to balance the goddess and warrior energies.

"Many people think that compassion equals weakness, but they couldn't be more unaware of the truth. Compassion takes enormous courage and strength. Where there is love, there can be no fear."

Kezia removed her drum from its place of reverence on the wall. "Now, let's journey to release you from your past life patterns."

With Abby under one arm, and my garden journal under the other, I walked down my lawn to the edge of the lake. Once positioned on our chaise, with our backs to the water, we surveyed the property, the journal open on my lap.

"Too many perennials, Abs," I concluded. She looked up at me and yawned. "The former owners were crazy about colorful borders—so that's not my fault. But we need to do some serious clearing work here. Daylilies, hostas, iris, peonies. Allium. Coreopsis and lavender. Sedum, asters, and daisies. Almost all of it pre dating us. I just don't want the clutter any longer."

The disorganized plantings detracted from the glorious view of the lake and its surrounding foliage. I opened my case of watercolor pencils and turned to a new page in my journal. Abby stretched across my feet, alert for trespassing wildlife.

I concentrated on Emily Dickinson as I worked. Famously reclusive, Dickinson was profoundly influenced by Emerson's *Nature*, and his 'transparent eyeball.' 'Into the woods we return to reason and faith,' he had written. When we connect with nature, Emerson explained, we absorb the experience as part of what we see.

Dickinson, like Emerson and Thoreau, was a walker in the woods, and wrote poetry to release the ecstasy she felt from her encounters with the natural world. She grew up in a house that overlooked a cemetery, and often connected the garden with death in her writing. Death symbolized transition to a new life. Flowers and bulbs would always arise with heartfelt hope in the spring.

Emily Dickinson was an important member of the Transcendentalism movement. Although she never attended meetings or discussions, she sought, through her poetry, to develop her personal relationship with the universe. Her herbarium—a book of over four hundred pressed plants from her garden and nature walks—survives to this day.

Known as 'the Myth of Amherst,' Dickinson was an introvert, and traveled only within the world of her imagination. She became increasingly detached toward the end of her life, and reveled in the freedom that came with solitude and silence. She claimed that ordinary socializing had become painful, and that her home and garden served her as a microcosm of human relationship and activity.

The concept of home as a sanctuary and refuge from the outside world was personally familiar. After my divorce was finally over, I had found the money driven energy of Fairfield County to be intolerable. I had moved my life, and my law practice, up to the woods and hills of Litchfield County, and had started over. When people asked me what I preferred about the northwest corner of Connecticut, my answer was always the same—more trees than people.

Releasing the past, and all of its pain and fear. Kezia and I had journeyed first to clear my former marriage, and then on to surrender any remaining toxic energy related to my family. "Keep only the lessons and the love," Kezia had advised me, "and leave the rest behind." My younger sister Kate and I had grown up surrounded by conflict; raised by our deeply damaged father, and Audrey—our narcissistic mother—who amused herself by setting her two daughters against each other. I was always happiest reading in my room, drawing and painting outside, or riding my bike. Kate preferred blasting 'tunes' and hanging out with her friends. I eventually decided that we were too different to ever be kindred spirits, and had stopped trying to build a relationship with her.

But I had since learned about psychic imprints. Energy overlays. A living person can impress her own feelings and impulses on a vulnerable individual, just as a ghost can.

If Kate was truly a victim of Audrey's low vibrational influence, then Kate wasn't living her truth—she was living Audrey's. So who was Kate, really?

Sophie was right—the fact that Kate had dated my boyfriend after he had just dumped me was still a childhood energy block that needed to be cleared. I had always dreamed of having a supportive sister like Jo in *Little Women*. This explained my relationship with Angela—rock solid, dependable Angela—who in nearly thirty years had not once caused me to question her loyalty.

Was Kate even capable of being a true friend like Angela? I decided to concentrate on our similarities. Kate loved to garden. We both grew up enjoying our beach vacations. Most of all, we were each devoted to our animals.

How would I teach Kate about psychic vampires like our dear mother, when she hadn't asked for help?

I decided to trust that when my sister was ready to heal, she would let me know.

Abby had fallen asleep in the sun. I finished my drawings and collected my terrier. I would call the Bridge Hollow Garden Club and donate most of my perennials to the town. I knew that Luke would want to help me plan my new landscape.

CHAPTER TWENTY-ONE

Pall Bearer

"**H**ey Em," Denise's voice had that hushed tone that no one ever wants to hear. "Judge Conroy died this morning."

Horace J. Conroy. A famed criminal lawyer in his late fifties when he was appointed to the Superior Court bench. I had been his first clerk, hardly a year out of law school. The Judicial Department, in its unfathomable wisdom, had assigned Conroy to the civil jury docket. As a new judge he had known almost nothing about the civil side of litigation, but we had worked well together, and ultimately we achieved the best stats in the state for moving cases. Judge Conroy had subsequently been promoted to the Appellate Court, but we had stayed in touch.

"The funeral is on Saturday, here in Westport," Denise continued. "I just heard. Are you OK?"

My past was certainly catching up with me. "A little shocked, I guess. Who called you?"

"The Administrative Judge in Bridgeport. He was looking for you."

"Why?"

"They're expecting you," Denise replied. "Conroy wanted you to be a pall bearer."

Judge Conroy's funeral was held at a small Catholic church

near the center of town. The pews were packed with people that I had known from the Clerk's Office in Bridgeport nearly twenty years before. Judges, prosecutors, public defenders, court reporters, clerks—and lawyers.

"Today is an episode of *This Was Your Life, Emma Carbury*," I muttered to Luke. "I worked with so many of these people. Dated a few of them, too."

"Really?" Luke replied, interested. "Can you point out an example?"

"Emma!" One of the court reporters called to me, "Good to see you after so long—just sorry about the reason. Where have you been?"

"Northwest corner. Are you still working?"

"Oh forever," she laughed. "Not much has changed."

Another woman stopped and smiled at me. "Emma, isn't it? Irene from Family Services. I remember you so well. You called Judge Conroy 'Your Eminence' all the time."

"Which he loved!" A tall man in a dark blue suit said. "Chuck Duncroft," he announced, holding out his hand to Luke. "How's it going Emma?"

"Exhibit A," I murmured to Luke, and he grinned. It suddenly occurred to me that either, or both, of my ex husbands could show up for this event. I prayed for good vodka at the reception.

The Administrative Judge in Bridgeport had been a State's Attorney in my time. He took my arm. "We'll be assembling right after the service, Emma," he said quietly. I nodded.

The eulogies. I focused on being present in the moment, not noticing anyone in the congregation—alive or otherwise—and clearing any memories of my experience at the courthouse. Various friends and colleagues spoke of Conroy's military service, his devotion to his wife and family, his love of sailing. And his delight in being a judge.

Then the organ fired up, and a woman in a green dress rose to sing *When Irish Eyes Are Smiling.* I suddenly began to cry, as did many of the people sitting around us. Luke nudged me gently, and then took my hand.

"Kind of a second dad," I whispered. "Lots of closure going on here." I had remembered Conroy's first day on the job. He'd accidently pushed the panic button on the bench, and five state troopers had stormed in on a surprised group of lawyers, all sitting quietly in court during the call of the civil jury calendar. Conroy's face had been nearly purple with embarrassment.

Then I reminded myself what Sophie had said about the new age of energy that we were entering. "All the old fear and pain is being dredged up for us, Emma, so we can understand it, and clear it, and raise our vibrations. We're all going through a fire of some sort, and remember that with fire comes transformation. Trust in the flow; don't fight it or judge it. Focus on kindness and forgiveness, finish the old cycle and move on. The folks who didn't choose to participate in this big change are leaving the planet. Don't mourn them—just think of it as contract fulfilled for each one who makes the transition."

I was the only woman around the casket as we lifted it into the hearse for the short trip to the cemetery. The funeral director had wisely put the two youngest and strongest men on my side of the coffin. I felt thankful that Judge Conroy had been short and slight.

We were carrying the casket to the gravesite when it happened.

Something made me glance to my right. Horace Conroy was standing next to the priest. He smiled and gave me a two thumb's up, just as he had always done. I was so startled that I stopped moving. The man behind me stepped on my foot, my heel was driven deep into the ground, and the entire procession halted while the funeral director hurried over to retrieve my shoe and replace it on my foot.

When I looked up again, the good judge was laughing. So was everyone else.

"Levity at a burial," Luke remarked, as the priest took over with his final remarks. "Novel approach. I hope someone had a camera."

"Yes, well, the leading man was certainly amused," I replied, still attempting to recover some poise. The recently departed was now standing by his widow, who was dropping flowers into the open grave.

"Has he said anything to you?"

"Not yet. But he's sure to be lingering near the martinis when we get to the beach club."

"Aha. Good to know. If he mentions any of your old boyfriends, I'd like a transcript."

Email from Peggy in Saratoga entitled: "Ken dumped; Geraldine devastated."

Dear Emma,

You wouldn't believe how hot it is up here! There are no leaves on the trees, and it's eighty-five degrees. I packed a whole trunk full of winter coats and nothing with short sleeves. Figures.

Gossip is rampant! First up is the big news—Ken was just told that he has thirty days to remove his horses from the Prudeau's farm. Only three of his clients are going with him. Everyone else opted to stay and work with the Prudeau's new in-house trainer. All those years building up his business—for this!

It seems there are a whole host of reasons for The Booting. Chronic non-payment of rent, plus an allegation that one of his grooms was dealing drugs on the premises. Ken is scrambling around for temporary housing for the four horses he has left, out of the twenty-six that he started with. That's what you get for pissing off the rich owners. Geraldine is tearful over the decision she has to make, and the Prudeaus are particular cronies of hers. However, the temptation to show Ken how loyal she can be is too great. She'll bring the straight guy out of him yet.

The word is that Geraldine only took Fitz back long

enough to lull him into a false sense of marital security, while her lawyers geared up for battle. Their divorce is getting down and dirty. She has blamed Whitney for the breakdown of the marriage, and has effectively ostracized Whitney from the horseshow world. Whitney told me on the phone yesterday that she's moving back in with her mother. So, I guess that's it for Whitney and Fitz, at least for the time being. I always thought he was a nice guy, but such a weenie.

I love this town, and I love the Saint Clement's Horse Show, but this year has been a definite downer thus far. Will I be enjoying the pleasure of your company at Old Salem?

XO Peggy

I was happy to see that Suzie Marino had returned to class the following week. Her mother's ghost, as usual, walked in behind her, and sat down at the back of the room.

"Those of you who took my Evidence course last year are already aware of the emphasis placed on evaluating the character of witnesses who are testifying in court."

There were murmurs of assent from the throng.

"Today we are going to discuss the concept of character in a different context—when it is applied to our leaders in government. As part of the assignment you were asked to watch two movies. First up, *The American President* with Michael Douglas and Annette Bening. Who wants to begin with a general synopsis?"

Piper raised her hand. "The film is a romantic comedy set in the 1990's. It starts around Thanksgiving time, and ends at the State of the Union in an election year—so two plus months altogether. One of the main themes is the fact that President Andrew Shepherd, regardless of his position as the most powerful man in the world, can't do a blessed thing without a posse of support staff badgering him, or getting in his way somehow."

Adam nodded. "Not to mention the ever present media, panting for new storylines."

"And the Senate Minority Leader, Bob Rumson, who wants to beat Shepherd in the next election," Matt added, "is just drooling over Shepherd's very public romance with a liberal lobbyist."

"The leader of the free world can't drive a car on his own, use credit cards, or make a phone call—no one believes that it's Shepherd on the other end," Suzie laughed, "and he sure as heck can't go out on a date."

"Why not?" I asked.

"Because it opens the door for attacks on his character," Maddie answered. "Something he avoided in the previous election."

"His wife had just died," Heather explained. "And the Republicans couldn't run the campaign the usual way, for fear of making the media feel sorry for Shepherd."

"OK," I said, moving them along. "The President of the United States meets Sydney Ellen Wade—a lawyer turned hired gun for the environmental lobby. Sydney is trying to push an aggressive new bill through Congress—one which would reduce fossil fuel emissions by twenty percent. Shepherd, in order to appease the Global Defense Council and get them off his back, makes a deal with Sydney. What's their agreement?"

"Coercing Congress to vote for the fossil fuel package," Kim answered.

"If Sydney can get twenty-four votes by the State of the Union," Jon added, "the President promises to get her the final ten that the GDC needs for the bill to pass."

"Good. But what is Shepherd's real agenda?"

"His crime bill," Ed replied. "The President assumes that the environmental bill won't pass at twenty percent—probably not even at ten—and that Sydney will be wasting her time."

"Meanwhile, Shepherd thinks he can drive the crime bill home without addressing gun control." Henry added, rolling his eyes.

"He's protecting his precious sixty-three percent job approval rating," Cassie remarked.

"So really, what are we saying?"

"Getting reelected is more important to Shepherd than either bill," Rob answered.

"Excellent. So what happens?"

"Against all expectations, Sydney gets the votes she needs for the environmental bill," Megan said. "But Shepherd's approval rating has tanked to the low forties."

"The press knows when Sydney spends the night because her car is still parked at the White House in the morning," Suzie explained. "The Republicans accuse her of everything from flag burning to sleeping around for votes, in order to trash the President."

"But Shepherd won't engage in a character debate," Adam replied. "He's sure that this will all just go away."

"And the moral majority goes nuts," Matt said, "because when Sydney sleeps over, Shepherd's twelve year old daughter Lucy is just down the hall."

"Shepherd makes the argument that he's a single adult; that his personal life is not the business of the American people." Kim added. "He points out that Jefferson and Wilson both went out on dates during their administrations—and Wilson got remarried while in office."

"But Shepherd's Chief of Staff reminds him of the ugly truth. Which is?"

"That neither of those men had to be President on television—or in more modern terms—the Web. In the United States, the people get to decide what is, and what is not, their business," Henry quoted. "We have the right, and the responsibility, to question our leaders."

"And the environmental bill?"

Heather smirked. "Shepherd caves to pressure from his staff, and decides to throw it in a drawer—so he can get the votes he needs for the crime bill."

"As a result, Sydney is fired from her lobbyist job," Maddie said. "She dumps Andy Shepherd as she walks out the White House door, on her way to her new job in Connecticut."

"Now let's talk about Lucy Shepherd."

"When we first meet her, she's having trouble—ironically—in her social studies class," Adam said.

"They're studying the Constitutional Convention," Piper laughed. "The teacher has set up a mock Congress, each student is playing one of the delegates, and they're expected to debate the issues."

"Lucy is not enjoying the assignment, right? Why do you think this storyline was included in the movie? What was the point?"

"I think it was to remind Shepherd of who we are, how we got here," Cassie said, slowly, "and what we won't tolerate from government. Tyranny, corruption, and self serving leaders. It's all about We the People."

"I agree," Suzie added, a little grim. "Even so, we make fun of our leaders—they all seem to be the same in the final analysis—but somehow we expect Shepherd to be different."

"Is he?"

"By the end of the movie, yeah, he gets it," Jon remarked. "He tells the press that being President of the United States has everything to do with character. He refers to America as 'advanced citizenship,' meaning, I suppose, that the people have to be involved for it to work."

"It's more than that," Rob argued. "It's about protecting the other guy's right to advocate the polar opposite of your personal position. Remember that whole bit about free speech and the American Civil Liberties Union? The Republicans are attacking the fact that Shepherd is a member."

"Why would that be a problem?"

"Too ultra liberal?" Suzie asked, in return. "I'm not sure."

"Shepherd's point is that every politician should be a member," Matt said. "Defending the Bill of Rights is the ACLU's reason for being. Why would any American object to upholding the Constitution?"

"Maybe it's the old argument about 'American family values' that people mix up with Constitutional rights," Megan said, thought-fully. "Which usually translates to who you can, and can't have sex with. It's as though the seventeenth century Puritans are still alive and kicking sometimes, isn't it?"

"The film ends with Shepherd walking into the State of the Union Address," I said, laughing. "He has announced that he is rewriting the flawed crime bill to include hand gun restrictions, and he's sending the environmental package to the Hill. Sydney is back. What do you think the final message is?"

"Oh that's easy," Piper giggled. "They get married. Sydney helps Andy get reelected and she becomes First Lady. Lucy gets a really cool stepmom. We have cleaner air."

"And safer streets, right? Now, for our purposes in this U.S. History class, what can we take away from lessons learned by Andy Shepherd in those two months?"

Adam raised his hand. "We have to fight the battles that need fighting, no matter what it costs."

"The impact of fear and blame," Suzie suggested. "And how politicians use it to win elections."

"Governing may be about choosing," Henry noted, "but the choices our leaders make can never be self serving."

"What about that line that kept coming up throughout the movie?" Kim asked. "Shepherd says in his speech to the Daughters of the American Revolution that we can no longer claim to be part of a 'great society'?"

Matt grinned. "Oh yeah. It's the thing that is left 'hanging out there.' Shepherd was avoiding the hand gun issue."

"What do you think?" I replied.

"That the whole concept of the Land of the Free is suspect," Ed volunteered. "And probably has been for over two hundred years."

"We started out with the right idea," Matt said, sadly.

"But lost it pretty early on," Cassie finished. "We need to get better people in D.C."

"Let's hold that thought, and move on to the next movie. *Protocol* with Goldie Hawn. Now, why do you think that I picked such a whacky comedy for our discussion today?"

"Because screwball silliness aside," Suzie answered, "the issues that are raised are actually very serious."

"Good Suzanna. Why don't you start us off with a plot outline?"

"*Protocol* was filmed in the mid 1980's. Goldie Hawn plays Sunny Ann Davis—a cocktail waitress at a seedy bar with a safari theme in Washington, D.C. Sunny is definitely down on her luck. Her car is a mess, as is her love life, and the bar is not doing well financially. She's originally from a small town in Oregon, lives with two gay guys, and has a perky, naïve attitude toward life.

"Sunny is standing in front of an embassy event when she happens to stop a shooter who is bent on assassinating the Emir from a Middle Eastern country called Ohtar—only Sunny thinks it's our President who's threatened. So she jumps the shooter, bites his hand, ends up getting shot in the ass, and becomes a global celebrity overnight.

"Ohtar is strategically important, because of its proximity to the Gulf, and its situation between two rival nations. The U.S. wants permission to build a military base there. And the Emir is very grateful to Sunny for saving his life."

Kim took over. "So Michael Ransom, who is a Middle East Desk Chief from the State Department, shows up in Sunny's hospital room to help her with her press conference. The powers that be, watching her on television, decide that Sunny is potentially an asset in their efforts regarding Ohtar, and they encourage the President to get up from his nap and call her while she's live on every news channel across the country."

"By the way, who *was* our President in the mid eighties?"

"Ronald Reagan," the throng replied.

"Excellent. I was just about your age at the time, and very idealistic. Now, who can remember the various interest groups that Sunny's 'cornball' speech reached from the hospital?"

Jon waved his hand. "Senior citizens, gays, working women, animal lovers, law and order types, small town folks, bar flies, and baseball fans."

"Sunny announces that she doesn't consider herself a Republican or a Democrat," Cassie said. "She claims to be just an American."

"Which the press loves," Maddie added.

"So in one day the cocktail waitress in the skimpy emu costume becomes special assistant to the head of the Protocol Department. What is protocol?"

"The customs and regulations dealing with the ceremonies and etiquette of the diplomatic corps," Adam read from his notes.

"Sunny is excited and honored—at first," Heather reported. "But she soon learns that the people around her say one thing, and mean another. Her new boss is Ambassador Marietta St. John, a sophisticated double-talking dynamo of a woman, who informs Sunny that she should expect new sights, sounds, and exotic fragrances in her future. Sunny, according to Mrs. St. John, should be prepared to do whatever her country needs of her."

"For a bonus point," I laughed, "who can tell me what *Protocol* and *The American President* have in common—besides idealistic young women who get trampled by both the U.S. Government and the media?"

"Gail Strickland," Piper answered brightly. "She plays Ambassador St. John in *Protocol*, and much later on, the wife of the Chief of Staff in *The American President*."

"Well done," I said, tossing her a bag of Hershey's kisses. "What are Sunny's new duties in the State Department?"

"The Protocol entourage keeps her busy meeting high profile foreigners and dragging them around to various national monuments," Cassie replied. "There's an emotional scene with the Queen of Dubai and her ladies in waiting—heads covered in veils—in front of the Declaration of Independence."

"*We hold these truths to be self-evident,*" I read, "*that all men are created equal, that they are endowed by their Creator with certain unalienable Rights, that among these are Life, Liberty and the pursuit of Happiness. That to secure these rights, Governments are instituted among Men, deriving their just powers from the consent of the governed. That whenever any Form of Government becomes destructive of these ends, it is the Right of the People to alter or to abolish it, and to institute new Government, laying its foundation on such principles and organizing its powers in such form, as to them shall seem most likely to effect their Safety and Happiness.*"

"Sunny is beginning to notice what's going on from that point in the story," Jon said. "She comments that the Founders really knew how to say what they thought, and she wonders what government ever talks about happiness in the modern world."

"There's another poignant bit later on," Piper remembered, "when Sunny is standing on the steps of what I assume is the Jefferson Memorial, contemplating the Declaration and its meaning."

"Meanwhile," Henry added, "in Ohtar, the people are preparing for a new queen. A billboard of the Emir next to a veiled woman— with Sunny's blue eyes—is being painted in the city."

"Eerie," Megan shivered. "With her face covered like that, she could have been anybody."

"So finally the Emir comes to Washington for an unofficial visit," I prompted. "And Sunny is instructed to show him a very good time. There's a humorous bash at the safari bar, and then Sunny is ordered to return to Ohtar with the Emir."

"Ambassador St. John tells Sunny that it's all about simple trust," Cassie said drily.

"Sunny still doesn't understand that she's being set up," Rob continued, "until she is standing in the hot desert sun, covered in robes, staring at her own eyes on the billboard."

"So she whips off her native garb," Heather said, "and marches into the Emir's presence. He has a fit that she is dressed as an American, and then drops the bomb."

"Her country used her as bait to get their military base in Ohtar," Jon said. "Sunny was exchanged for balance of power in the Middle East."

"At that point the Revolutionaries attack—enraged by the imminent wedding—and the rebel forces overthrow the Emir's government. Our heroine is back in D.C., and the globe is buzzing with the drama of 'Sunnygate'. Did she know, or didn't she? Now what?"

"Michael Ransom resigns," Ed began, "and tells the press what he thinks—that Sunny was duped."

"Sunny also quits," Maddie said. "Predictably, Ambassador St. John attempts to smarm her with nonsense about the welfare of the American people—that the department sold her down river for the good of the country. St. John is concerned, no doubt, about Sunny's testimony at the hearings to come."

"And Sunny reminds St. John—pretty sharply, that Sunny is also one of the people," Henry remarked.

"And of her individual rights as an American. So what happens at the hearing?"

Suzie grinned. "Sunny refuses to name names. She tells the chair of the committee that ultimately she was responsible for her sojourn in Ohtar—that she should have known better. Sunny explains that until she accepted the position she had never read the Declaration of Independence, or the Constitution. She had no idea how the government worked. But the experts did, she says; they knew what it all meant."

Kim added: "She reminds everyone on the committee that ultimately it's about We the People—and that means every American. Anything and everything that our government does—selling arms and spending money and negotiating with foreign big shots—has a direct impact on the lives of We the People."

Unity Consciousness. "Her argument is that if people don't take time to keep track of what their leaders are up to, and don't care, then the people get what they deserve, right?"

"Sunny announces that from now on she's going to be watching them," Cassie said. "Like a hawk."

"Then she marries Michael Ransom, runs for Congress and wins," Adam concluded.

"So what have We the Class gleaned from the adventures of Sunny Ann Davis?"

"That referring to the U.S. as the Land of the Free is pretty ridiculous these days." Matt remarked, returning to his earlier theme.

"Why?"

"Because all the star spangled glory of the Spirit of 1776 seems like a myth now," Rob replied. "What happened to us? How are we any better now than the Brits were back in the eighteenth century?"

"We're big bullies," Megan added. "And our taxes are way higher now than they were then."

Madeline held a finger up. "But we have representation."

"Uh huh," Ed rolled his eyes. "And no matter who we elect, they all seem exactly the same. Where's all the tax money going? Why is everyone working harder for less? How come it feels like we're all being managed with smokescreens—so that we're diverted from what's really going on?"

"No choices," Cassie agreed. "It's all an illusion."

Suzie sighed. "And who even has the time, or the energy, for the pursuit of happiness?"

I listened as the discussion continued, but ultimately did not comment. I knew that in time my students would learn how the return of the sacred feminine energy to the earth was making mammoth positive changes in government all over the planet—for everyone.

CHAPTER TWENTY-TWO

Suzie's Story

Email from Peggy entitled: "Know a good lawyer?"

Hi Emma,

I would never dream of dumping this on you under normal circumstances, but Whitney really is in a jam. Geraldine's lawyer had her served with a notice of deposition, which is to be held in two weeks. She's pretty upset. Will you please help her prepare for this?

Don't you just adore friends who put you in difficult positions?

Love, Peggy

Whitney was staying with her mother in Easton. She drove up to see me at my office later that week.

"What's happened to privacy in this country?" She moaned. "Why do I have to talk about my sex life to a room full of lawyers with some female recording every word? And Geraldine, no doubt, glaring at me the whole time! This is a nightmare!" She looked at me, miserable. "Can't I just run away?"

"Ducking a depo is serious trouble. I wouldn't recommend it," I replied. "Were you served with a subpoena *duces tecum* as well?"

"The thing that says I have to bring phone bills and credit card receipts? Oh yeah."

"What are they fighting over, anyway? Does Fitz want part of her practice?"

"No! All they've got jointly is the house in Westport, which is mortgaged. She brings in two times what he makes, but she told him that if she's forced to support herself, it will seriously curtail her personal spending."

"Meaning horseshows. So the purpose for this deposition is just spite?"

"She told Fitz that she wants to torture both of us. She wants me run out of the county."

"Getting you dragged into her divorce will keep you *in* the county, though. She's just thick. Has Fitz been deposed yet?"

"That's the real joke. Geraldine told Fitz that she's afraid to depose him. She doesn't want to hear what he has to say."

"So rather than embarrass the client, Geraldine's lawyer wants to skewer you on the record."

"Exactly. How come there are privacy laws about everything under the sun—except sex? I'm a single adult. I've broken no laws. Connecticut is a no-fault state. Why do I have to do this?"

"Because no one's brought this issue to the Supreme Court and won, I guess. I agree with you. Morality has no place in the law."

Whitney sighed. "I know I was stupid."

"Look, we've all done crazy things for the wrong man. And I am seriously the last person to judge you. Let's go over what you're going to say. I don't want to enter an appearance because I know all of the parties involved, but I can help you with answering questions and avoiding traps."

"Good news Emma!" Stan Mullins was exuberant on the phone. "I think we've settled our motorcycle noise problem with the Grudbergs."

"That's great, Stan. How did you manage it?"

"Believe it or not, the kids pulled it off. Grudberg's niece—Suzie

Marino—talked to her cousin, and Rick approached my daughter after school. He's thinking about getting his own horse, and boarding with us. We're going to work out an arrangement with his father, so his garbage collection fees will be offset with board money."

"I'm so pleased, Stan. That sounds like a positive solution for everyone."

"We've heard that Suzie is in your history class. Did you say something to her?"

I was careful. "Not about this case. But I *have* introduced the virtues of mediation and cooperation into our group discussions. Perhaps that's made an impression."

"Well, however you got through to her, my family and I—along with the horses—are very grateful."

"Psychometry," Kezia said at our next shamanic session, "is the ability to read the energy of an object."

"Personal items in particular?" I asked.

"Any object can absorb energy, which can be analyzed intuitively," she answered. "Have you ever gone antiquing, and been suddenly attracted, or repelled, by an object?"

"Definitely. Which is precisely why I always buy reproductions." I smiled to myself, thinking of Luke.

"Probably wise. Aside from the fact that antiques, if genuine, are often fragile and expensive, the real issue is that these objects are carrying other people's energetic baggage imprinted on them—sometimes centuries of it.

"However, back to our main topic, which is symbols and signs. Being aware of synchronicities. Learning to understand the extraordinary meanings of everyday items. Recognizing psychic information that comes in for us constantly. Signs are part of a whole other language. Like dreams—only we're awake."

"I recognize many of them," I said, "especially when they're repetitive. But I've learned not to assume that I understand the message."

"Why?"

"Because I'm so often wrong!"

"Then you weren't reading the information intuitively," Kezia replied.

I felt frustrated, and apparently my face registered same.

"Get out of your head, and into your gut," Kezia said. "Do some deep breathing, drop down to your still center, and let the answer come in. You'll know when you're on target."

"For example," I responded, still slightly annoyed. "I've booked a week on Nantucket this summer with Luke and my cousins. Now everywhere I look I see symbols of Nantucket. Bumper stickers, magazine articles, television programs. Someone's wearing a sweatshirt. Even when I open a book these days—there's some reference to Nantucket. The island is in my face all the time. But I already know that I'm going—so where's the gift?"

"The Universe may be validating your choice of locations, or it may be showing you something that you aren't aware is happening—perhaps behind the scenes." Kezia smiled at me.

Psychic people can be maddeningly smug at times.

"Fine," I replied.

"Information comes in from many sources," Kezia continued, "since we have helpers around us all the time. Spirit guides, ascended masters, angels—even deceased relatives and pets. Their energy is a much higher frequency than ours. They are coming from a place of pure love, and their task is to help us do the same."

"Tough job," I remarked.

"It *will* get better, you know, Emma," she said. "In many ways it already is. Look at you and your law partner—you've stepped away from highly contested litigation and are manifesting clients who want mediation. A definite move in the right direction."

"But I find that I'm exhausted by the people who aren't getting it. Their agitation is too much for me. I'm tired of pretending that I take litigation seriously. The whole process is insane and I just can't stand being in court anymore. The contention is becoming physically painful. *I just want peace,*" I barked with finality, surprised at my anger.

"As within, so without," Kezia quoted, gently. "Don't worry, you won't have to do it much longer."

I stared at her.

"Intuition is merely every person's innate ability to tune into higher energetic vibrations from the Other Side. When you combine intuitive messages with free will," Kezia reported, "you'll find yourself making better decisions. Information can come from anywhere—even other people. The trick is to know what resonates with you. We've already talked about Discernment—trusting your gut. Everyone is on his or her own path, dealing with their particular fears, so they may often confuse agendas. Just listen to your inner voice. You'll always know what's right for you, and you'll cease to rely on the opinions of others. Messages will come in more often when you listen."

I sighed. The path of least resistance again. I struggled with that concept daily.

"Symbols, on the other hand, come to us psychically," Kezia explained, "either in dreams, or through visualization. For example, when you think of Nantucket, what do you see in your mind?"

"The shape of the island. The harbor from the water. Rose covered cottages. Sometimes one of the lighthouses."

"Just have confidence in what is coming to you. This will bring more balance to your life—and who couldn't use more serenity? You'll learn by doing. Remember that free will also involves our thoughts and emotions. We have a choice regarding how we react to any given situation. Have you considered what you *really* want for your life—beyond a mediation practice?"

I shook my head. "Not since the divorce, anyway."

"I invite you to do so now. If you are sending confused signals out to the Universe, I guarantee that the answers will come back the same way. Be careful what you ask for. When you learn to trust in the flow, without resistance, you are home free."

"What do you mean?"

"Positive belief and positive actions manifest positive rewards. Have faith in the power of living your truth. Relax and let life unfold naturally. And learn to love yourself.

"For now," Kezia continued, briskly. "I'm going to bring over some items for you to touch. Let's see what messages you get."

Suzie Marino made an appointment to meet with me at my office in town the following week.

"I have two reasons for seeing you," she said, looking nervous. "The easy thing first. My mother's estate has to be addressed, and I would like you to represent me, please. My grandmother said that she can cover your fees. I have a retainer check for you."

"I'd be happy to look after you in probate court, Suzie." I paused. "You're eighteen now—correct?"

"Two weeks ago," she said. "That's why I waited. I didn't want my dad involved."

"I see."

"The other reason is tougher for me to talk about. It involves my dad—and Esther MacInerney."

I glanced over at the corner of the room, where the ghost of Suzie's mother was standing by my bookcase. She was frowning, and shaking her head.

"Go on."

Suzie's face contorted with anger. "Mom *never* had a boyfriend. That was just a rumor that Esther spread around town to distract everyone from what was really happening."

Suzie's expression was a mirror image of the ferocious rage on her mother's face.

"Esther and your dad are having an affair?"

Claudia's ghost had moved toward her daughter, and was standing right behind her. I caught a strong odor of cigarette smoke as I visualized the protective circle around Suzie and myself, and added energy to it. Suzie's mother telepathed *Stop that!* to me, but I ignored her.

"They were. Around the time that Mom disappeared. Esther's a really nasty woman, Ms. Carbury. She knew that I saw through her, and she threatened me—a bunch of times—to keep quiet."

"What did she say to you?"

"Basically that she'd hurt me—bad—if I ever opened my mouth about her relationship with my father. She knew I'd be at all the games—that's where she cornered me. Varsity basketball. Henry and I have been dating for a while."

I grinned. "I *had* gotten that impression."

"He's a good guy. And a good friend to me, which is the total opposite of what I ever got at home."

Claudia scowled. Not a healthy mother/daughter relationship then.

"So anyway, Henry and Matt and some of the other guys from the team—well—they've been helping me out—uh—with the Esther situation."

"The tea in her pool, the effigy on the tree—et cetera?"

Suzie looked surprised. "How did you know?"

"Partly from observing your reactions to the issues that come up in class," I told her. "Also, the fact that all of the incidents followed discussions that we'd had from American history. Seeing you and your group at the cemetery on Halloween was the real tip-off."

Suzie was terrified. "I don't want to get my friends in trouble. Especially not Cassie and Matt. Are you going to tell anyone?"

I shook my head. "I can't now—I'm your lawyer. Confidentiality. And well planned on your part."

"I honestly never thought of that," Suzie replied, taken aback. "I just felt somehow that you'd get it. Even applaud what we were doing."

"Hmm. Well, let's just say that I understand feeling trapped and unsupported, and wanting to hit back. But the illegal behavior needs to stop now. Are we clear?"

"OK, that's fair. Besides," Suzie shrugged, "Esther's buried herself just fine on her own—thanks to Carlie's article. She won't be bothering me any longer. My work here is done." Her eyes welled up. "You know, Ms. Carbury, I never did believe that Mom had run away. Something kept telling me that she was still here, somehow. I've felt creepy for the whole year. And weird stuff keeps happening to me."

"I'm not surprised," I said grimly, looking up at Claudia's ghost, which began to circle Suzie's chair. "Do you feel like giving me some examples? I promise that I'll take you seriously."

"I keep smelling her perfume everywhere for one thing." She made a face. "Opium. Which I never liked. And cigarette smoke. Mom tried to quit for years. Also she loved Madonna—used to sing *Holiday* and *Crazy for You* all the time. I keep hearing those songs in my mind. It's driving me nuts. I get headaches nearly every day, and I've had trouble sleeping since she disappeared. When I finally do doze off, the dreams are pretty scary sometimes. She talks to me, and she's angry. Mostly about Dad. I've lost a lot of weight, I keep breaking out, and lately I have problems focusing in class. It's like I'm in a fog sometimes.

"Then there are other things—and some of them have followed me to my grandmother's. Lights flashing on and off when I'm alone. The radio in my room has a mind of its own, and so does my alarm clock. My garage door remote won't work for me half the time, and other days the door just goes haywire—up and down for no reason. The DVD player in the family room is nearly always on the blink, and my laptop's been doing some really funky things. The worst was a few months ago. I tried to do Mom's horoscope online—I was curious. Then suddenly the screen went blank—just crashed. Stayed that way for hours."

Suzie glanced down at her fingers, which were locked together in her lap.

"Take a few deep breaths," I advised her. "Hold them for the count of four, and then release—slowly."

She did so, and some of the color returned to her face.

"There's more. Last fall Esther dumped my dad, and started sniffing around Town Hall. The Conservation Commission Chair—Leonard Abel? I'm positive that she's doing him now."

I began to see daylight.

"The hardest part," Suzie concluded, tears leaking down her face, "is that I think my dad caused that explosion. The one that killed Esther's husband. And if that's true," she paused, "then he probably murdered my mom as well."

Claudia Marino's ghost stopped pacing, stared directly at me, and nodded her head.

I stood up. It was time that Suzanna Marino received some relief from contact with her parents.

"Grab your bag, Suzie. I'm going to take you to see a friend of mine. Julie Sullivan's mom—Sophie."

Suzie's eyes opened wide. "The ghost hunter?"

I held my office door open for her. Claudia glared at me, and followed her daughter out into the hall. "That's the lady. She's a powerful witch, and she's going to help clear up a lot of your questions. You'll feel better, and you'll be able to sleep again. Trust me."

CHAPTER TWENTY-THREE

Eleanor and Franklin

Dana and Wesley had been divorced for three years, and had decided to give their marriage a second try.

"But we're going to be smart this time," Wesley announced. "We want to hammer out all of the old problems so they don't come up again."

Dana nodded. "We each made a list," she informed me. "Here are your copies."

I perused these documents. "Where would you like to start?"

"Housework," Dana said, firmly. "Wesley is fifty-eight. He labels specific domestic tasks to be exclusively 'female.' He won't even consider changing the sheets on the bed, for example. Or scrubbing out a pot. He doesn't believe in hiring cleaning ladies, so for seventeen years I did the floors, the commodes, the tubs and sinks. His cooking skills consist of boiling water for pasta, and hitting the power button on the microwave."

"What about you?" Wesley retorted. "You won't get your hands dirty! You'll have nothing to do with spreading mulch or raking leaves. You expect me to be in charge of both cars, and I never once saw you take out the garbage in all the years we were together. Do you even know how to start the lawn mower?"

"I have a thought," Dana sneered. "Why don't you hire someone to take care of the yard? You've got more money than God. Think of all the extra time you could spend at the lodge!"

"Here we go! And what about your quilting bees, or whatever you call them? Ridiculous women gabbing for hours—to accomplish what, exactly?"

"You know very well that we auction off our work to raise money for the church."

"All those busybodies at the parish hall. Smells like a high school cafeteria. Why don't you get a job?"

"The next item on my list is the television," Dana continued, as though he hadn't spoken.

"What about it?" I inquired.

"It's always on! In the morning, when he gets home, even on a beautiful day!"

"I like the company," Wesley said. "Beats what I have to put up with from you."

They snarled at each other.

"Do you have a specific wedding date in mind?" I asked.

My Book Club met for the June meeting at our law office in Westport. We were discussing the first volume of Blanche Wiesen Cook's superb biography of Eleanor Roosevelt.

"Ladies, grab your pizza and let's get going!" Angela announced. "This is our last discussion until September, and we're concluding our study of power-house First Ladies. As Emma is our expert on the Roosevelt family, she's got the talking stick."

"Not so much of an expert," I protested, taking two slices of the all veggie variety, "but I *am* a longtime fan of Eleanor Roosevelt—of her courage and decency, if not necessarily of her politics." I picked up my notes. "This volume covers the period of her parents' marriage and Eleanor's birth in 1884, until 1933, when FDR first takes office as President. Many people don't realize that ER was born Anna Eleanor Roosevelt. She and Franklin were distantly related, and her father, Elliott, was FDR's godfather. Elliott's older brother was Theodore Roosevelt, twenty-sixth President of the United States, from 1901 to 1909.

"Ted and Elliott's branch of the family were pioneers in the creation of philanthropies in New York. Their father, Theodore Senior, helped found charities that aided the poor and homeless, the blind, children in need of medical care, the SPCA, as well as various museums in the city. He was generous with both his time and his money. These causes no doubt acted as a strong background for Eleanor's lifelong commitment to alleviating the misery of others.

"Despite the fact that Eleanor was born into privileged New York society, her childhood was ghastly. Her family on both sides, according to Cook, was ravaged by alcoholism and self destruction. ER's mother, Anna, was a society beauty who was completely unprepared for the challenges of married life, and valued looks and social standing above all else. Eleanor was a disappointment to her mother, who often joked about her daughter's appearance in public, and called her 'Granny' because she never smiled.

"But in my opinion, it was ER's charming father, Elliott, who was the real problem. Like all children of alcoholics—and I can personally attest to this—Eleanor did all she could to protect her father's image. At the same time, ER never gave her mother any credit for what Anna must have suffered from her husband's behavior. Eleanor claimed to be 'perfectly happy' whenever she and her father spent time together, but the truth is that Elliott Roosevelt was an emotionally damaged man who lived for the sporting life—hunting, drinking, and later, taking mistresses.

"There are two childhood incidents that particularly help us to understand ER as an adult. First—Eleanor is left outside her father's club for six hours, holding several of his dogs on their leashes, while her father goes in for a drink, and is later carried out."

"That got to me too," Angela remarked.

"More important is the tragedy aboard the *Britannic*. Eleanor is two and a half. The family is bound for Europe, but on the first day out their ship is rammed by an incoming steamer. The carnage and screaming is terrifying, and understandably, little Eleanor is fearful of being dropped by a seaman into her father's arms—he is far below in a life boat, and annoyed by her behavior. The horror of this experience was compounded, Cook says, by the fact that when ER's parents finally did sail for England, they left Eleanor behind with relatives."

"Abandonment," Dottie concluded. "Emotional and physical. And betrayal."

"Absolutely," Tina agreed. "They should have helped her to clear that memory by taking her with them the second time."

"So the child was left with the sense that had she only behaved better, her parents would not have gone without her." Angela remarked.

"That incident was a foreshadowing of what happened with Franklin and Eleanor's marriage later on," Denise commented.

"It certainly sets the stage," Eliot said. "Everyone's behavior toward Eleanor is always her fault."

"We get a great many divorce clients who feel the same way," Tina added.

"Her father's issues continue to alarm the entire family," I said, picking up the theme. "Elliott tries everything to straighten out, but nothing sticks. His brother Ted arranges to have him institutionalized, with his wife's approval. The press is relentless. Meanwhile, the shame of Elliott's antics is destroying his beautiful wife, who is becoming more and more remote—and desperate. Anna dies of diphtheria at the age of twenty-nine, when Eleanor is only eight.

"At this point, all of Elliott's efforts to rehabilitate die too. Eleanor and her two younger brothers, Ellie and Hall, go to live with their maternal grandmother, Mary Hall. Eleanor begins to idealize her father. She dreams of them going off as a family together; even wondering if her brothers will become their children."

Dottie frowned. "Yuck. Poor little girl. How totally inappropriate—and dysfunctional. And of course it never happens."

"No. Her brother Ellie, who is four, dies the following spring. Cook reports that Eleanor lives almost entirely in a dream world with her father. Elliott goes on his final binge, becomes delusional, jumps out of a window, and is dead on August 14, 1894. Eleanor is not quite ten. She is not permitted to attend his funeral.

"Eleanor lives with her maternal grandmother and her mother's siblings until she is sent to Allenswood in 1899, when she is fifteen. This is a small, exclusive boarding school—located outside London—and founded by Mademoiselle Marie Souvestre. Allenswood operates in a pseudo collegiate environment, and takes the education of young women seriously. Cook describes it as 'feminist and progressive;' turning out several generations of outstanding women. Creativity and imagination are encouraged, as the students are taught to think for themselves and aspire to a better future.

"Eleanor flourishes at Allenswood, and later claims that Souvestre was one of the most important influences in her life. There she is finally free, according to Cook, to acknowledge her own emotions and to be herself. Eleanor develops her love of literature and language. She is fluent in French, and an excellent athlete. Most important, because of the teachings of Marie Souvestre, Eleanor is now dedicated to a life of independence, public service, and self fulfillment.

"After three years, eighteen year old Eleanor Roosevelt returns to New York society. Haunted by the fact that she is not the belle that her mother had been, her time as a debutante is pure agony."

"I'm not surprised," Eliot barked. "After all that serious education in England, living an intellectual life, ER is dragged back to Manhattan, draped in satin, and wearing a sign around her neck that says 'open for marriage.' I would have spent the evenings in the ladies' powder room—throwing up."

"Enter Cousin Franklin," Tina said, laughing.

"They reconnect at the big horseshow at Madison Square Garden in 1902," Denise remarked. "FDR is a Harvard junior. He proposes to her in the fall of 1903."

"At this time Eleanor is also beginning her volunteer work in the Lower East Side of New York—a theme of social reform that continues throughout her life."

"Let's get to the secret romance with FDR," Dottie urged. "His mother has always fascinated me—the ultimate Queen Bee, with an unusually strong and certainly unhealthy dependence on her only son."

I nodded. "Sara Delano Roosevelt, known as Sally—or simply SDR—is a powerful force, who holds the purse strings for most of their marriage. Franklin learns at a young age to keep his mouth shut around his mother, which infuriates and often humiliates Eleanor."

"And once she finally hears of their engagement, Sally has them wait a year more, and hauls FDR off on a cruise, hoping he'll forget Eleanor," Denise noted.

"Regardless of Sally's efforts, they marry in 1905."

"But Sally remains a thorn in ER's side. With Franklin, and later with their children. The problem is apparent very early on, and it triggers ER's insecurities from childhood—probably because she always dreamed of having a normal, united family. Why does Eleanor pick Franklin, of all people?" Angela demanded. "By every account he is a spoiled mama's boy—pompous, flirtatious—an emotional and intellectual lightweight. She is way too good for him."

"Cook says that Eleanor sees his potential."

"She also says that FDR reminds Eleanor of her father—the idealized version, anyway," Denise added. "She is attracted to his neediness."

"Yes," Tina sighed. "Charm plus chemistry. That's a tough combination when you're nineteen."

"Eleanor suppresses her own interests and feelings in the wake of Franklin and Sally's lives—always on the periphery, never one of them. She gives birth to six children—the first FDR, Jr. dies in infancy. She supports FDR's political career, while he refuses to participate in domestic matters. In 1910 they move to Albany for his stint in the State Senate, and she becomes a political wife. This time marks the beginning of ER's public career. They move to D.C. in 1913 when Franklin is appointed Assistant Secretary of the Navy during the Wilson administration.

"According to Cook, Eleanor's first years in Washington entail the mind numbing and seemingly endless tradition of 'calling' on the other wives of D.C. politicians. Remember Dolley Madison and her efforts. Eleanor meets everyone, records her ten to thirty visits a day, and reports everything she sees and hears to FDR. As we know, she continues this practice on a global scale while he is president, and unable to get around as she can.

"The First World War erupts in Europe in 1914, which creates new avenues for Eleanor and the other Washington wives to be useful. The world is changing, and women are changing their public roles as well. Eleanor learns to drive and volunteers for the Red Cross. At this point ER's and Franklin's social interests begin to clash."

"And that's when it happens," Eliot announced.

I nodded. "Lucy Mercer, hired as Eleanor's social secretary in 1914, becomes the new love of Franklin's life. We all know the famous story of Eleanor finding Lucy's letters in FDR's luggage, when he returns from Europe in September 1918 with double pneumonia and flu. But Cook makes it clear that ER has suspicions long before that time—she just denies them."

"Thereby confirming her childhood fear of abandonment and betrayal," Dottie added. "How horrible."

"To feel unwanted in one's own home?" I asked, grimly. "It's far better to be alone."

"Apparently Eleanor has the same mindset," Denise said, "because she offers her husband his freedom."

"Which he refuses. Divorce would end his political career. Furthermore, Sally would cut him off financially."

"How satisfying for Eleanor," Angela noted sarcastically.

"Yes. From that time on, Cook reports, their marriage is transformed into a partnership. ER begins a long process of introspection, and change, remembering, perhaps, lessons learned from Marie Souvestre at Allenswood. Her journey enables her to enjoy her personal freedoms and a more independent life."

Eliot sniffed. "What you're really saying is that Franklin's affair actually released Eleanor from the limitations of her marriage."

I considered this. "Yes, I think I am. Transformation always begins with some kind of crisis, doesn't it? Eleanor is able to find new avenues outside their relationship to feel happy and fulfilled. The planet begins the long recovery from the Great War. ER becomes an advocate for progressive change—what Cook calls 'a new world of action and activism'—particularly championing improved working conditions for women. At this time Eleanor becomes involved with a strong group of brilliant feminists, with whom she remains friends for the rest of her life."

"I particularly enjoyed the passage about living in balance," Tina remarked. "These women are committed to an elegant existence of work and love and art, in unity with nature."

"I made a note of that too," Denise said. "It seems to me to be the ideal formula."

"Then, as we all know, FDR contracts polio in 1921, and loses the use of his legs."

Eliot sighed. "So Eleanor is thrown back into the marital saddle—helping Franklin keep his spirits up."

"For a time," I agreed. "But Cook tells us that Eleanor and Franklin are infrequently together after 1923. During the twenties Eleanor becomes financially independent for the first time in her life. She earns money from lectures, writing magazine articles, and making appearances on radio shows. She teaches at the Todhunter School. She resumes participating in outdoor sports such as riding, hiking, and swimming. As a result, she is able to pursue her own interests and causes, and to be in charge of her life.

"Eleanor becomes a major political force in the U.S., although she never acknowledges that her contribution is of any value."

"She didn't want Franklin to feel threatened," Dottie said. "Her work was always about keeping his name out there, while he recuperated."

"I don't believe it!" Eliot scoffed. "Mrs. Roosevelt had power, and she enjoyed it."

"I love Cook's comments regarding ER's work on the Equal Rights Amendment," Angela laughed. "And the quotation from Thomas Jefferson—that women should be excluded from the deliberations of pure democracy—to prevent deprivation of morals and ambiguity of issues."

"And John Adams never did 'remember the ladies,' as his wife begged him to," Dottie added.

"Most men just don't want women to have power," Tina concluded. "But that will have to change—and soon."

"As tough as it is today—imagine the battle that Eleanor and her cronies fought over eighty years ago," Denise said.

"Political women were in effect blown off—not taken seriously," Angela noted. "Equal representation does not guarantee equal power."

"In 1928 FDR is elected governor of New York, and Eleanor becomes First Lady of the Empire State," I continued. "Cook tells us that ER encourages her husband to run, when most of the people around him are against it. Eleanor struggles with the fact that at that time, there is no accepted place for a political wife. So she creates her own role. She and Franklin agree that she will be the governor's wife, and continue her teaching, and her activist's agenda. ER is determined to have a life apart from her marriage."

"And presumably FDR respects her wishes," Tina added.

"Yes. He never publically gives her credit for her ideas, but he certainly listens to her advice," Dottie remarked, "in many areas. Even when they disagree, the same principles are important to them. They are decent people."

"And finally, in 1932, FDR is elected President of the United States. Cook writes that Franklin's famous inaugural speech—'let me assert my firm belief that the only thing we have to fear is fear itself....' was actually borrowed from a line of Thoreau's—'Nothing is so much to be feared as fear.'

"Eleanor doesn't want the job of First Lady, and panics at the thought of losing her independent lifestyle. As a result, ER completely recreates the role of the President's wife in the modern world. And she accomplishes this with great courage—by remaining true to herself, and being sincere."

"Phenomenal, Emma—thank you so much," Angela said. "We now have the background regarding a very complicated, and important woman. Comments?"

"Eleanor Roosevelt's life was a lesson in self re-creation," Dottie noted, "if that makes any sense. She and her family faced constant upheavals, and each time she was determined to learn, change, and grow."

"And while she was evolving, ER was working to transform the rest of the world," Denise added. "In an era when women had barely won the right to vote."

"She was tough, she believed that action was the antidote to fear, and she was committed to a peaceful world community," Dottie said.

"I hope we get there someday," Eliot remarked.

"What about their marriage?" Angela asked. "Would any of us be happy with a political partner—instead of a passionate relationship?"

"No," Denise said, quickly. "The loneliness would be too much for me."

There was a moment of silence among us. I felt a wave of anxiety—and a flashback to my divorce.

"They each found outside avenues," Angela said carefully, "and kept the marital unit intact."

"For political reasons, though, don't you think?" Dottie said. "If FDR had become a country squire in Hyde Park, instead of running for public office, would they have stayed married?"

"Possibly," Eliot said. "They were wealthy people, remember. It was not as though Eleanor had to cook dinner every night, or do the laundry. The kids had nurses—there were plenty of servants. She had the time and the funds to pursue her own interests."

"All the better for us," I replied, a little impatient.

"I agree," Angela said. "I feel that I have grown just from reading her story."

As the others packed up to depart, I sat still in my chair—thinking of Eleanor and Franklin Roosevelt, and the personal sacrifices that each had made for their political ambitions. I felt a tremendous surge of gratitude toward them for their visions of public service to human dignity—and powerful social change.

CHAPTER TWENTY-FOUR

Playhouse Ghost

"Emma!" Carlie shouted, hurling herself into my office on Tuesday morning. "I got accepted!"

"To the summer journalism course at Yale?" Carlie beamed. "Congratulations! That's great, honey, but I'm not surprised."

"Because of my article, you mean?"

The *Hartford Courant* had picked up Carlie's report on Lavandula, LLC and the connection to the Cameron Manor explosion and Claudia Marino's murder. Within hours it had appeared all over the Web.

"When do you go to New Haven?"

Carlie glanced at the letter in her hand. "It's the third week in August—six days—at the *Yale Daily News* building on campus. We're going to participate in workshops, attend lectures, and be mentored by Yale students on staff—while we pitch, investigate, and write our own stories. At the end of the week we help produce an issue of the paper."

"Sounds pretty intense. You'll get great experience and make important contacts, plus it gives you an opportunity to really check out Yale."

"Yeah," she agreed. "It's my top choice for schools." She paused.

"My dress for Junior Prom is ready. I'm going to get it from the tailor's this afternoon."

"Is Max all set with his tux?"

"Yep. And the flowers are ordered." She grinned. "I checked."

"Excellent. How's he doing?"

"Much more level. Probably because Jim is completely changed since the de-ghosting. Well," she laughed, "he's still kind of a jerk, but in a much nicer way. Max told him off in front of the entire hockey team, and I think Jim's got a better attitude toward girls now."

"Sounds positive."

"Definitely. He asked Megan to the Prom, and she won't take *any* crap from guys."

"This farm is gorgeous Emma!" Whitney exclaimed, staring at the enormous grass pastures, with the groves of trees beyond them, and the Litchfield hills in the distance. "Is Luke sure that he wants me to be barn manager here?"

"We're both sure! I've seen you with the horses, and Patty and Ryan can't handle all the work on their own—new boarders are coming in all the time. When can you move into the apartment?"

"Is this weekend OK? I got my brother and his friends to agree to help. And I've borrowed a truck and trailer to bring my horse up."

"Perfect." I took a breath. "Do you mind if I ask?"

"Fitz?" Whitney shrugged. "He disappeared—right after my deposition. Turns out he'd already started seeing someone else anyway. It's my own fault, and I accept total responsibility for my behavior." She let out a long sigh. "I knew he didn't have much of a backbone. Anyway, I'm glad to be up here in this beautiful area, so far from it all. I need the peace and quiet. Maybe I'll meet a nice farmer's son."

"That's the spirit! Let's give Joy her treats."

The Bridge Hollow Country Playhouse was preparing for the opening night of Oscar Wilde's comedic masterpiece, *An Ideal*

Husband. I met Jerome Forester in the greenroom for our conference, having replaced Esther MacInerney as counsel for the theater. "Take a look, Emma," he said grimly, indicating the glass cabinet filled with two centuries of theater memorabilia.

Hugh Murdoch's pocket watch was missing.

"This is the first time that *An Ideal Husband* has been performed here since Murdoch murdered Fenella Cameron in 1921. I have a bad feeling about this," Jerry said. "The disturbances have escalated in the last few months, and since the cast arrived for this show—it's been total chaos. Dress rehearsal is Thursday night. I'd really appreciate it if you and your friend Sophie were present. In fact," he said, making a face, "I'll call her myself. We want to hire her services. Just in case anything—er—extraordinary happens."

After Jerry left I stood quietly in the greenroom, gazing at the space for Hugh Murdoch's watch, and the card beside it. The gold pocket watch had been found next to Fenella's body by her sister Pauline—in the room that had been Esther MacInerney's office, until someone—possibly Chief Marino—had caused Cameron Manor to explode. It occurred to me that Murdoch's initials had spelled HAM, and giggling, I picked up my purse and turned to leave.

Suddenly I was enveloped in the aroma of lavender. The smell was so concentrated and pungent that I could barely breathe. Grabbing my briefcase I ran into the hall and felt immediate relief. Noise emanated from the stage area, where last minute details were being added to the set. The corridor was deserted—the actors would not arrive for another two hours. Then I heard a door open. I scurried across the passage to the restroom and watched as Bill Wheeler, the Stage Manager, moved quickly out of one of the star dressing rooms, and headed toward the backdoor.

I called Jerry from my car.

"I may be way out of line here, but my instincts are usually good. My advice would be to have someone keep an eye on Wheeler from now until the play opens."

"I could hire someone undercover," Jerry mused. "Say he's an extra stagehand or something."

"Whatever you think is best." Then I told him about the lavender. "It takes a lot to scare me, but being nearly suffocated in an herbal fragrance really came close. Have you called Sophie?"

"Just did. She'll be there Thursday night. I'm sorry you were attacked Emma—I'm even more worried now."

"Please don't be. I take it as a sign that we need to get this problem addressed—and cleared out—now. Action is always the best antidote to fear."

Back in the office I reviewed my notes from Sophie's workshop on the common uses for lavender.

Lavandula is grown primarily for the production of its essential oil, which has antiseptic and anti-inflammatory properties. It has been used to soothe insect bites, headaches, and burns, and when diluted with witch hazel, it may be applied to the face to treat acne.

Lavender is also harvested for use as a condiment, and blended in teas.

Bunches of lavender repel insects, and it is often added to sachets to freshen linens.

In modern times lavender is used extensively in aromatherapy, to aid relaxation and sleep. More recently, the dried flowers have become popular replacing rice as wedding confetti.

Thursday afternoon my cell phone rang as I was returning from lunch.

"We got him Emma!" Jerry Forester was ecstatic. "Bill Wheeler. You were right. The private investigator we hired followed him for two days, and caught the man this morning—tampering with the lights—after they'd been set for the dress rehearsal. We went through his office and found a stash of stolen items, including Clare Rowler's Cartier wristwatch from *Over Heath and Glen*."

"How about Murdoch's pocket watch?"

"Nothing yet. But we're still searching the theater. Tough to do with all of the activity—getting ready for Saturday night."

"I can imagine."

"You're still coming for tonight's rehearsal—correct?"

"Absolutely. Sophie and I will be there at six."

An Ideal Husband was first staged in London in 1895. The action of the play is completed within two days, and has been acclaimed as a brilliant portrayal of English aristocracy, politics, and marriage in the late Victorian era.

At the center of the plot are Sir Robert Chiltern and his wife, Gertrude, as well as Robert's sister Mabel, and Robert's best friend—Arthur, Lord Goring. Sir Robert is a rising star in Parliament who is admired for his integrity. Gertrude is a woman of the very highest principles—passionate regarding women's politics, and a determined supporter of her husband's career. Arthur, in contrast to his two friends, is an example of dandified gentry with no purpose—or so the audience is led to believe. Mabel is a smart and funny ingénue who is attracted to Arthur.

Enter Laura Cheveley. An Englishwoman who lives abroad, Mrs. Cheveley is deeply involved in European affairs of every description. She was once briefly engaged to Arthur, is a despised former schoolmate of Gertrude's, and is currently in possession of an old letter of Robert's, the publication of which would destroy his career, and his marriage.

Although *An Ideal Husband* has been hailed as a social commentary with anti-aristocratic sentiments—highlighting hypocrisy and political corruption—the main theme of the play explores the moral conclusion that no one should be judged by his or her past.

Sophie and I took seats in the fifth row, and waited.

As dress rehearsal began I followed along with my copy of the script.

Act One opens as Lady Chiltern greets her guests at the top of the staircase, over which hangs a chandelier, illuminating a French tapestry representing the Triumph of Love. Gertrude is surprised that Lady Markby is accompanied by Laura Cheveley, who Gertrude knew, and disliked, by another name when they were at school together.

Sir Robert Chiltern enters, and Mrs. Cheveley immediately engages him in conversation, clearly with the purpose of getting him alone long enough to introduce her blackmail scheme. She tells Sir Robert that politics are her only pleasure, to which Sir Robert expresses his belief that a political life is a noble career. Mrs. Cheveley replies breezily that it is a clever game. She has just let it be known that she was an intimate of the late Baron Arnheim, startling Sir Robert, when Lord Goring is announced.

"Any action yet?" Luke whispered, sitting down. Sophie shook her head.

Sir Robert learns that Arthur and Laura are previously acquainted. Mrs. Cheveley and her prey move offstage, and Lord Goring saunters over to speak with Mabel Chiltern. They engage in several flirtatious exchanges. Mabel announces that she doesn't like Arthur at all this evening, whereupon Arthur counters by telling Mabel that he likes her immensely. Mabel replies that she'd prefer that Arthur show his admiration in a more obvious manner.

The players were interrupted suddenly, as the huge reproduction French tapestry was ripped from the wall and flung down the stairs. It thudded onto the stage and sent waves of dust into the air. The actors scrambled to sanctuary.

"We have lift-off!" Luke exclaimed. Sophie moved out to the aisle to speak to Jerry. Onstage several men were running to repair the set.

"Did you see anyone?" Luke asked me.

"Yes," I replied, as Sophie returned. "But it doesn't make sense."

"I agree," Sophie admitted. "I told Jerry that I want to keep watching for a bit more. If my theory is correct, we're going to have to change the strategy for tonight."

Mrs. Cheveley corners Sir Robert with her threat of exposure. She requires him to publically support the Argentine Canal Company proposal currently before Parliament—a scheme which Chiltern vehemently opposes—or she will publish Robert's letter to Baron Arnheim from nearly eighteen years before, and ruin him. As a young man Robert had been secretary to an influential politician, and had sold a Cabinet secret for a huge sum of money. Everyone has to pay for what they do, Mrs. Cheveley assures Sir Robert. He has to pay now.

Lady Chiltern is mystified to learn from Laura Cheveley that her husband now intends to support the Argentine Canal speculation, and plans to announce his decision to the House of Commons.

Mabel and Arthur have another interlude. Mabel sits on the sofa and catches sight of a diamond brooch that is lying there.

The actor playing Mabel held out her prize, confusion registered on her face.

"That doesn't look like a pin," Luke remarked, drily.

It was Hugh Murdoch's missing gold pocket watch. There was a brief lapse, as the watch was given to the director, who then passed it to Jerry.

Sophie touched my arm. "I know how to handle this now," she said. I nodded.

"Pick up from Mabel's line," the director shouted.

Mabel exclaims about the brooch, but Arthur shows her that it can be transformed into a bracelet as well. He then requests that Mabel not mention the jewelry to anyone, and puts the brooch in his letter case. If anyone should write to her about it, he says, she is to let him know about it at once. He explains his strange behavior. He had given it as a gift to someone many years earlier.

Gertrude and Robert return, and Arthur leaves. Gertrude tackles her husband regarding Mrs. Cheveley. Gertrude tells Sir Robert that Laura was a negative influence on anyone she ever knew, and was sent away from school for being a thief. Gertrude is adamant that people must always be judged by their past actions.

Robert attempts to convince his wife that he has changed his mind about the proposed Argentine Canal scheme. Sooner or later, he assures her, one must compromise in politics, as circumstances may change.

Gertrude is horrified by this alteration in her husband. Circumstances can never change principles, she retorts. It is never necessary to do what is not honorable. Power is nothing in itself, she tells him. Only the power to do good is what matters.

Sir Robert, devastated by his wife's renouncement of his principles, implores her to consider the question as no more than a political rationalization. In return, she begs him not to kill her love for him—to continue to be an ideal.

"Poor Robert!" Sophie murmured. Luke and I both looked at her, but did not respond.

Gertrude begins to suspect that Robert is not telling her everything. She begs him to relay any secret disgrace, so that she can separate from him immediately, thereby alleviating further pain. Sir Robert assures her that there is nothing in his past that he is keeping from her. She then convinces him to write to Laura Cheveley, declining his support from her fraudulent plan. Gertrude reads his letter, and sends it off immediately, announcing that she feels she has saved him from a great danger. Now he will always be worthy of love.

Act One closes on Sir Robert sitting alone in almost complete darkness.

Act Two opens the next morning at the Chiltern home. Robert has told Arthur the entire story. Arthur then attempts to persuade Robert to relay the business to Gertrude, as she will no doubt learn of it on her own. Robert is terrified of losing her love, and is clearly bitter about the choice that he is being forced to make. But Arthur will not back down.

Sir Robert extols the late Baron Arnheim's philosophy of power. Power over the world, he explains, is the one thing worth having, and only the rich ever possess it. He declares that it had required terrible courage for him to yield to the temptation and sell Cabinet information to the Baron.

Robert then decides to fight the thing out. He wires to the Embassy at Vienna to inquire if there is any information that can be used against Mrs. Cheveley. He thanks Arthur for allowing him to unburden his secret. The great thing in life is to live the truth, he says.

Gertrude returns and Robert goes out. Lord Goring sees his chance to speak with Gertrude. He suggests that perhaps she is a bit rigid in some of her views on life. He encourages her to make allowances for weakness in everyone's nature. Nobody is incapable of doing a foolish thing, or a wrong thing, Arthur says. Life must be filled with charity and love, in this world, and possibly in the next world as well.

Arthur tells Gertrude that if she ever finds herself in trouble, she should come to him at once. Lady Chiltern is amazed at his seriousness, and Mabel enters the room.

Mabel and Arthur make a date to ride in the Park the following morning at ten, and Arthur exits. Then Mabel announces to Gertrude that she has had yet another marriage proposal from Tommy Trafford, who is Sir Robert's secretary.

Suddenly there was a loud sound of sharp staccato rapping on the wall behind the actor who was playing Mabel. She jerked her head slightly, but remained in character, and subsequently left the stage.

"I'm beginning to see a pattern here," Luke whispered. I smiled at him.

Lady Markby comes in with Mrs. Cheveley. They are calling to see if Laura Cheveley's diamond brooch has been found. It is described as a snake with a ruby on its head. Tea is brought in, and Gertrude indicates that she would like to speak to Mrs. Cheveley alone. Lady Markby exits. Gertrude is stiff with judgment, while Laura appears amused.

Gertrude flatly tells Laura that she would not have been asked to the party the previous evening if Gertrude had known her identity.

Gertrude announces that life has taught her that a person who has once been guilty of a dishonest deed may be guilty of it again, and therefore should be shunned.

Laura Cheveley replies that she has come to render Gertrude a service. Make your husband do as I tell him, she informs Gertrude. Gertrude, horrified, orders her to leave the house, just as Sir Robert enters.

Mrs. Cheveley then breaks the news to Gertrude. Her husband is a fraud. Laura gives them until noon the following day to accede to her demand, or the whole world will learn that Sir Robert once sold a Cabinet secret to a stockbroker. She leaves.

The Chilterns are left alone. Gertrude stands still in shock, and Robert attempts to tell her the story. But she will not listen. Do not touch me, Gertrude tells her husband. She feels soiled forever. He was once her ideal, but that is now dead. She deplores the mask that Robert has been wearing for years.

I felt a sickening jolt of fear, and then a shudder ran through me.

Robert pleads with Gertrude. It is the imperfect who are in need of love, he tells her, and that above all, love should forgive. If only women would cease to make false idols of men, he exclaims, men would have the courage to show their wounds, and tell of their weaknesses. Finally he cries out that she has ruined his life, and leaves the room.

Lady Chiltern rushes toward him, but she is too late. Act Two closes with Gertrude sobbing on a sofa.

I picked up Luke's left hand with my right and squeezed it. He turned to me and smiled gently in response.

Act Three takes place in Lord Goring's house. Arthur is in evening dress and obviously about to go out. His butler brings in his letters, one of which is in a pink envelope. The note is from Gertrude. She needs him, she trusts him, and she is coming to him. Arthur realizes that Gertrude has learned Robert's secret, and decides that he will make her stand by her husband. He is distracted by the entrance of his father, Lord Caversham, who refuses to be put off. Lord Caversham reminds Arthur that he ought to get married. Arthur sends him to the smoking room to wait.

Arthur tells his butler that a lady is coming to see him, and that the butler should show her into the drawing room. He is at home to no one else. Mrs. Cheveley arrives unexpectedly, and not understanding his mistake, the butler admits her and puts her in the drawing room. There Laura finds Gertrude's letter to Arthur.

Sir Robert Chiltern enters. Robert tells Arthur that Mrs. Cheveley has destroyed his marriage. The telegram has arrived from Vienna, and he has learned that nothing is known against Laura Cheveley. She has a high position in society and Baron Arnheim has left her most of his enormous fortune. The butler appears, Arthur takes him aside, and learns that a lady is now in the drawing room. Thinking that the lady is Gertrude, Arthur allows her to overhear his conversation with Sir Robert through the door.

Robert exclaims that his life is crumbling about him. Arthur reminds Robert that he loves his wife, more than anything else. Robert tells Arthur that he used to feel that ambition was all that mattered, but now he realizes that it is love, and only love. But Gertrude, he says, does not know what weakness is. She is pitiless and cold and without mercy.

But Arthur assures his friend that Gertrude will forgive him. About to leave, Robert begins to tell Arthur of his plans regarding the Argentine Canal debate in the House of Commons that night. Then they both hear a noise in the next room. Robert goes to the door and is horrified to find Laura Cheveley standing there. He remonstrates with Lord Goring, who is flabbergasted. Sir Robert leaves, thinking that he has been betrayed by his best friend.

Arthur assumes that Laura is there to sell him Robert Chiltern's letter. He is surprised to learn that she is willing to give it to him, if Arthur marries her. Arthur declines, and Laura admits that she has always detested Gertrude Chiltern, and hates her now, more than ever. She went to the Chiltern's house merely to inquire about her lost brooch, and the scene that occurred was forced on her by Gertrude's rudeness and sneers.

Lord Goring produces the brooch, and snaps it on Mrs. Cheveley's arm as a bracelet. He taunts her with the fact that ten years previously he had given the jewel to his cousin as a wedding gift, and that it had been subsequently stolen. He knows now the identity of the thief.

Mrs. Cheveley attempts to remove the bracelet, but she is unaware of the location of the spring. Enraged, she curses at Lord Goring. Her mask of civility has dropped, her face is contorted with anger and she looks dreadful. Arthur tells her that he will have the servant ring for the police unless she produces Robert's letter. She does so, and Arthur burns it in front of her.

While Arthur is getting Laura a glass of water, she steals Gertrude's letter to him. With bitter triumph in her voice, she alerts Lord Goring to this fact. He rushes toward her to grab the letter, but Mrs. Cheveley rings the bell, and the butler enters. Laura leaves the room, her face illuminated with evil elation. Act Three ends.

Act Four opens in the morning room at the Chiltern home. Lord Goring is full of interesting information and looking forward to sharing it. He is told that Sir Robert is at the Foreign Office, Gertrude is upstairs, and Mabel has just returned from riding. He also learns that his father, Lord Caversham, is waiting in the library for Sir Robert.

Lord Caversham enters, and relays that the leading article in *The Times* covers Robert's speech from the previous evening. Chiltern has denounced the Argentine Canal speculation. *The Times* lauds Sir Robert as a brilliant orator and a rising star in government with impeccable character.

Lord Caversham then resumes the subject of marriage, and encourages his son to marry Mabel Chiltern. Lord Caversham informs Lord Goring that he does not deserve Mabel. Arthur agrees.

Enter Mabel. She is annoyed that Lord Goring broke their

appointment to ride in the Park, and refuses to acknowledge his greeting. Lord Caversham exits the room and they are alone. Mabel announces that she is about to leave as well, when Arthur stops her. He has something very particular to say to her. Mabel asks if it is a proposal, and Arthur admits that it is. Arthur tells Mabel that he loves her, and asks if she loves him in return.

Sophie and I glanced at each other. She got up and began moving toward the stage, the file from Carlie's research on Fenella Cameron's murder in her hand.

Mabel laughs and announces that she adores him.

Arthur takes Mabel in his arms and kisses her.

Just as Sophie reached the steps, the giant chandelier overhead began to sway violently. Everyone in the auditorium gasped. The actors pulled apart, looked up, and raced from the center of the stage.

That's when I saw her. The tall, thin ghost of an elderly woman was standing on the staircase, looking down on the scene below. Sophie advanced until she reached the bottom stair.

"Miss Cameron?" Sophie said out loud. "Miss Pauline Cameron, correct?"

"Pauline?" Luke whispered. "The sister? The one who found Fenella's body?"

I nodded.

The ghost scowled. *Who are you?*

"I'm here to help you," Sophie replied. "I'm here to send you to Hugh Murdoch. He's been waiting for you—all this time."

Not after what I did.

"Yes," Sophie said, firmly. "It's been nearly one hundred years. He forgives you. He's waiting," she repeated.

Pauline's ghost took a tentative step forward. *Is that true?*

"Absolutely. It's time for you to go to him, Miss Cameron. Your place is with Hugh." Sophie was quiet for a moment, and I knew that she was asking safe passage for Pauline's spirit—back home to the Other Side.

Pauline and Sophie both looked up at the top of the staircase. The chandelier had stopped swaying and suddenly sparkled even brighter. Pauline turned and disappeared through the doorway.

Sophie smiled and gave us two thumbs up. I thought of Judge Conroy, just as the entire cast ran onstage, and a loud burst of applause erupted from everyone in the house.

The director took his seat, and the dress rehearsal resumed.

Jerry beckoned us out to the lobby. I passed Carlie several rows behind us, writing furiously in her notebook. She followed us through the doorway.

"I don't get it!" Carlie exclaimed.

"Hugh Murdoch did *not* murder his fiancée," Sophie replied.

"Fenella's sister Pauline did," I added.

"And he still swung for it?" Jerry was shocked.

"Circumstantial evidence," I told him. "They found the watch—no doubt planted by Pauline—they heard the stories, he had no alibi—and that was it for Hugh Murdoch."

"So much concentrated negativity," Sophie said. "The mansion, the theater. The pocket watch. This property needs a serious clearing."

Luke looked troubled. "Why didn't Murdock testify in his own defense?"

Sophie pulled out the research file and laid the three photographs on a table. Next to Hugh Murdoch's sensual good looks, and Fenella's glamorous beauty, Pauline as a young woman had been quite plain. Her nose was large, her lips thin, her jaw square and mannish—and her complexion was pitted and blemished.

"I think Murdoch knew that Pauline was in love with him, and that perhaps he had led her on at some point. He felt that Fenella's death was his fault, and he wasn't going to exonerate himself."

"You mean that he had a conscience?" Carlie scoffed.

"Men do, you know," Jerry laughed. "Some of us, anyway."

"It's best not to judge people, remember," Sophie said, and Carlie sighed. "Sir Robert has taught us that tonight."

"What about the lavender?" Jerry asked. "We've been smelling it all over the theater."

"Adult acne," I replied. "Pauline used lavender oil on her face to treat acne. She must have reeked of it."

"Poor thing," Carlie remarked thoughtfully, looking at the photographs of the two sisters. "No wonder. She was jealous of Fenella."

Back onstage, Sir Robert has arrived home. Arthur and Gertrude tell him that his letter to Baron Arnheim has been burnt. Mrs. Cheveley, bitter over her defeat, has sent Gertrude's letter to Robert, implying that Gertrude is having an affair with Arthur. Sir Robert confronts Gertrude with the letter. Gertrude explains, and they reconcile. Lord Caversham announces that the Prime Minister intends to offer Sir Robert the vacant seat in the Cabinet. Robert consents to Mabel and Arthur's engagement. Lord Caversham tells Arthur that if he doesn't make Mabel an ideal husband, he will be cut off with a shilling.

But Mabel is adamant. She doesn't want an ideal husband. It sounds too much like something from the next world, she explains. Lord Caversham asks Mabel what she wants Arthur to be. Whatever he likes, Mabel replies.

Gertrude tells Robert that she loves him, and that a new life is beginning for them.

The director yelled Curtain! and called the cast together for notes.

"Sophie," Luke said, as we collected our belongings and moved back out into the lobby, "we have a situation here in the park as well. The surveyor that the Garden Club hired is complaining of disturbances on the grounds, and mysterious interference with the equipment." He grinned at her, one eyebrow raised. "Are you available?"

Sophie laughed, and pulled a datebook from her purse.

CHAPTER TWENTY-FIVE

Nantucket

The Steamship Authority fast ferry docked, and I proceeded with the others down to the lower level to retrieve our bicycles.

"Everybody make sure you've got all your stuff," Leslie shouted over the noise of the loudspeakers. Greg and the rest of her clan moved quickly down to the parking lot. Joan struggled with Kellie and their bicycles. Ashley had already mounted hers and was exhibiting signs of bolting. "Cell phones need to be ON!" Leslie shrieked.

I shoved my straw hat into the basket on my mountain bike, three bags slung over various parts of my anatomy. Luke followed close behind. "Just out of curiosity, Emma, what have you got in there?"

"Clothes, books, paints," I told him. "Why?"

Luke just grinned, and pulled the largest one from my right shoulder.

Leslie had already ducked into the car rental office. She reappeared almost immediately. "The station wagon is ready, Em. They need you to go in and sign. OK troops. Maps." She pulled a pen out of her canvas bag. "Here's the house, right by Surfside Beach, which is due south of town, on the Atlantic. We're looking at Broad Street. I've highlighted the course that you'll take on your bikes. Kellie will go with you. Trish, you're in charge. Everyone stick together. Stay alert, and be careful. There are places where there is no bike path, and you're on the road. Gabrielle and Ben, I don't want to hear about any nonsense. Sara, is your phone on?"

"Yes Mom."

"Well done. Forward, march." The five elder offspring disappeared into the vacationing throng.

"All right. Next shift. Greg—you and I are going to take the shuttle to Surfside with a bicycle each. Emma—you, Luke, Joan and Ashley will go in the car with the luggage and the remaining bikes. Clear?"

"Admirable," Luke remarked.

"Oh that's nothing," Greg laughed. "You should see her run the ER. The other doctors live in terror."

The house I had rented was about a quarter mile from the beach. It had an upside down floor plan, and a view of the ocean from the deck off the kitchen.

"This place is huge!" Gaby yelled from downstairs. "Dibs on the blue room."

"Your rooms have been assigned," her mother replied crisply. "Get your shoes back on. You're coming with me to buy food."

Joan emerged from the master bedroom on the upper level. She had put on fresh lipstick and was polishing her nails. "I have my things in here, Emma."

"Well, you can take them right back out again," her sister snapped. "Emma and Luke are getting that room. You're downstairs with the rest of us, in the corner by the patio. And what's with the makeup, Joan? We're at the seashore, for God's sake."

I made a quick exit into the kitchen, where Trish and Sara were going through the cabinets and making a shopping list. "We need paper towels and Cascade," Trish called, her head under the sink. "Oh, and napkins. Emma, the men went to arrange for the kayaks to be delivered. Is there anything you want from the store?"

"We're fine, thanks. Where are the rest of the kids?"

"They've already gone to the beach. Gaby's determined to get a

287

killer tan here, and she's worried that this is the only nice day that we'll have all week."

I left the domestic arrangements in their capable hands and took my bike out for a tour of our neighborhood. It seemed as though most of the property owners in this area had foregone the usual manicured gardens, and had left their landscapes *au naturel*. The only additions were the inevitable hydrangea bushes, their flowers huge in deep blues and purples. I rode south from the house and took a left into the beach parking lot. Many of the families were already packing up for the day. I spotted my younger relatives in a clump of soggy towels near the lifeguard stand. Ashley jumped up and grabbed my hand.

"I found a crab!" She whispered fiercely.

"It was washed up, dead," Gaby added. "Ben and Kellie are snorkeling." She pointed to a spot in the water where I could just make out two air tubes, one blue and one pink.

I flopped on my back on the sand. Several small propeller planes flew in and out of the little island airport just east of us. A wisp of cloud covered the sun briefly and then moved on. Ashley and Gaby amused themselves by filling buckets and then dumping them on my feet.

"Emma! Dinner's almost ready. Come on." I opened my eyes and looked up into Leslie's amused face. "Have a nice nap?"

"What time is it?"

"Nearly six. I've taken the kids back in the car already. Your bike is on the rack. Lifting you is a little tougher."

"So what are we having for dinner?" I asked, feeling guilty.

"Luke's doing the grill, and I'm in charge of potatoes and salad. Joan, needless to say, has been sunning herself on the deck all afternoon, and only came in once to ask if there was any ice tea."

"We might as well have brought my mother," I grinned. "Though I'm hardly one to talk."

"You arranged this adventure," My cousin replied. "But there *does* appear to be a streak of spoiled females in this family, I agree. I'm afraid that Gabrielle is the next generation."

Early Sunday morning Trish and I rode our bikes into town on a quest for large quantities of baked goods.

"Check out the éclairs!" Trish exclaimed. "They're really big."

"Stupendous. But I don't think that the ride home in your backpack will do them any good. How about doughnuts? They have glazed, chocolate frosted, and raspberry jelly."

"OK. Also some cranberry scones, muffins—and maybe a bunch of bagels." Her cell phone buzzed. "Mom says we need to stop for cream cheese on the way back."

After breakfast Luke and I reviewed the guide to island activities.

"There's a lecture at the Maria Mitchell Association on Tuesday," he noted, flipping through the book. "The topic is the osprey population. We could go to the Life Saving Museum, or go look at some art galleries. What about the Whaling Museum?"

"The harpooning scenes upset me. You and Greg should go."

"Well then, how about we take the Shuttle into town and rent a Jeep, and just tool around the island? Maybe have lunch in Sconset?"

"Deal. I think we've earned some quiet time together," I said, kissing his cheek. "You're a real hero for doing this, Luke."

Luke laughed. "I'm enjoying it."

"Even Joan?" I asked, picking up my camera.

"She doesn't bother me. Her focus appears to be on baiting her sister. Too bad, really."

I sighed. "It *is* too bad. Leslie and I grew up with the same problem—envious, competitive little sisters."

The key to enjoying Nantucket in July and August is avoiding the center of town as much as possible. Food shop early, and if one must eat out, it is best to do it on a weekday. Bearing this in mind, Luke and I packed a picnic lunch and left the house to my cousins.

"I'd forgotten what the crowds were like during the high season,"

I mused. "I've been coming here in early September for years. It's a completely different island."

"The kids are all back in school then," Luke replied. He glanced at me. "But you still love it, don't you Emma? You're always talking about Nantucket—always painting it. Would you come here more often, if you had a choice?"

"Definitely. Why?"

We pulled into the village of Siasconset, on the southeastern side of the island, and Luke found a parking space. "I've been negotiating to buy a house here in Sconset, that's why," he said, laughing at the look on my face. "I just want to make sure that you like it, before I commit to a contract."

The house was situated three blocks away. "The beach is an easy walk, as is the market," the real estate agent said. "Not so much of the sea breezes perhaps, but you also avoid the vacationers. It's no fun having strangers peering into your windows all summer—I can tell you from experience."

I barely heard her. The weathered shingle house with white trim, about seventy years old, was a mass of gables and porches, with a roof walk, and an outdoor shower. A detached two car garage was visible at the end of the driveway. "You can see the Atlantic Ocean from those windows," the agent pointed, "and from the roof walk. It's a half acre of land, so some privacy from the neighbors." She seemed to sense that mine was the deciding vote. "The bank of hydrangeas and other foliage around the property provides adequate screening for the season. As far as I know there are no rental properties on this street. Shall we go in?"

Luke was unusually quiet. The sales agent continued her commentary as we explored the downstairs—all hardwood floors, with a fireplace in the living and dining rooms, a big dated kitchen with pantry, a powder room, a screened porch area, and a laundry room just inside the back door. "This room could be used as a television and library area," the woman said. "Or an extra guestroom. The house is gas heat, so comfortable year round. The second floor," she continued, climbing the stairs, "has five bedrooms and three baths. There is plenty of closet space," she announced, opening doors. "The attic is big and could be turned into additional sleeping space for summer guests. There are lovely views on all four sides of the house."

I looked at Luke. "Lots of work to be done," he said, his face registering as little emotion as possible.

"Why don't I leave you alone for a bit," the agent said, pulling out her cell phone. "I'll be on the porch when you're ready."

"I have many clients here on Nantucket," Luke explained, once she'd gone. "I fly over fairly regularly. I've been thinking about buying a second home in Sconset for a while, and then you came into my life, and you're so in love with the island. It just all came together. Several of my clients have barns on their properties—we can bring the horses over here, if we like. So? What do you think?"

"I think we're going to have a blast redoing this place," I said, working hard not to stammer. "I've been dreaming of a house like this for about half my life."

"So I'll tell Caroline that it's a deal!" Luke exclaimed, heading for the front door. "That's great, Emma! I can't wait to get started on that garden." He paused. "You haven't noticed any uninvited guests here, by the way?"

"Nope. Nice and quiet."

"That's a relief! Did you see the name of the house on the quarterboard outside?"

I shook my head, still dazed. "What is it?"

"Sconset Joy."

Monday night after dinner, I took my journal out to the deck and sat at the table facing the beach with the ocean beyond.

A little over two days on this blessed island and I am almost completely relaxed. So far, the weather has been ideal, so the kids spend all their time at the beach, and only reappear in the evenings.

This rental house has gotten the thumbs up from everyone. There is a constant flow of fresh air. The common rooms are open and bright. In the immediate distance are scattered gray shingle houses with roof walks and big porches. We are surrounded by rosa rugosa, bayberry bushes, sea grass and some straggly pines. There's a huge land reserve area behind us, and the colors are amazing when the sun is coming up.

The kids brave the ladder to our roof walk at night. They bike to the bakery every morning, loading us up on sugar for the day. Then Luke and I take off. I feel like a little girl again, riding over rutted sandy roads—my backpack stuffed with a towel and my watercolor field kit. I sling my white artists' umbrella over one shoulder, and pedal away happily. I've already read two books.

This morning Luke and I went out in the sea kayaks with Greg and Ben. We launched from the beach and stayed parallel to the shore for quite a distance. I was acutely aware that paddling in the Atlantic is very different from the Long Island Sound. The water is a clear green, cool but not cold. The waves make kayaking much more challenging.

Everyone for the most part is getting along. Joan expects the rest of us to wait on her because she is now a 'hard working single mother.' Leslie is barely able to be civil to her at times. There have been a few dramatic clashes between Gaby and Ben. Leslie quickly herds them outside, thereby avoiding property damage.

I've done a good amount of painting, although it's tough on the beach. The sun dries the washes too fast. I attempted a study of some rose hips and dusty miller today. Yesterday I worked on seawater rolling up and then receding on wet sand. I cheated a little with watercolor pencils to get the textures that I wanted.

All of this close family contact has changed Luke somehow. The paralyzed acceptance that I observed when he was coping with his sister and brother is now gone. When we're with Leslie's clan he is reasonable and pleasant about everything, and brilliant at being part of the group without forcing any boundaries. But when he's had enough, he says so, and we make our quick exit. We've had sex on the beach three nights in a row—the last two times were his idea.

Everyone is a teacher, Kezia told me. So what is Luke learning from me? How to heal from the past? Must have been tough—a creative, sensitive guy growing up with those two corporation-bound hard-asses—never missing an opportunity to prove to him that kindness and compassion equal weakness.

I now understand what all of my past boyfriend clearing work has been showing me. Having someone to love is huge—but the real test is finding the courage to allow that person to love you back. Once you know your own value—it's easy to be patient until you find a person with a similar vibration.

Luke now owns a home on Nantucket. We're meeting with the contractors to get started on the kitchen and bathrooms later this week. It's unbelievable—I'm still in shock, and yet, it's happening. Luke's so enthusiastic about his new island garden that he's basically given me free rein with all the interior decisions. Two years ago I was a tourist with a camera and a borrowed bike. We do get what we wish for, eventually.

I had just spread my towel down by the water the next morning, when my cell phone rang. Angela.

"How is your Nantucket adventure going?"

I sighed with contentment. "It's heaven, Ange. As we speak I am sitting just above the waterline with my toes digging into the wet sand, watching my cousins bodysurf. The sun's really strong, and I have my straw hat jammed on to my head so the breeze that comes off the Atlantic won't send it to the mainland. We've been eating well—too well—and the only thing that saves me from resembling a humpback whale is the dozens of biked and kayaked miles that I log per day."

"Sounds idyllic. Is Luke enjoying himself?"

"He seems to be. The men are good about taking Ben on various outings. They've been in the water around most of the island."

"You and Leslie are smart to provide them with a diversion."

"Experience is the best teacher."

"That it is. Call me when you're back."

On Wednesday evening Luke and I decided to take a break from the family and dine in town. When we arrived back at the house Greg was sitting in a chair in the backyard. Gaby was flying her new kite—a gray and white shark. Raised voices could be distinguished through the windows.

"I wouldn't go in just yet, if I were you," Greg warned. "There's been an altercation of sorts."

"Any injuries?" I asked.

"I think I heard some face slapping just now." Greg opened a second bottle of beer and poured it into his glass. "It's the mother of all catfights."

"You didn't leave Ben in there with the women!"

"He took off on his bike half an hour ago." Greg took a gulp of beer. "He's the smart one."

"What happened?"

"The best I can tell, Joan said something to Trish that made her cry, and then Leslie let Joan have it."

"Hence the slapping. Shouldn't we go in and put a stop to this?"

"No way. I'm good here, thanks," Greg replied. He offered Luke the rest of his beer, and Luke pulled up a chair.

The mayhem was taking place on the lower bedroom level, for which I was moderately grateful, as there were fewer breakable items. I located my cousins in the big triple bedroom. The scene was set as follows: Leslie and Joan were standing in the middle of the room, shouting at each other. The left side of Joan's face was considerably pinker than the right. Trish was sitting on the farthest bed, sobbing miserably. Kellie was jumping up and down on the second bed and only the lower half of Sara was discernable from underneath the third bed, the safety to which Ashley had presumably retreated.

I flicked the ceiling lights on and off to get the attention of the cast. There was a momentary lull in the proceedings.

I used my best courtroom voice. "Ladies. Your attention please. What's the problem here?"

Leslie pulled herself together. "My sister is a goddamn bitch, that's the problem. Where the hell does she get off telling my daughter that she's not pretty?" There was an ominous snarl in her voice.

Joan rolled her eyes. "I didn't say that. I just said that she wasn't as pretty as her younger sisters, that's all."

"Oh, *that's all*, is it? I'd like to push your face in, you miserable, vicious shrew!"

"*Excuse* me?"

"You heard right. No wonder your husband left you for some younger babe!"

Uh, oh.

"Girls, let's go upstairs and give your mothers some breathing room. Sara, pull Ashley out by her feet if you have to. Trish, here's some tissue. Kellie, kindly stop jumping on that mattress for which I am legally responsible. Let's go."

"Oh and by the way Joan," Leslie sneered as we hurried out the door. "I hope you checked your baggage for *bugs*. You wouldn't want *this* house to be infested as well, *would* you?"

Postcard to Carlie, picture of waving sea grasses with Great Point Light and the Atlantic Ocean in the background:

Hi Carlie!

Tomorrow is our last full day on Nantucket, and we are making the most of our remaining time here. Luke and I packed a picnic lunch and took Trish and Sara on a Jeep tour of the island. We saw Sankaty Light, the rose covered cottages of Sconset, Dionis Beach, the very impressive Cliff Road estates, and Madaket, with its wild surf and seals playing in the waves. Also the interior—the cranberry bogs, Altar Rock and the moors off Milestone Road.

You'll love the new Sconset house! I already have a room in mind for you.

See you Saturday night. Please kiss Abby and Joy for me.

Love, Emma

That evening Luke and I had dinner early at my favorite Italian restaurant in town.

"How about a drive out to Madaket to watch the sun set?" He suggested. "I can show you some of my clients' properties on the way."

The waves were coming in with an impressive crash. The sun was leaving huge bands of orange and pink behind as it slowly sank into the sea. We stood quietly at the edge of the beach, enjoying the antics of the seals.

"You're a homeowner here now, Luke," I reminded him. "How does it feel?"

"We're *both* homeowners now," he replied. "And the feeling is indescribable."

Then suddenly, Luke was down on one knee in the sand, a light blue box tied with white ribbon in his hand.

"Will you marry me Emma?"

I smiled at him. "And why should I want to do that?"

"Mind-blowing sex for the rest of your life. Guaranteed."

This was not rocket science.

"Yes," I replied. "Yes I will."

Luke stood up.

"I was thinking about a honeymoon in Ireland," he said, grinning.

"Only if you promise to carry my easel," I replied, and Luke moved in for one of his knee-wobbling kisses.

There would be plenty of time to talk about the pre-nup on the trip home.

To love oneself is the beginning of a life-long romance.
OSCAR WILDE

RECOMMENDED READING

American Creation, Triumphs and Tragedies at the Founding of the Republic by Joseph J. Ellis, Alfred A. Knopf (2007).

Founding Brothers, The Revolutionary Generation by Joseph J. Ellis, Vintage Books (2002).

Founding Mothers, The Women Who Raised Our Nation by Cokie Roberts, William Morrow (2004).

Ladies of Liberty, The Women Who Shaped Our Nation by Cokie Roberts, William Morrow (2008).

Bunker Hill, A City, a Siege, a Revolution by Nathaniel Philbrick, Viking (2013).

Unruly Americans and the Origins of the Constitution by Woody Holton, Hill and Wang (2007).

Martha Washington, An American Life by Patricia Brady, Penguin (2005).

First Family, Abigail and John Adams by Joseph J. Ellis, Alfred A. Knopf (2010).

Abigail Adams, A Biography by Phyllis Lee Levin, St. Martin's Press (1987).

The Words We Live By, Your Annotated Guide to the Constitution by Linda R. Monk, Hyperion (2003).

The Hemingses of Monticello, An American Family by Annette Gordon-Reed, W. W. Norton & Company, Inc. (2008).

Founding Gardeners, The Revolutionary Generation, Nature, and the Shaping of the American Nation by Andrea Wulf, Alfred A. Knopf (2011).

A Rich Spot of Earth, Thomas Jefferson's Revolutionary Garden at Monticello, by Peter J. Hatch, Yale University Press (2012).

The Discovery of Freedom, Man's Struggle Against Authority by Rose Wilder Lane, Fox & Wilkes (1993).

American Renaissance, Art and Expression in the Age of Emerson and Whitman by F.O. Matthiessen, Oxford University Press (1941).

American Bloomsbury by Susan Cheever, Simon and Schuster (2006).

The Gardens of Emily Dickinson by Judith Farr with Louise Carter, Harvard University Press (2004).

Clan MacLaren by Darby Lee Patterson, Bolton House (2011).

The Scottish Highlanders by Charles MacKinnon of Dunakin, St. Martin's Press (1984).

A Concise History of Scotland by Fitzroy Maclean, Thames & Hudson Ltd (1970, 1993, 2000).

Mhòr and More, Hill Walks in Uist by Martin Margulies, The Islands Book Trust (2011).

A Clearing in the Distance, Frederick Law Olmsted and America in the Nineteenth Century by Witold Rybczynski, Scribner (1999).

Genius of Place, the Life of Frederick Law Olmsted, Abolitionist, Conservationist, and Designer of Central Park by Justin Martin, DaCapo Press (2011).

The Spirit of the Garden by Martha Brookes Hutcheson, University of Massachusetts Press (1923, 2001).

Across the Open Field, Essays Drawn From English Landscapes by Laurie Olin, University of Pennsylvania Press (2000).

Quiet, The Power of Introverts in a World That Can't Stop Talking by Susan Cain, Crown Publishers (2012).

How to Thrive in Changing Times by Sandra Ingerman, Red Wheel/Weiser, LLC (2010).

Like a Tree, How Trees, Women, and Tree People Can Save the Planet by Jean Shinoda Bolen, M.D., Conari Press (2011).

The Book of Psychic Symbols by Melanie Barnum, Llewellyn Publications (2012).

Halloween, From Pagan Ritual to Party Night by Nicholas Rogers, Oxford University Press (2002).

Ghosts, True Encounters with the World Beyond by Hans Holzer, Black Dog & Leventhal Publishers, Inc. (1997).

Ghosts Among Us, Uncovering the Truth About the Other Side by James Van Praagh, HarperCollins (2008).

Visits From the Afterlife by Sylvia Browne with Lindsay Harrison, New American Library (2003).

ABOUT THE AUTHOR

Author Karen A. Stansbury practiced law in Connecticut for twenty-four years. After enduring twenty years of courtroom litigation she became certified in mediation, hoping for a more peaceful life. She began posting helpful articles on her website, encouraging clients to choose a less stressful path to problem solving. Writing novels using real cases was the next logical step. Now she does it full time.

When Karen isn't writing or traveling, she's painting watercolor landscapes, or riding, or kayaking, or rowing, or biking, or gardening. She lives in Litchfield County, Connecticut.